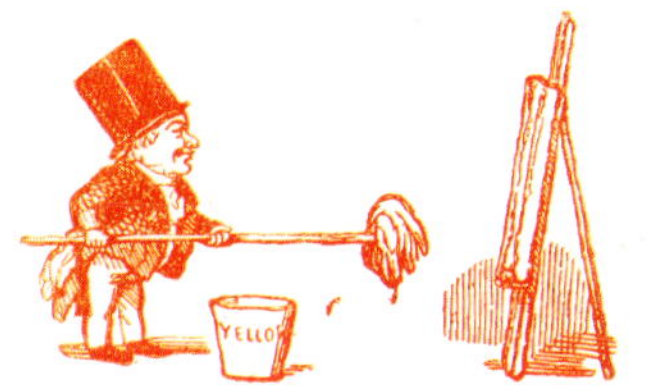

The Life of J. M. W. Turner

AF473655

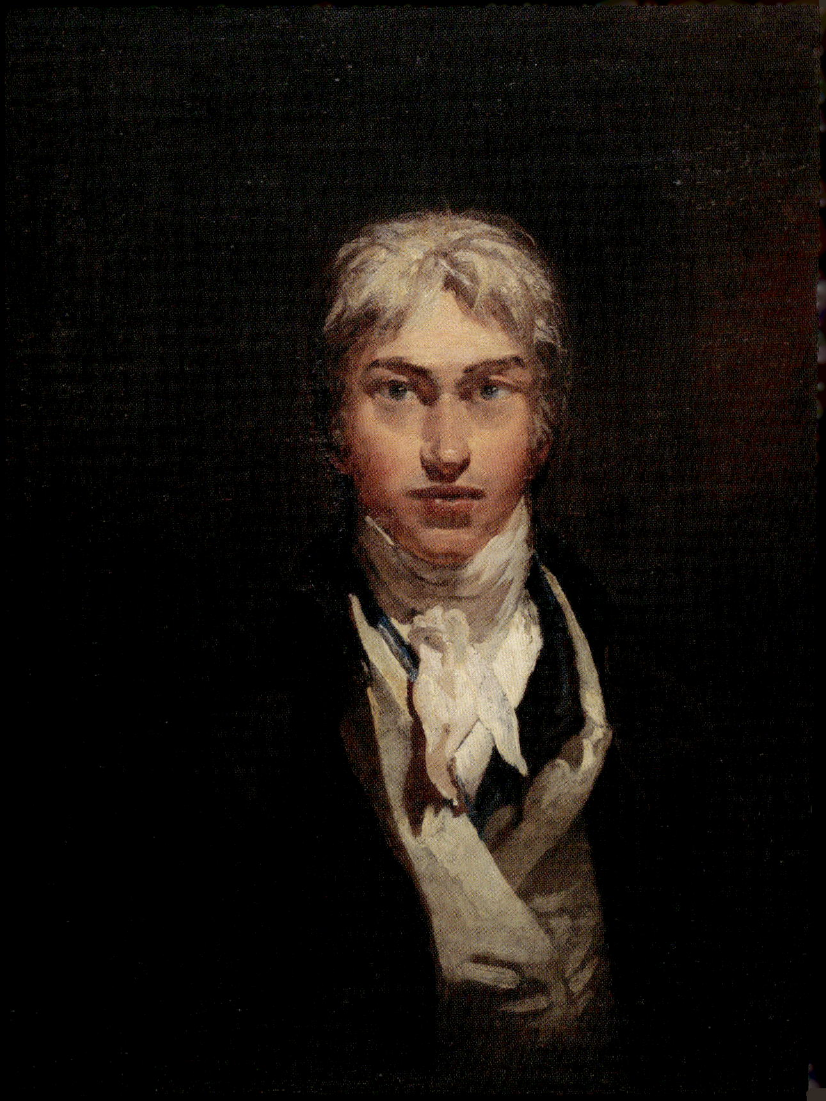

THE LIFE OF J. M. W. TURNER

WALTER THORNBURY

Selections chosen, edited, and introduced by
IAN WARRELL

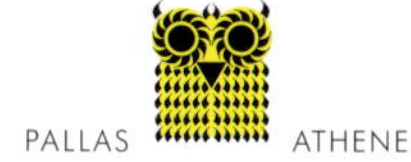

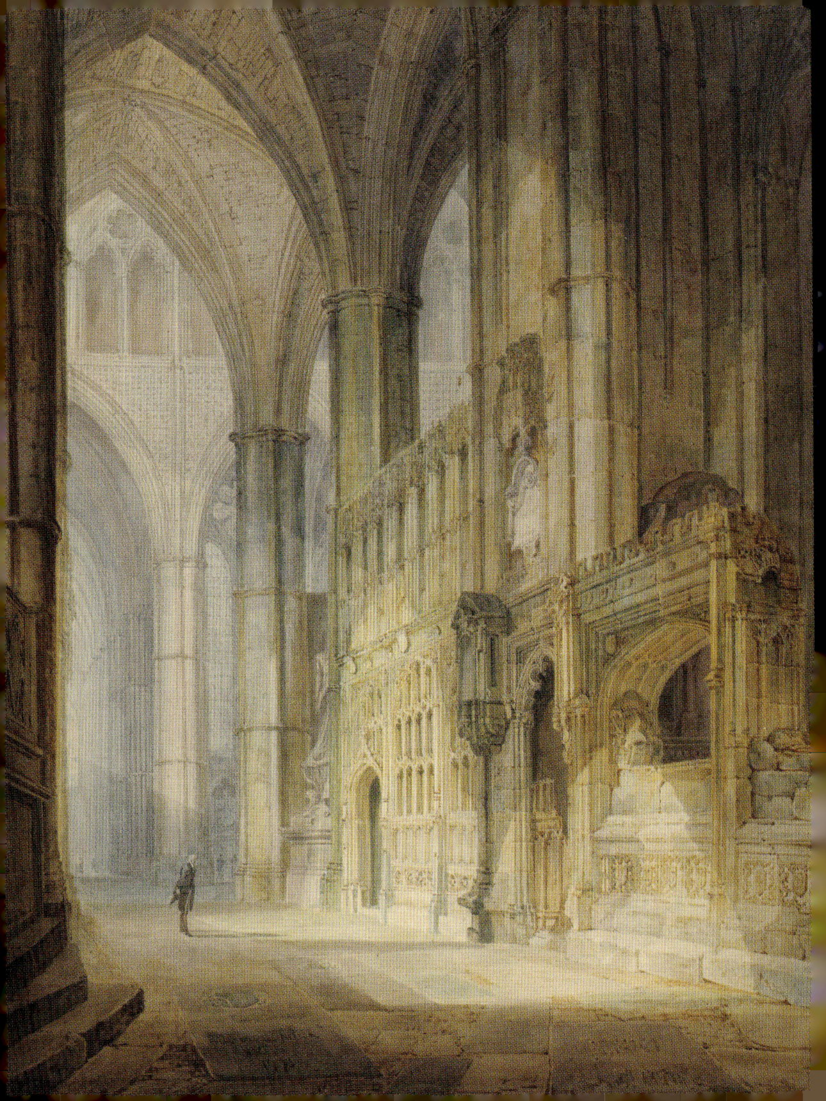

CONTENTS

Opposite: St Erasmus in Bishop Islip's Chapel, Westminster Abbey, 1796

CONTENTS

Overleaf: Staffa, Fingal's Cave, 1832

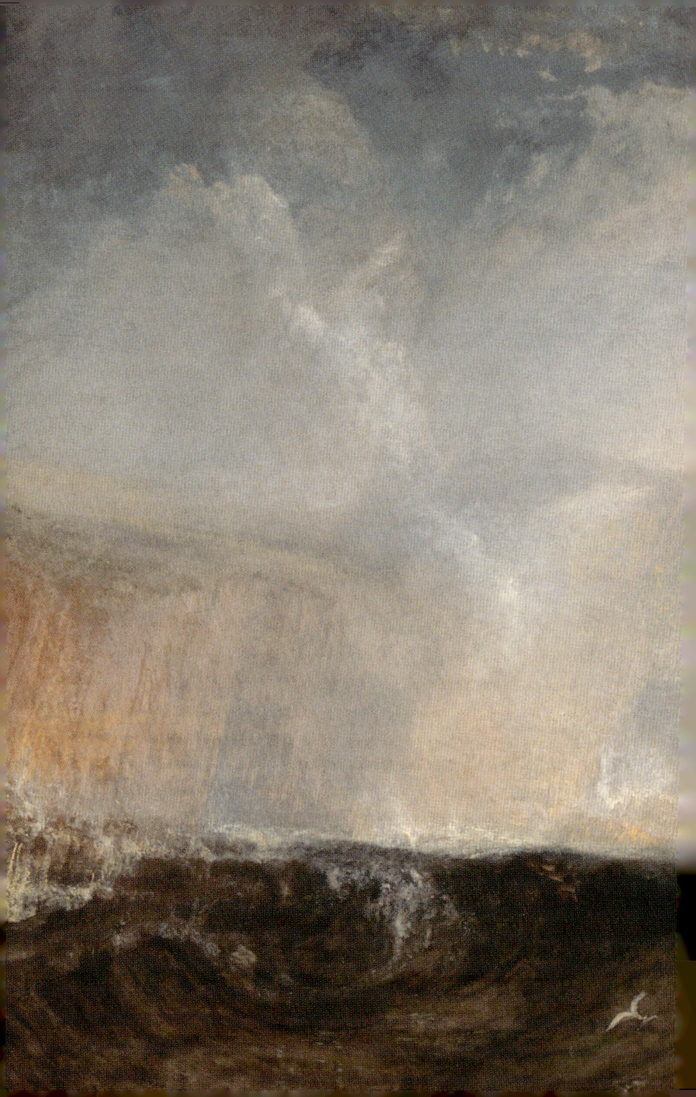

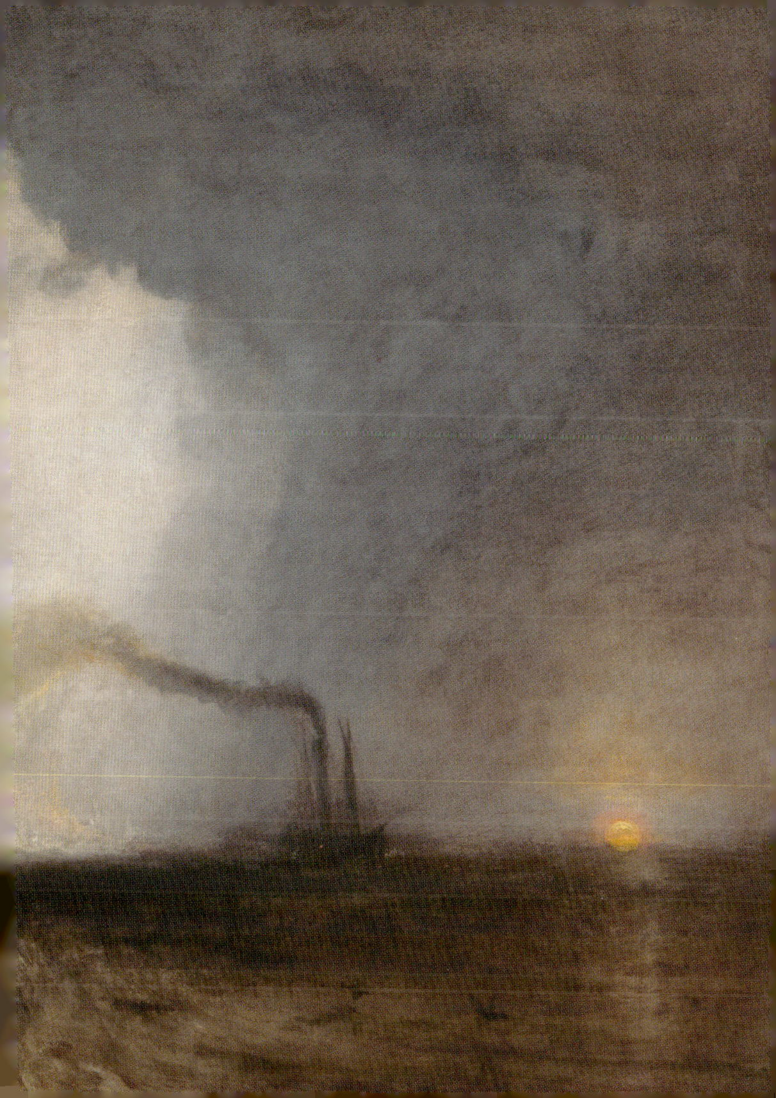

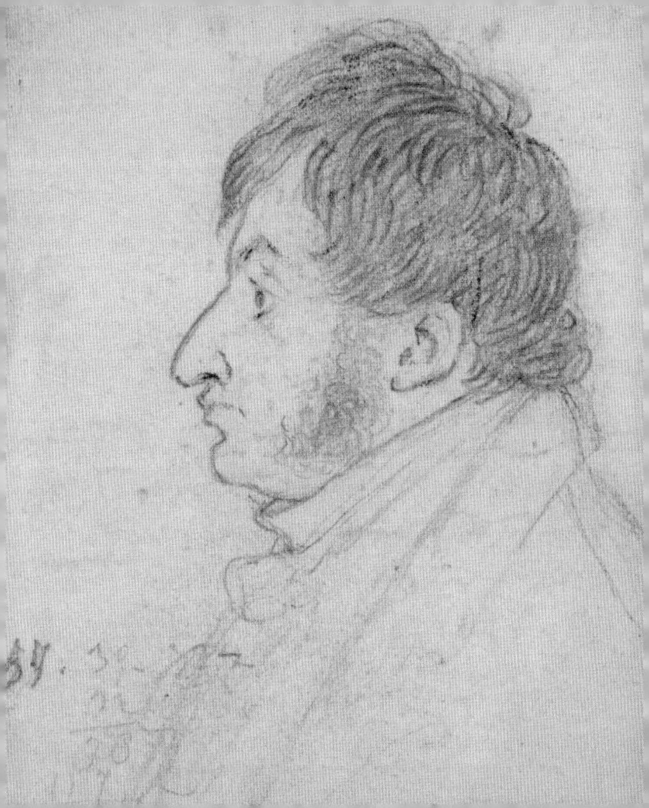

INTRODUCTION

ON AN OVERCAST DECEMBER DAY, right at the end of 1851, the body of Joseph Mallord William Turner was buried in the crypt of St Paul's Cathedral, after a service attended by the foremost names of the London art world, but no discernible family members. He was thought to have been seventy-nine years old, but was actually seventy-six, having been born in 1775 (perhaps on 23 April – notably both St George's Day, and Shakespeare's birthday). Contemporary notices of his death routinely described him as the 'father of the Royal Academy, and in spite of the peculiarities of his latter manner, one of the most eminent artists of his age'.

But the *Daily News* cautioned that 'We have properly not yet arrived at the time when a just estimate can be formed of this artist's great talents. That he founded our present school of landscape, by mingled example and influence, there is no shadow of a doubt' (23 December 1851). On the same day, the *Saint James's Chronicle* proposed that Turner had 'lived long enough to see his greatest productions rise to uncontested supremacy, however imperfectly they were understood when they first appeared in the earlier years of this century; and, though in his later works, and in advanced age, force and precision of execution have not accompanied his vivacity of conception, public opinion has gradually and steadily advanced to a more just appreciation of his power.'

It was common knowledge that Turner had retained many of his most successful paintings, notably *Dido Building Carthage* (1815) and *The Fighting Temeraire tugged to her last berth to be broken up, 1838* (1839), along with some of his commercially popular views of Venice, as well as many larger canvases that failed to attract buyers while on display at the Royal Academy exhibitions. So even as the news broke of his death, there was excited speculation about the fate of the collection stored haphazardly in his gallery on Queen Anne Street, and whether some of the pictures might have been left to the nation.

Such uncertainties about the nature of Turner's legacy were, however, only a fragment of the bigger mystery: who exactly was Turner, and what was he really like? Despite his prominence at the Royal Academy, where he had served as Deputy President in recent years, as he noticeably aged, he had increasingly lived privately. Consequently the chief perceptions of him were that he was secretive, anti-social, eccentric (like his boldly coloured paintings), penurious, yet sharp in business matters. By 1851 many of those who had been his closest friends or patrons had already died. So it was only gradually that the trajectory of his life was once again uncovered in obituaries and personal recollections.

His origins, as the son of a barber in Covent Garden, appealed especially to the mid-Victorian taste for rags-to-riches narratives, and this modest, but not impoverished background was sometimes exaggerated for effect. In fact, as Martin Myrone has recently demonstrated, Turner's social position was actually not exceptional among his artistic peers. Unlike most of them, however, Turner's precocious talents were spotted and nurtured quickly, so that he gained regular employment as a draughtsman, entered the Royal Academy schools, and soon after, at the age of only fifteen, submitted the first of the over 250 works he showed in the Academy's annual exhibitions.

Instilled with professional values by his father, Turner was already involved in the print trade by 1794, producing watercolour designs that were translated into black and white book illustrations. This type of work became the mainstay of his output throughout his career, so much so that he was able to dictate the terms to publishers, who competed to secure work from him (though this was always a risk financially in a volatile market). As he gained in experience, he became an exacting taskmaster, habitually revising tiny details while seeking to perfect each engraved image. His designs were often the main attraction, even when paired with a celebrated writer like Sir Walter Scott, who was bluntly told that by employing Turner's images his poems would sell considerably more than double what they might do on their own.

From 1793 (and more consistently after 1796) Turner had begun exhibiting oil paintings, alongside his technically inventive watercolours, which eventually gained him recognition as an Associate of the Royal Academy in 1799. By then he was receiving commissions from wealthy aristocratic patrons, such as William Beckford, John Julius Angerstein and the Duke of Bridgewater, along with Lord Elgin, whose meagre and onerous terms, seeking the artist to join his team for his controversial trip to Greece, Turner was able to decline.

A couple of years after becoming a full member of the Academy in 1802 (then the youngest to receive this accolade), he opened his own gallery on Harley Street, later expanded around the corner at Queen Anne Street. There he was able to promote his latest paintings along with his ambitious series of mezzotints known as the *Liber Studiorum* (which in 1851 many believed would be his most significant artistic legacy). It was there also that he displayed his experimental naturalistic canvases, inspired by the *plein air* studies painted during his excursions on the River Thames from 1805 onwards, some of which found favour with Lord Egremont, later a close friend.

In addition to his home and gallery in central London, Turner's success enabled him to construct a small villa – Sandycombe Lodge – close to the river at Twickenham, which became a regular retreat until the mid-1820s. Further afield, at Farnley Hall, near Otley, in Yorkshire, he became a regular guest of Walter Fawkes, a progressive-minded landowner with an interest in history, who proved to be the most enthusiastic collector of Turner's art. It was apparently while visiting Farnley that Turner conceived the first of his series of paintings evoking the rise and fall of the Carthaginian empire (see pp. 106–7, 116–17).

In the meantime the long wars with France were settled by the peace following the Battle of Waterloo in 1815, which enabled British artists to travel on the continent more freely. Turner took full advantage of this, as was plain in his resulting oil paintings, and in numerous carefully crafted watercolours for the book trade. His exposure to Italy in 1819, both in terms of its dazzling light and its cultural associations (particularly the landscape paintings of Claude Lorrain), consolidated his achievements and gave a new impetus to his work, which was further augmented in a later stay in Rome in 1828–9, plus three visits to Venice (1819, 1833 and 1840).

Since the mid-1810s Turner had made use of new pigments, which gave his palette a much higher tonality, most notably in terms of his preference for yellow. By the

1830s his vivid colours (previously confined to his watercolours) were a distinctive trait recognised by exhibition viewers and mocked by critics, who also increasingly took him to task for his blurred means of representing the natural world. Famously, a picture of the Scottish island of Staffa that had remained unsold after its first exposure in 1832, was eventually bought in 1845 by an American client, who complained about its indistinct appearance.* Hearing this, Turner conceded that 'Indistinctness is my fault' (a comment that has often been corrupted to read 'Indistinctness is my *forte*'). To compound the perplexing strangeness of Turner's exhibited subjects, which ranged across mythology and aspects of contemporary life and industry, he often supplemented his titles with extracts seemingly from an unpublished epic poem titled *Fallacies of Hope*.

Turner also embraced a certain indistinctness when it came to his personal life, keeping its details obscure even from close friends. In his later twenties he had begun a relationship with Sarah Danby (1760/66–1861), the widow of a composer. She had two daughters with Turner, which he acknowledged in his will of 1829: Evelina (born *c.* 1801) and Georgiana (*c.* 1811–1843). But by the mid 1830s, Turner had long been estranged from Mrs Danby. It was then

* Yale Center for British Art, New Haven, CT (see pp. 10–11)

that he became a regular visitor of the Margate lodgings of Sophie Caroline Booth (1799–1878). Twice-widowed, she was a practical helpmate, but also a loyal companion in the artist's final years (both in Margate, and finally in Chelsea) away from the controversies of the art world, where his paintings were increasingly derided.

In the absence of any certainty about Turner's meanings in these later creations the young John Ruskin (1819–1900) came forward as both defender and interpreter, publishing in 1843 the first volume of *Modern Painters,* which was succeeded by a further four volumes by 1860. During these years Ruskin's writings made a sustained and passionate case for the originality and richness of Turner's art, simultaneously acclaiming him as a supreme genius who had been cruelly overlooked by the world. Though Turner himself evaded opportunities to endorse Ruskin's books, they likely ensured significant sales to new collectors before the artist died. It was inevitable, therefore, that many people assumed that Ruskin would be the one to research and deliver a full biography of Turner.

There had, in fact, been earlier attempts at setting down impressions of Turner's character, most notably that by Edward Dayes, among sketches of other contemporary artists, which was published posthumously in 1805. Its most memorable but decidedly unkind assertion must have wounded, and partly explains Turner's aversion to having his portrait painted: 'The man must be loved for his works; for his person is not striking, nor his conversation brilliant.'

Following Turner's death, there was a renewed interest in his life calling forth a useful *Memoir* in 1852 from Peter Cunningham (1816–69), who had worked for Sir Francis Chantrey (1781–1841), one of Turner's greatest friends and a rival fisherman. The text appeared in *Turner and his Works* by John Burnet (1784–1868), an engraver who had well-founded opinions on the artist, despite not having collaborated with him directly. Another 'Biographical Sketch' was included in Henry Bohn's *Liber Fluviorum; or, River Scenery of France* (1853), this time by Alaric Watts (1798–1864), who would have come into contact with Turner during the years he edited the *Literary Souvenir.* Extracts from most of these sources, as well as Charles Robert Leslie's *Autobiographical Reflections* (1860), and the personal recollections of David Roberts, were clipped and published by John Timbs (1801–75) for his *Anecdote Biography* in 1860.

As the 1850s went on attitudes to Turner were bound up in the long-running dispute over his will, and its various codicils, relating to an estate valued at £140,000, which was challenged by his distant cousins. Regrettably, Turner's chief object of reserving his lifetime's financial capital in order to establish a charity for 'decayed English artists (Landscape Painters only) and single men', was ultimately thwarted. But in 1856 it was settled that around one hundred finished paintings, plus the contents of his studio, would join the National Gallery collection as the Turner Bequest (yet only if his stipulation that two of them were hung between paintings by Claude Lorrain). The gallery at that stage only occupied the west side of its current building in Trafalgar Square, so initially the paintings were shown first at Marlborough House, and then at South Kensington (along with the Vernon and Sheepshanks bequests of British pictures). But in order to honour the terms of Turner's will within ten years of his death, a room was found in the National Gallery itself in the autumn of 1861. The arrangement was overseen by Ralph Wornum (1812–77) the Gallery's Keeper, who was simultaneously publishing commentaries for a set of engravings of Turner's paintings, appearing each month in the *Art Journal*.

By then the arts pages were buzzing about the imminent publication of a 'long-expected' biography of Turner by 'that ever entertaining writer Mr Walter Thornbury' (1828–76). This book (from which extracts are reprinted here) remains one of the most important (and indeed entertaining) sources for contemporary recollections of the artist; but as we will see, it is a problematic text that proved highly controversial from the moment of its publication. Thornbury started his career as a journalist in Bristol, exploring antiquarian subjects, which he drew on once he began to publish historical novels. As well as fiction and history, he expanded his range to write on art for the *Athenæum* and many other contemporary journals. From 1856 his books were being issued by the London firm of Hurst and Blackett. Towards the end of 1860 he had published a two-volume survey of *British Artists from Hogarth to Turner*, though curiously the text contained nothing about the latter, other than a portrait, despite Thornbury having contributed the entry on Turner to the latest edition of the *Encyclopedia Britannica*.

Thornbury was definitely a young man in a hurry, and had quickly established a reputation as someone 'who is said to write a book every week, and to issue three-volumes additional on the first Monday of every month' (*Illustrated London News*, 12 October 1861). Inevitably his style, judgement and methods of assembling texts, at short notice, raised eyebrows. For admirers of Turner, it was presumably troubling to read the reservations in October 1861 about his most recent production, *Cross Country*, of which the *Saturday Review of Politics, Literature, Science and Art*, felt that, of the last nine chapters, 'there is scarcely one which Mr Thornbury would not have done well to omit' (26 October 1861).

This lacklustre review appeared less than a fortnight

before *The Life of J. M. W. Turner, R. A., Founded on Letters and Papers Furnished by His Friends and Fellow Academicians* was published on Friday 8 November. Like the previous year's *British Artists*, the book's title page anticipated the coming year of 1862, and was no doubt issued in advance to capitalise on end-of-year sales. However, in this case, some reviewers noted that its publication coincided with the new presentation of the Turner paintings at the National Gallery, which might suggest it was hurried through the press a little faster.

Nevertheless, as Thornbury's Preface made plain, the origins of the book date from four years earlier, in 1857, when he had approached Ruskin to establish whether he intended to write the biography that many hoped he would deliver. As that was not to be, Ruskin offered some guidance, which Thornbury cunningly incorporated at the start of his book:

> Fix at the beginning the following main characteristics of Turner in your mind, as the keys to the secret of all he said and did:—Uprightness, Generosity, Tenderness of heart (extreme), Sensuality, Obstinacy (extreme), Irritability, Infidelity. And be sure that he knew his own power, and felt himself utterly alone in the world from its not being understood. Don't try to mask the dark side.

These final remarks proved to be advice that Thornbury

took very literally, despite vowing that he was seeking to demonstrate the 'injustice' of Frederick William Fairholt's earlier assertion in the *Art Journal* (1 April 1859)

> that all reminiscences of Turner are decidely unpleasant, in person and in manners, and worse than all in habit; his parsimony was excessive. Altogether, it is best to know him only by his works, and keep an ideal Turner for the mind to dwell upon.

(Ironically, Fairholt had continued, 'Many anecdotes of his "ruling passion" float about in artistic circles, it is almost to be hoped no one will collect them for the press.') In pursuing his defensive role Thornbury believed he had written with a

> stern and undeviating regard for truth … I have tried to paint the man as I really believe he was – an image of gold with clay feet … a great disappointed man, whose ambition was never satisfied, and who in despair of all other pleasure sought out nature, and in her presence felt his only real happiness.

As the title claimed, the ensuing book was compiled from recollections of friends and colleagues, as well as original documents, pieced together in a rather undisciplined and repetitive fashion within a meandering, and much-disrupted chronological framework. Aside from his advisory letter, no further correspondence from Ruskin is included in the book, though extensive quotations from his writings on Turner's paintings constitute a key element of the text (described by one critic as an 'inexhaustible spring'), including a close paraphrase of his celebrated chapter from *Modern Painters V* (1860), contrasting the boyhoods of Giorgione and Turner.

Among those who proffered information, Turner's affable associate, the painter George Jones (1786–1869) shared his unpublished memoir, and further insights came from one of the few people to accompany Turner on his travels, Hugh Munro of Novar, who was the most important collector of the artist's later works. An unacknowledged (and essentially appropriated) contribution came from Dante Gabriel Rossetti's brother William Michael, who helped Ruskin assess the works on paper in the Turner Bequest, and generously allowed Thornbury to consult (though not to publish) his painstaking transcriptions of the poems Turner had jotted down in his sketchbooks. Curiously, in one of the early reviews, the *Daily News* implied, seemingly mistakenly, that Thornbury had benefitted from 'a personal acquaintance with Turner', but that is nowhere apparent in the text; not that this falsehood deterred the publishers from selecting this quote in their advertisements during the next couple of months.

Despite its obvious structural flaws, the book was

successful in fleshing out the earlier life of Turner (including his mother's mental health), chiefly with second-hand anecdotes relayed by Henry Syer Trimmer (1806–76), the son of the artist's childhood friend. Conversely there is arguably an imbalance towards stories emanating from the last decade of Turner's life, which lends an undue emphasis to his shabbiness and eccentricity, as well as his increasing partiality to wine, a particularly damning characteristic in this strict temperance era. More shocking still were the allegations Turner had produced four illegitimate children, the intimation that his last housekeeper (Mrs Sophia Booth) at Margate and then Chelsea was his mistress, together with the accusation that he spent debauched weekends down in Wapping and Rotherhithe (see pp. 235–6).

The more common criticism of Turner's miserliness was something Thornbury repeatedly claimed he was seeking to refute, even as he regurgitated narratives appearing to substantiate this kind of behaviour, some of which verge on anti-semitic stereotyping. Turner's reputation for penny-pinching is further underscored by the descriptions of the mean and decrepit outward appearance of his house at the end of his life. These are exaggerated to become a metaphor for the man himself, much as Dickens used Scrooge's warehouse in *A Christmas Carol* (1843). Thornbury was not a subtle *pasticheur*, but like

Autolycus, that 'snapper-up of unconsidered trifles', he barely disguised what he borrowed. As well as the inevitable comparisons with the hero-worshipping adulation of Ruskin and Thomas Carlyle, in refashioning Turner as 'a character in a novel' (as the *Tablet* asserted on 25 January 1862), he frequently channelled Dickens (specifically comparing the architect William Porden to the pompous Seth Pecksniff in *Martin Chuzzlewit*), as well as drawing on Thackeray in his use of a 'mock-heroic dramatic style', invoking *Vanity Fair* as the 'curtain rises' at the start of the biography (see the *Morning Post*, 6 January 1862).

Thornbury's book was widely promoted, not just throughout the British Isles, but advertisements in publications like *Thacker's Overland News for India and the Colonies* (11 November) ensured it had an international profile. Similarly, numerous syndicated extracts from its pages further heightened interest. If some of the initial reviewers welcomed this more complete image of Turner, the majority felt that such aspects of the artist's life should 'never [have] been brought to light' (*Bell's Weekly Messenger*, 16 November). As Susanna Berger has noted, several of them delighted in detecting parallels between the 'florid, extravagant' colours, and the blurred and 'experimental' impressions created by Thornbury's style and the controversial indistinct paintings of Turner's later years. Coincidentally, it was actually Thornbury's book that first distorted the celebrated phrase mentioned earlier to 'Indistinctness is my *forte*' (possibly accidentally, or as a result of his journalistic instinct for punchy effect).

The first long assessment of the *Life of J. M. W. Turner,* in the *Liverpool Albion* (11 November), highlighted the unflattering contrast between the 'superficial' meagreness of Thornbury's style and that of Ruskin (Turner's 'chief worshipper and ear-splitting trumpeter'), a theme that was repeatedly taken up in subsequent reviews, even amongst those who disliked Ruskin's 'flash rhetoric'. In an article entitled, 'The Turner Bubble Burst', for example, the critic of the *Press* bemoaned 'The incontinent gossip in which [Thornbury] indulges dispels for ever the mystery which too long has shrouded the character and genius of Turner ... What, we would venture to ask, can Mr Ruskin say to all this?' (14 December 1861). In fact the sense that the art critic had shirked his responsibility to become Turner's biographer pervades critical responses to the book, culminating in the *Westminster Review*'s judgment that Ruskin 'has laid himself open to the imputation of having wilfully frustrated the chief end for which he was created' – that is, as Boswell to Turner's Dr Johnson (April 1862). Because Ruskin had promised in the closing pages of *Modern Painters* to challenge any 'unjust' conclusions propagated by Thornbury, the journalist naturally expected him to deliver a 'torrent of his matchless sarcasm and most merciless invective'. But Ruskin was away in the Alps at the time, and, publicly, remained mute about the book, despite telling his father it was a 'dreadful book … in every sense – utterly bad in taste and writing.'

Further reviews confirmed and expanded on Ruskin's opinion, many of which observed sharply that, while Thornbury was crudely dismissive of previous biographers (mocking John Timbs especially for resorting to scissors to 'cut out a dozen or two of trite or erroneous Turner stories'),his own text was evidently heavily dependent on them, sometimes substantively so. This became a long-running issue over the winter in the pages of the *Athenæum* (to which Thornbury was affiliated), manifested as a steady stream of letters addressing errors and shortcomings in the book from patrons such as Henry McConnel, the notable engraver John Pye, or distinguished public figures including William Hookham Carpenter, the Keeper of the British Museum Print Room.

As the *Morning Post* reported at the start of January 1862, the most grave and contentious charges against Thornbury came from the publisher, conchologist, and former editor of the *Literary Gazette,* Lovell Augustus Reeve, who accused him of plagiarism, citing specific instances that challenged the 'literary honour and honesty of the author'. By that date it was clear that Thornbury was unable to address these concerns because he was travelling in Egypt, leading the newspaper to quip that the public could no doubt expect him to produce 'Chats with Cheops', or 'Oddities of Osiris' on his return.

Parallel to this, George Jones was assiduously gathering corrections in his own copy of the *Life of J. M. W. Turner* (now in Tate Britain), including review cuttings, along with important responses from Munro of Novar, who was able to expand on Thornbury's garbled account of his 1836 journey to the Val d'Aosta with Turner, as well as relaying details from artists such as Daniel Maclise or Clarkson Stanfield that contradicted details given by Thornbury. Most famously Munro's annotations repudiated the idea that the latter artist had proposed the subject of the *Temeraire* to Turner (page 204). Like other friends, Jones was horrified by the damage done to Turner's reputation in its prurient discussion of the 'night-side' of his character (as it was described in the *Art Journal* in December 1861).

Jones's loyal accumulations were possibly propelled by the much-repeated assumption that a corrected second edition of the *Life* would soon be necessary. However, an awareness of his activities caused rumours, reported in the January edition of the *Art Journal*, that he and other executors were in possession of unpublished documents, 'which illustrate, in a new way altogether, the details of Turner's life'. From which, the columnist deduced that an alternative biography was under way 'which will render Mr Thornbury's nugatory, by upsetting all his facts, conclusions, and theories'. Like many admirers of Turner, offended by the now tarnished idea of their hero, the writer was hopeful they would be able to 'rejoice greatly, if these letters and papers do, in any degree scatter the dark clouds which rest on his memory'.

Almost a month after the *Yorkshire Gazette* remarked on Thornbury's continuing absence and the weekly fresh onslaughts made on his book, a riposte from the author at last appeared in the *Athenæum* on 22 February 1862. Instead of conceding any ground, Thornbury adopted a high-handed tone in responding to the 'quibbling attacks', belittling Pye and Reeve in a way that would probably now be deemed tantamount to gaslighting. Dismissing casually the charges of plagiarism, he promised to rectify any errors in a future edition, and concluded, 'I cannot, however, but feel that no generous critic would judge harshly of one or two trivial mistakes that may be found in a work containing so many thousand facts.'

However, this did not settle the matter. Pye continued to justify his claims of plagiarism until the *Athenæum*, on 15 March, refused to publish any more 'disagreeable correspondence' concerning the book. Even that did not draw matters to a close because in April substantial reviews of the *Life* appeared in both the *Westminster Review* (noted above) and the *Quarterly Review*. The latter was penned by Lady Eastlake, a sophisticated art world insider, who had visited Turner in his gallery in 1844. With her characteristic tartness, she dismissed much of the book for its 'spongy tumidity' (meaning its unnecessary padding with extraneous matter) or its irrelevances, which she termed 'twaddling reminiscences, traditions, and remarks about them'. As a mid-Victorian woman, it is fascinating to see that her outrage at Thornbury's unearthing of Turner's 'wallowing' at Wapping was not horror at the activity itself, if indeed she believed it to be true, but that this damaging hearsay was published on such slight evidence (having already demonstrated that Thornbury's use of even published sources was unreliable). Moreover she questioned whether it was actually of public interest: 'Are the lives of eminent men to be written with the aid of the detective police?' On the issue of plagiarism, she widened the debate to illustrate passages of Thornbury's text in which detail and phrasing are suspiciously comparable to extracts from Wornum's commentaries in the Turner Gallery series published by the *Art Journal* (1859–61). As the *Sun* had previously observed on 23 November, Thornbury had grudgingly acknowledged his dependence on Wornum in the Preface, but had mentioned this 'painstaking writer of the day with uncalled-for acerbity'.

Surprisingly the unremitting paper trail of unease and controversy, prompted by the book's publication, did not diminish the public's curiosity about Turner. Thornbury's stock may have been dented but he continued to put out a historical novel each year, settling into married life in 1872. Perhaps the greater casualty was Ruskin's, whose idealistic love of Turner was severely dulled and his authority somewhat undermined. The *Westminster Review*, for example, had proposed that 'Only one thing occurred during [Turner's] lifetime which seriously injured him in public estimation, the foolish attempt of Mr Ruskin to make him act at once as the apostle of Nature and as a martyr for the sake of Art.'

Hurst and Blackett continued to promote the book in 1862, doing so by co-opting a quote from the review in *Blackwood's Magazine* in January: 'Henceforth nobody can have any excuse for re-opening this subject. Mr Thornbury has collected a mass of information large in quantity and fuller in detail than Turner's incommunicative and secretive character could have justified any one in expecting.' As is often the case, the selected extract neatly overlooks the largely negative content of the rest of the review.

Significantly, this was a review that clearly rankled more than any of the others with Thornbury himself. This is clear from his Preface to the considerably revised, one-volume edition of the biography, written in 1876 shortly before he was admitted to Camberwell House Lunatic Asylum, suffering from overwork. In justifying his exposure of 'those small frailties which the polite biographers of fifty years ago used so discreetly to suppress', he mocked those who had sought to protect Turner's reputation. As expressed in the piece in *Blackwood's Magazine* (which he quotes without naming his source), they objected to the version of Turner he had presented, which seemed

> a figure only adapted for twilight and the shadows; an unhappy soul, whom common charity is content to accept as a great painter, without special inquiry into his character, but whom the cruelty of friends forces forth into public ignominy, by way of proving his right, had not circumstances forbidden, to take his place among the greatest of men.

Unrepentant, Thornbury opined that,

> If biography is to consist, as it too often does, of undisguised eulogy, such as could only flow from the pen of an enraptured executor; if it is to be a garish picture without shadow; if it is to increase our knowledge of human nature by suppressing all that is painful, incongruous, or inconsistent; if it is to be no truer than a funeral sermon, or more reliable than one of the fulsome dedications of the last century, then can no honest man condescend to write biographies.

Ironically, by the time the second edition of his book was

published he had died from typhus, and others were writing *his* obituary.

After reading the extent of the opprobrium directed at Thornbury and his *Life of Turner*, you may reasonably be wondering why the book still deserves an audience today. Indeed at the 2003 conference dedicated to Turner in Birmingham several art historians considered whether it might be possible (advisable even) to write about Turner without calling on material from the biography. This of course has not proved possible, and for good reason because, as Selby Whittingham has noted, 'Thornbury did not make things up, but repeated the stories he laboriously collected uncritically, and that makes his work as a source invaluable'. The book is also richly peppered throughout with incidental details, which as well as giving a vivid impression of Turner the man, have also proved especially helpful to conservators and scientists like Dr. Joyce Townsens and Rebecca Hellen in their research into Turner's studio practice and the materials he used. Furthermore, as James Hamilton has sagely observed, Thornbury's access to material not previously published and individuals who did not otherwise record their connection with the artist, mean that he is essentially 'the Old Testament of Turner studies – chronologically unreliable, vague, muddled and repetitious, but containing a few searing truths, many inaccuracies and lots of good stories'.

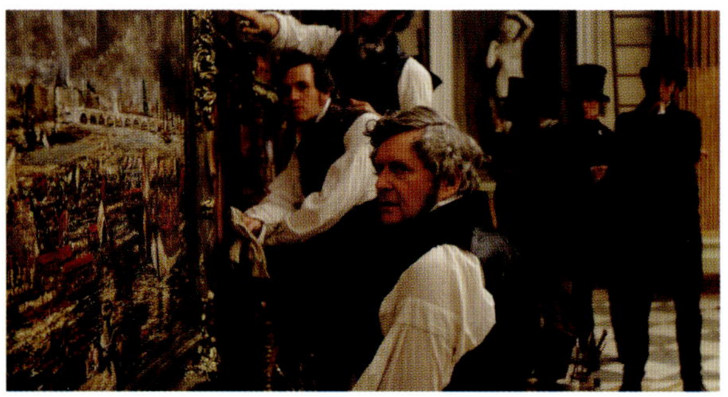

'"He has been here," said Constable, "and fired off a gun."' The scene on Varnishing Day at the Royal Academy (see p. 175) as portrayed in Mike Leigh's 'Mr. Turner', with James Fleet as Constable

That last point was, no doubt, the reason that the film-maker Mike Leigh was drawn to the book when preparing his visionary *Mr Turner* (2014), and why (without becoming the 'film-of-the-book') he structured his narrative around several of its most notable incidents that recent biographers have also assimilated into their accounts of Turner's life, most poignantly the discovery of Turner in his final days, living under the pseudonym of 'Mr. Booth' at Chelsea. For fundamentally Thornbury was a canny and frequently engaging storyteller, even if he sometimes dealt in illusions and embellishments. And unlike Ruskin's Turner, who the *Morning Post* aptly asserted was 'an entirely imaginary being', the Turner Thornbury brought into the light has endured as something of greater substance, a man for our times perhaps, who transcends his flawed humanity through his paintings. Thus, while the initial critics, often reluctantly, admitted the frailties of the artist, they steadfastly clung on to what they cherished most about his art, which was invariably his ability to recreate light. Indeed, as the *Sun* concluded in its piece on 23 November 1861, Turner

> is one among the world's great teachers, and the sunshine which he loved so well while living, and on which his dying gaze still rested, is typical of the enduring splendour of the artist's fame.

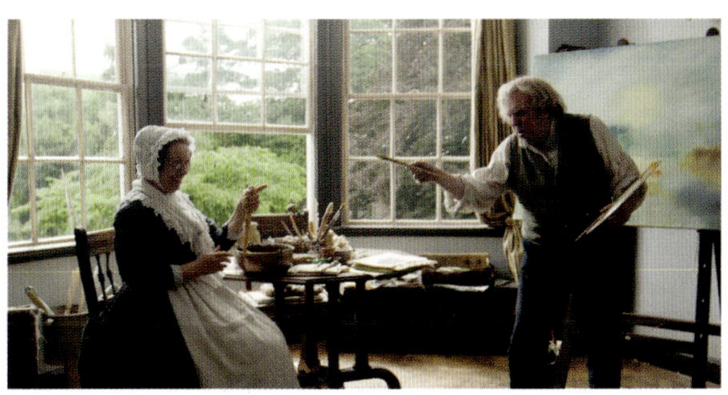

Turner (Timothy Spall) in Chelsea with Mrs. Booth (Marion Bailey). He is painting Norham Castle: Sunrise (see pp. 264–5)

Susanna Berger, '"When sobriety and taste were cast to the winds". A study of George Walter Thornbury's The Life of J. M. W. Turner, R.A.', *The British Art Journal*, Winter 2012/13, vol. XIII, no. 3, pp. 81–8

Imogen Holmes-Roe (ed.), Turner. *In Light and Shade*, Manchester 2025

Evelyn Joll, Martin Butlin, and Luke Herrmann (eds), *The Oxford Companion to J. M. W. Turner,* Oxford 2001

James Hamilton, 'Turner and Thornbury' in *Turner: A Life*, London 1997, pp. 333–8

Rebecca Hellen, '"Three Days or more..." Turner's Varnishing Day practice and the physical evidence', *The British Art Journal*, Winter 2014/15, vol. XV, no. 2, pp. 47–53

Andrew Loukes, *J. M. W. Turner*, London 2024

Nicola Moorby, *Turner and Constable. Art, Life, Landscape*, New Haven and London 2025

Franny Moyle, *The Extraordinary Life and Momentous Times of J. M. W. Turner*, London 2016

Marjorie Munsterberg, 'Ruskin's Turner. The making of a Romantic hero', *The British Art Journal*, Spring/Summer 2009, vol. X, no. 1, pp. 61–71

Felicity Myrone, 'J. M. W. Turner and his World: John Platt (1842-1902), a Late Victorian Extra-illustrator, and his Collection', *eBLJ*, 8 (2009), pp. 1-52

Martin Myrone, *Making the Modern Artist. Culture, Class and Art-educational Opportunity in Romantic Britain*, New Haven and London 2020

William Michael Rossetti, 'Turner's Life and Genius: Review of Mr Thornbury's Book, 1861', in *Fine Art, Chiefly Contemporary: Notices Re-Printed, with Revisions*, London and Cambridge 1867, pp. 291–323

Eric Shanes, *Young Mr Turner. The First Forty Years, 1775-1815*, New Haven and London, 2016

Sam Smiles, *The Late Works of J. M. W. Turner: The Artist and his Critics*, New Haven and London 2020

Ian Warrell, 'Exploring the "dark side". Ruskin and the problem of Turner's erotica', *The British Art Journal*, Spring 2003, vol. IV, no. 1, pp. 5-46 (plus Summer 2003, vol. IV, no. 2, p. 102); reprinted as *Turner's Secret Sketches*, London 2012, and with revisions 2020

Ian Warrell, 'Turner's "Staffa, Fingal's Cave"; exporting "indistinctness"', *The Burlington Magazine*, April 2025, vol. 167, no. 1465, pp. 330–41

Selby Whittingham, 'J. M. W. Turner, marriage and morals', *The British Art Journal*, Spring 2015, vol. XV, no. 3, pp. 119-25

Imogen Holmes-Roe (ed.), Turner. *In Light and Shade*, Manchester 2025

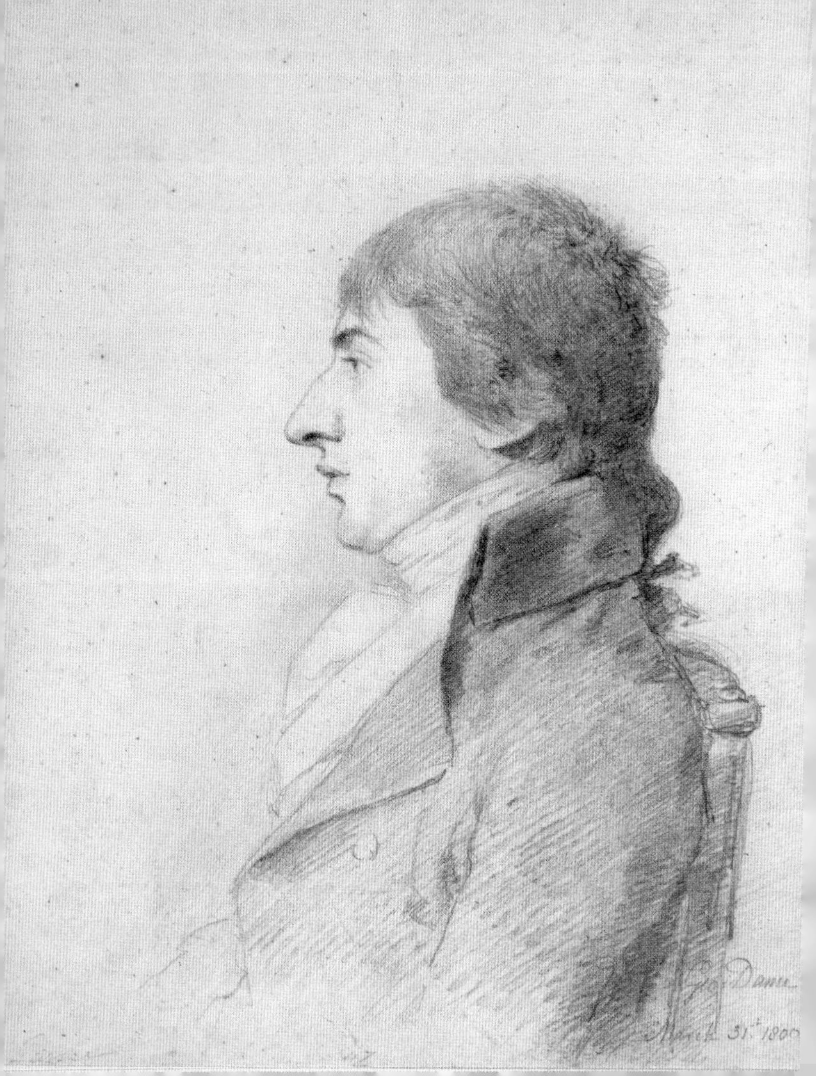
Geo Dance
March 31st 1800

THE CURTAIN RISES

JOSEPH MALLORD WILLIAM TURNER was born on St. George's Day (day ominous of greatness), the 23rd of April, 1775, and was baptised on the 14th of May following, in the parish church of St. Paul's, Covent Garden, where his name may still be seen in the register.

His father, William Turner, a barber, well known in the district of the Garden, lived at the west end of Maiden Lane, on the right-hand side, opposite the Cider Cellars (opened about 1730); at the time of the future painter's birth the studio of an Artist Society.[I, 1]

Turner mentioned his birthday as April the 23rd, in the first codicil of his will. In the parochial books of St. Paul's, Covent Garden, we find that his father was married (by licence) to Mary Marshall, also of the parish of Covent Garden, on the 29th of August, 1773.[I, 2]

Turner's grandfather and grandmother lived all their life at South Molton, in Devonshire. His father went to London early in life, became a hairdresser, and married a young woman whose surname was Mallord (or Marshall), from whom the painter derived one of his Christian names. An uncle of the painter settled in Barnstaple, and

Opposite: George Dance, J. M. W. Turner, 1800

became a wool-merchant. A descendant of this uncle is now principal clerk in one of the Barnstaple banks, and kindly furnishes me with these facts. He tells me he once called at the painter's house, but was refused admittance, as he believes all the painter's relatives were, if they ventured on a visit to the Gallery.[I, 4]

A family like Turner's, that produced a small tradesman, a bank-clerk, and a solicitor, must have at least been of as good yeoman rank as Shakespeare's. It is the middle classes indeed that have produced England's greatest minds.

As talent is said to come on the mother's side, I will begin with some account of Turner's mother, kindly furnished to me by the Rev. Mr. Trimmer, the eldest son of Turner's old friend and executor, the rector of Heston. Mr. Trimmer obtained his facts from an authority no less unquestionable than Hannah Danby, Turner's old housekeeper, who had them from the painter's father.

> She (the mother) was a native of Islington, but at Turner's decease they had not succeeded in finding an entry of her baptism. There is an unfinished portrait of her by her son, one of his first attempts.* I could perceive no mark of promise in this work, and the same remark might be extended to his first

* Untraced

landscape attempts. It is not wanting in force or decision of touch, but the drawing is defective. There is a strong likeness to Turner about the nose and eyes. Her eyes are blue, lighter than his, her nose aquiline, and she has a slight fall in the nether lip. Her hair is well frizzed—for which she might have been indebted to her husband's professional skill—and is surmounted by a cap with large flappers. She stands erect, and looks masculine, not to say fierce; report proclaims her to have been a person of ungovernable temper, and to have led her husband a sad life. In stature, like her son, she was below the average height. In the latter part of her life she was insane and in confinement. Turner might have inherited from her his melancholy turn of mind. I never saw her, never heard him mention her, nor ever heard of any one who had seen her.[I, 5–6]

A few years before his death, Mr. [Charles] Turner, the engraver, made a drawing of him [Turner Senior] which is a fair likeness. Turner, the son, hearing of the circumstance, said it must be destroyed; and the engraver, to pacify him, made a copy of it, which he gave up, and Turner destroyed it. At this time old Turner was decrepit.

As I knew him well, (Mr. Trimmer says), I will try and describe him. He was about the height of his

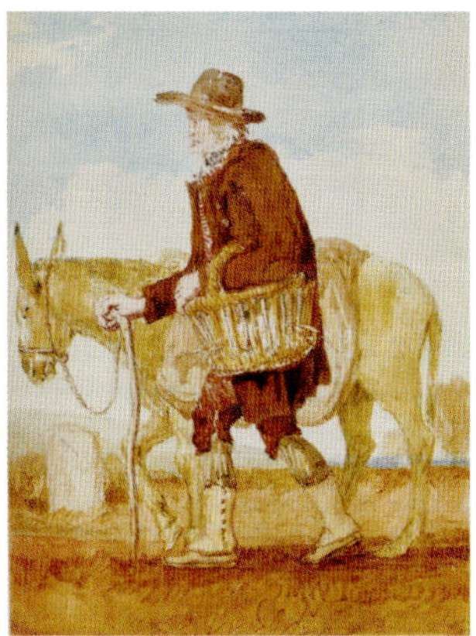

Old Man with a Donkey
(possibly a portrait of Turner's father), ?c. 1810–15

son, a head below the average standard, spare and muscular, with small blue eyes, parrot nose, projecting chin, fresh complexion, an index of health, which he apparently enjoyed to the full. He was a chatty old fellow, and talked fast; but from speaking through his nose, his words had a peculiar transatlantic twang. He was more cheerful than his son, and had always a smile on his face. When at Sandycombe Lodge, he was to be seen daily at work in his garden, like another Laertes, except on the Tuesday,

> which was Brentford market day, when he was often to be seen trudging home with his weekly provisions in a blue handkerchief, where I have often met him, and asking him after Turner, had answer, 'Painting a picture of the battle of Trafalgar' &c. &c. (I, 7)

MAIDEN LANE, COVENT GARDEN (LONDON VS. VENICE)

That narrow, smoky defile, Maiden Lane, now so sacred a place in the eyes of many Englishmen, does not perhaps seem to the 'outer barbarians,' or art Gentiles, a lane specially consecrated by great Mother Nature as a fit reception-chamber for one of her greatest minds, for one of those large-brained thinkers and doers that set their broad shoulders to the world's wheel, that keep it out of ruts, and urge it on at a nobler and more vigorous speed. (I, 7–8)

I remember the house well—I have been up and down and all over it. The old barber's shop was on the ground floor, entered by a little dark door on the left side of Hand Court. The window was a long, low one; the stairs were narrow, steep, and winding; the rooms low, dark, and small, but square and cosy, however dirty and confined they may have been. Turner's bedroom, where he generally painted, looked into the lane, and was commanded by the opposite windows. The house where I suppose he

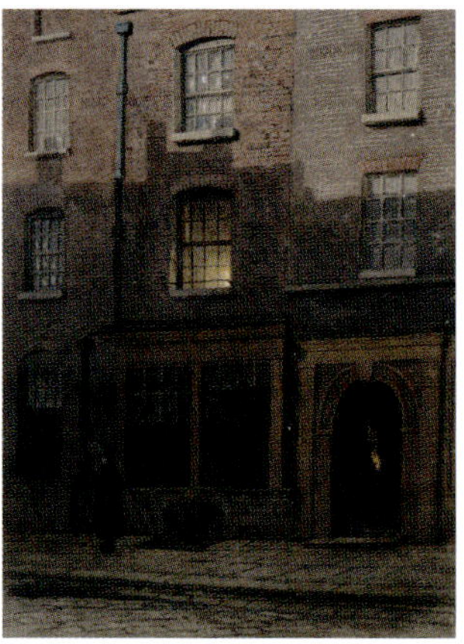

John Wykeham Archer, Childhood House of J. M. W. Turner, Hand Court, 1852

afterwards went to for more quiet and room, is at the end of Hand Court, and is on a larger scale, with two windows in front; but it must have been rather dark, though less noisy than his father's house.[I, 23–4 fn]

It was not a 'bright look-out,' as sailors say, for a child in the first scene of his life-drama. No beauty or loveliness surrounded him; the age, too, was poor, the religion faithless and half dead. The ebony dome—the dull red roofs—the squalid life—the low ideal, were far unlike, says a certain great poet, were far unlike such visions of beauty as Venice showed to the boy Titian and the stripling Giorgione.* For them there was a city of marble—nay! 'a golden city,' paved with fluid emerald; 'eternal sapphire above—fresh free winds around and apocalyptic sunsets ever in the distance;' ethereal strength of Alps, dream-like vanishing in high procession beyond the Torcellan shore, and blue islands of Paduan hills poised ever in the golden west.

But let us not think Heaven unkind in placing her genius in a Covent Garden kennel. Brave souls have broken from meaner homes than that; kind Nature, too, has so many compensations: Turner was not born either, we must remember, to be the joyous genius of a joyous age; but to be the sad genius of a sad age.[I, 9-10]

EARLY AMBITIONS

Turner's first ambition was, not to copy, but to go into the fields and make sketches. A son of [Thomas] Stothard, now living, perfectly remembers his father relating to him, that in early life he went one day to Turner's shop in Maiden Lane, to get his hair cut, when the barber remarked to him in conversation, 'My son is going to be a painter.' About this time he fell in with [Thomas] Girtin the painter.[I, 17]

There is an early drawing of Turner's, *Margate Church*,

* See Ruskin's 'The Two Boyhoods', in *Modern Painters V* (1860), Ch. IX.

executed by the artist when he was about nine years old.* The building is far from perpendicular. It is one of the boy's earliest works that I have yet heard of. I myself have not seen drawings of an earlier date than his eleventh or twelfth year.[I, 18]

BRENTFORD: THE COUNTRY EDEN

Turner received the elements of instruction at the Brentford Free School, as day-boarder. It was here his talent first showed itself. In his way to and from that seat of learning, he amused himself by drawing with a piece of chalk on the walls the figures of cocks and hens.[I, 7]

The green fields of Paradise to him were the fields round vulgar Putney and lonely, peaceful Twickenham. The birds must have been to him as little flying angels newly transformed, and the air seemed of sapphire brightness and transparency.[I, 20]

To these early days in the country Turner owed much … [What he saw] reached his young heart, stirred him to poetry, and roused his veneration, his sense of sublimity, and his love for the beautiful. I think that no place breeds so strong a reactionary love for poetry and art as London—the vast, the negative, the miserable, the loathsome, the great, the magnificent.[I, 22]

* Private collection

MARGATE

He is now thirteen, growing up short and thick-set, and with large but handsome features; clear grey-blue eyes and arched eyebrows; careless in dress, and generally a sturdy, determined, prudent boy, with an irresistible bias towards art. For I know not what reason, father determines now to send William to his third school, a Mr. Coleman's, at Margate.[I, 24–5]

Margate then must have seemed a wild, little seaside village, at a vast distance from London, and schooling, no doubt, was cheap there. Turner formed an acquaintance there with the pleasant family of a favourite schoolfellow. No wonder he retained to the end of his life an ardent love for the breezy piers and white-walled cliffs of that Kentish bathing-place; for it was there he first saw the sea, there he first learnt the physiognomy of the waves, and there, too, he first fell in love, that great revolution in the mind of youth, that temporary restoration to the lost Eden.[I, 25]

ARCHITECTS AND BLUE SKIES

All this time Turner is colouring prints and washing in skies for architects. When artist friends in after life used to express their wonder to Turner at his having ever worked, as a boy, at half-a-crown a night putting in Indian-ink skies to amateurs' sketches, he used to say, defensively, 'Well, and what could be better practice?' and he was right, for he acquired facility from those sketches, and he learnt the value of gradation from the habit of using only one colour. It prepared him to work for the engraver, who has but one colour, and has to make the most of it.[(I, 66)]

One of his chief employers at this time was Mr. [William] Porden, an almost unknown architect, who built part of the absurd Brighton Pavilion for the Prince Regent. Turner swept in gravel walks winding up to Porden's Grecian porches, floated blue skies over his composite pediments, and pencilled in grass-tufts and patches of docks for the foregrounds to his Corinthian mansions.

Porden was delighted with the lad's facility and quickness. The designs gained much by the setting. Perhaps dilettanti praised the style, and thought it prudent Porden's (for such suppressions have been). Porden, in full dress, comes one day to Hand Court, and blandly proposes to take young Turner as an apprentice without a premium.

Oily Mr. Porden! without a premium, indeed! Why, in seven years young Turner would have painted you drawings worth three times your premium. Go to! you are, I fear, an oily Pecksniff, trying to cheat a man, and all the time professing a deceitful kindness with a lying smile![(I, 47–8)]

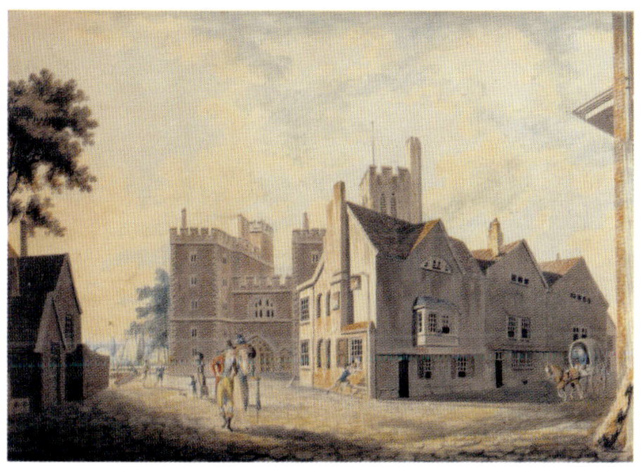

A View of the Archbishop's Palace, Lambeth, 1790
The first work Turner exhibited at the Royal Academy

THE ROYAL ACADEMY

At this same time, then, or soon after, Turner, must have become a student of the Royal Academy.[1, 56]

Turner goes, of course, through the usual ceremonies and forms. Draws a Greek statue a foot long, which he shades carefully, and sends in, after some two months' stippling, as a proof of his fitness. …

He must draw another Greek statue as good as the first—anatomy, and light and shade and outline, all correct; also, as ghastly companion, a correct drawing of a human skeleton. These accepted, he will receive the 'bone,' or exhibition-ticket, good for so many years; and then he will be a full-plumed Royal Academy student, entitled to compete for admission into the 'Life School'.[I, 57–8]

It was in 1790, that being the year after Turner entered the Academy, when he exhibited for the first time at Somerset House, which would make Turner fifteen at the time.[I, 65]

FIRST TOUR TO BRISTOL, 1791

It is to this period of Turner's life that we may safely refer some of the many visits paid to Bristol, to a Mr. Harraway [actually Narraway], an old friend of his father's, and a fishmonger and glue-boiler in Broadway.

Many of his large drawings executed at this time, and given to Mr. Harraway, are extant. They were executed at different periods, and show the various stages of maturity that his mind successively attained. The same family once possessed another rude and early drawing of Turner's, *Cote* [actually Stoke] *House, Durdham Down, the seat of Sir Henry Lippincotte*, with Sir Henry, Turner himself, and old Mr. Harraway all in the foreground. Perhaps the boy had been seen drawing down at the Hotwells, and was asked up, all red and smiling, to Cote House.[I, 43–44]

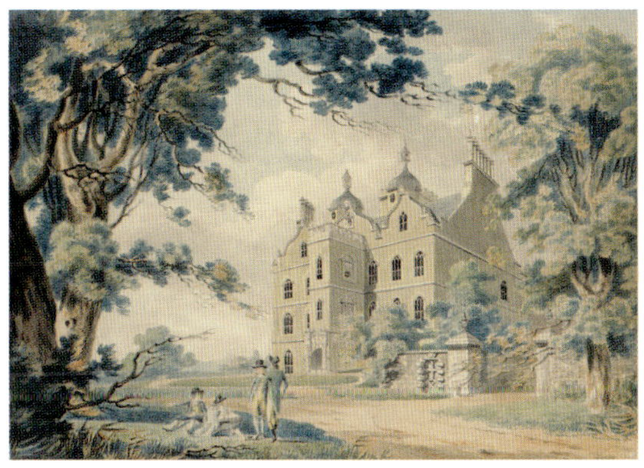

View of Stoke House, near Bristol, c. 1790

In one early tour Turner is said to have lived four or five days on a guinea. He once told a friend that in some of his early tours, the price of the drawing, thirty pounds, did not pay his expenses; upon which he took to a broader, quicker style. In his tours for Mr. Cadell [in the 1830s] he would never saddle the publisher with the expense of a post-chaise, but took the ordinary mail coach.[I, 77]

FIRST PAINTING IN OILS

It was in the parsonage at Foot's-Cray, the house of the father of Dr. Nixon, the present Bishop of Tasmania, that

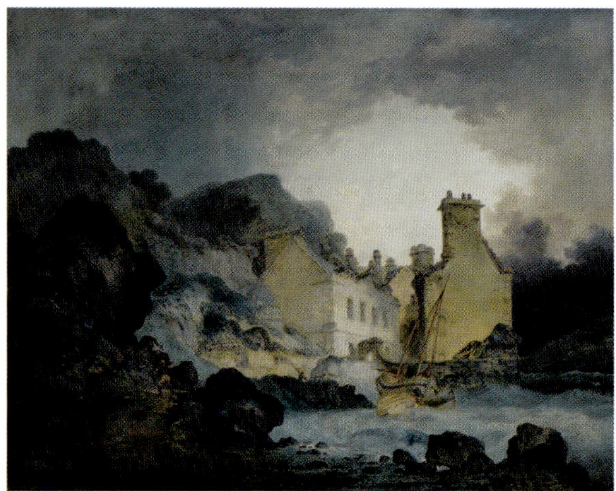

The Rising Squall, Hot Wells, from St Vincent's Rock, Bristol, 1792

Turner's first oil picture (according to this tradition) was finished. It was a view of Rochester Castle,* with fishermen drawing their boats ashore in a gale of wind. It is well drawn, says one who has seen it, and bears a strong resemblance to De Loutherbourg. It is carefully and thinly painted, with thin scumbles of semi-opaque colour, used

* Actually Hot Wells at Bristol. The painting was with Sotheby's, London, 2 July 2025, lot 28.

in so fluid a state as still to show where it has run down the picture from his brush. It shows us the experienced water-colour painter using a new and denser material timidly and with a hesitating hand, that was soon to grow more daring.[I, 77]

[This] was one of the earliest pictures that made critics think that a new poet had arisen.[I, 257]

TURNER AND GIRTIN AT DR. THOMAS MONRO'S 'ACADEMY'

Dr. Monro had many works by [John Robert] Cozens, which Turner must have studied and thought over much; and some of which I know Girtin copied by the Doctor's wish.

From Cozens, Turner learnt much, and indeed the poetry of his art descended from Cozens in lineal descent. [Edward] Dayes had made him minute and careful.[I, 85]

On winter evenings (for in summer the lads were out on the Thames or in the country sketching) Turner and Girtin repaired to the Doctor's costly furnished house, and spent an hour or two in sketching and in colouring. The 'good Doctor', as Turner always called him in after-life, was in the habit of giving them half-a-crown each for their night's drawing, and a supper afterwards.[I, 92]

THOMAS GIRTIN (1775–1802)

Girtin was in early life apprenticed to Dayes, an architectural draughtsman, who had no sympathy for his genius, and treated him as a mere means of making money. Dayes was a conceited, jealous man, who eventually got embarrassed and committed suicide, it was supposed, from envy at the progress of his contemporaries—Turner and his old pupil.

Girtin, naturally bold and reckless, began soon to find that he was more than paying back by work the premium paid for his apprenticeship. He refused to wash in any more skies for Dayes, and demanded in justice the cancelling of his indentures.[I, 102]

Like Turner, he also studied Cozens for gradations of tone and ærial effect (you always feel you can breathe in one of Cozens's landscapes). From Piranesi, Girtin got vigour; from Canaletti his firm staccato touch; but his sense of art began to lessen his desire for truth, while with Turner, the same sense only increased it. His boldness is often recklessness; his vigour, carelessness and disregard of form; his breadth, always admirable, is sometimes conventional, and obtained by the sacrifice of truth. Girtin was a great artist, but he was not a poet, as Turner was.[I, 105–6]

Girtin established a sketching-class, which was open to patrons and amateurs as well as to artists. For three years this little society of enthusiasts met on winter evenings for mutual improvement. 'No little coterie could be more respectable,' says a frequent visitor. How often the talent of the barber's son must have been discussed at these pleasant evenings. They met alternately at each other's houses. The subject was taken from an English poet, and each man treated it in his own way. The member at whose house they met supplied stained paper, colours, and pencils, and all the sketches of the evening became his property … Beautiful works of art were often produced in this impromptu way, and the first ideas of great pictures were often suggested in dreamy hints that had sometimes a charm greater almost than that of the completed truth. Turner would never join this club; he preferred working in solitude, and he could not at this time afford to sell a ten-pound sketch for a cup of tea and a slice of bread and cheese. Perhaps, too, he was at this time slow in execution, and found two hours insufficient to elaborate any thought worth painting.[I, 108–9]

But gradually the bony hand came nearer and nearer, pushing [Girtin] onward towards the clean square-cut grave. Fame might put by her crown—it was not to be for him.[I, 115]

Turner, who always loved to speak of 'Poor Tom,' must have pondered much on this death, and have set to work with greater vigour than ever to develop his own talent, that might so soon be quenched in the cold earth. His generous heart could never have felt envy at Girtin's talent, whatever foolish friends and small malignant enemies may have done to rouse his jealousy: he was incapable of such a base passion.(I, 115–6)

Turner painted his friend Girtin's portrait in oil.* It is, I believe, still extant, but I have never seen it. I know well the admirable stalwart likeness Cornish [John]Opie took of him.† It shows me the frank, generous nature of the hearty, kindly fellow whom Turner and every one would love; the strong black brow, the crisp dark hair curling down over it, the keen, far-seeing eyes, the bold chin, the bold features. And as I look at it I think of Turner's words in after-life: (I, 117–18) 'If Tom Girtin had lived,' he used to say, with true generosity and pathos, 'I should have starved.' All through his life, the sight of one of Girtin's yellow drawings made his eyes sparkle, and often would he earnestly declare that he would lose a finger willingly, could he learn how to produce such effects.(II, 35)

Of late years Turner often expressed to Mr. Trimmer and Mr. Field his high opinion of Girtin's power. 'We were friends to the last,' he used to say, 'although they did what they could to separate us.' How much regret and tenderness there is in these words.(II, 36)

* Untraced † National Portrait Gallery, London

EMBARKING ON TRAVELS IN ENGLAND

There was no county in England to which Turner was so much attached as Yorkshire. Here his first great successes were attained, and here he met his kindest patrons. It was here, too, on the wolds and beside the banks of the Wharfe that he first (after Wales) saw really wild scenery.[1, 150]

I go to few places in England but I seem to see Turner. I find him on the Derbyshire hills, and among the ruins of Yorkshire Abbeys. I meet his ghost on the banks of the Wharfe, and on the seashore at Dover. I come across him in the green hop fields of Kent, and in the marshes of the Thames. I see his short, stalwart spirit pacing about the Scotch moors, and around the pebbly margins of Scotch lakes. I never go on the Thames, and look at St. Paul's, but I seem to see him boat past me, and steer on to that old loved Chelsea. In Wales, at Oxford, in Sussex, in Wiltshire, I still cannot drive away the remembrance of him. He haunts Fonthill, Petworth, and Tabley; he meets one at every old castle and abbey in England; he has been on every river, and in every county. He did much to spread the fame of the beauty of our country.[1, 197]

Following pages: Norham Castle: Sunrise, c. 1797

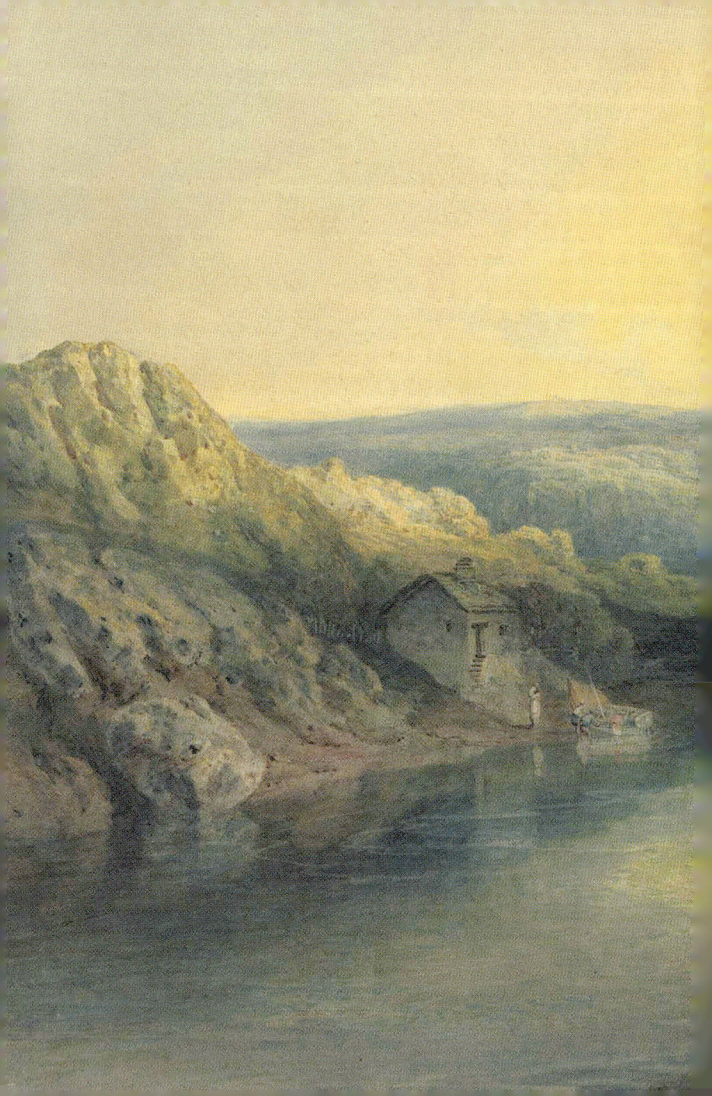

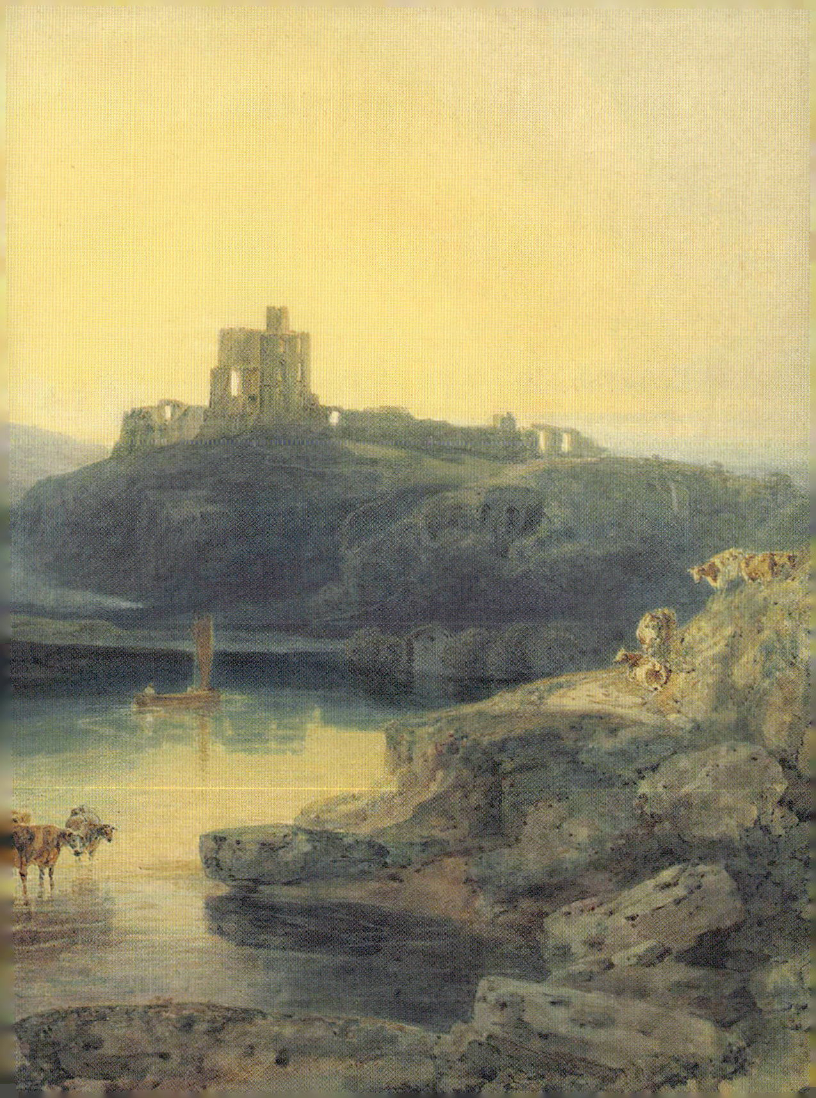

TURNER PORTRAITS, 1800

There is a current notion prevailing, that no portrait of Turner exists. Perhaps no great artist was oftener sketched; from behind pictures, from the ambush of dark corners of exhibition rooms, the busy pencil was perpetually recording him.

Mr. [William] Mulready drew him,* Mr. [Sir John] Gilbert drew him,† Mr. [John] Linnell drew him,† Mr. [George] Dance drew him,‡ Mr. Monro drew him, Mr. Fawkes drew him;§ and so, says Mr. Peter Cunningham, in his very inaccurate memoir, did Mr. [Daniel] Maclise** and Mr. Charles Turner.††

Yet the painter never sat willingly but once. He had a settled idea that if the public saw his portrait, they would think less of his pictures.

I know for certain that he sat to Dance for the portrait published in 1800, when Turner was R.A., and twenty-five years old. This portrait is one of a series of Academician portraits published by George Dance. It shows us a handsome young man, with rather large features, a full,prominent nose, a fine, strong-willed chin, and a rather

* Untraced † National Portrait Gallery, London ‡ Royal Academy, London (see p. 40) § Both Indianapolis Museum of Art, Indianapolis, IN ** V&A, London (and for posthumous medal, see p. 258) †† British Museum, London

sensual mouth, the lower lip of which is fleshy, and the upper lip beautifully curved. The eyebrow is arched, and the eyelids long, presenting a great depth between the eye and the eyebrow. The forehead is full, but rather receding, and is covered with a stray wisp of hair, as Turner always kept it. The hair, close and thick, and rather stubborn-looking, is long behind, and tied with a ribbon. He wears a white cravat, the ends of which bulge out in front of his waistcoat. The cape of his coat is of immense width, and the lapels are thrown back in a careless, but still rather cavalier way. Indeed, in this portrait, unless Dance's pencil has flattered. Turner looks a frank, handsome-hearted young man of genius, as far as appearance goes. The portrait might be as well that of a young general or a young statesman, for the expression is at once winning and commanding.[(II, 314–5)*]

Turner's own portrait, as painted by himself, is rather brown in colour, but fine in expression.* The forehead is high, the rather too large nose cleverly concealed by being taken full-face. The lip is full, but not unduly so. The chin is strong and Napoleonic. The young artist wears a huge cape to his coat; the fashionable double waistcoat, and a full white handkerchief, with pendent ends, round his neck; the colour is wanting in tenderness, and in trying for breadth the greys have been sacrificed.

Turner's iron-grey eye (it was really blue), says Mr.

* Tate, London (see p. 2).

Goodall, seemed to strike through you. There was a great consciousness of power in it. When animated. Turner's eyes were quite handsome, says an old friend. Turner's eyes were blue as enamel, and were round, staring, and bull-like as those of Frederick the Great's.[II, 320]

SUMMARY OF TURNER'S ART LIFE

Before I proceed further, let me divide Turner's art life into three periods.

Mr. [John] Ruskin divides Turner's art life in the following way, and the division cannot be gainsaid;—

In Turner's first period, 1800 to 1820, he laboured as a student, imitating various old masters.

In his second period, 1820 to 1835, he worked on the principles of art he had discovered as a student, doing what the theories of art then required, and producing beautiful ideal compositions instead of mere transcripts of nature.

In the third period, 1835 to 1845, he abandoned the ideal, reproducing his own simple impressions of nature, and associating them with his own deepest feelings.

In 1845 his health gave way, and his mind and sight began to fail. The pictures' of the last five years of his life (he died in 1851) are, of wholly inferior value.[I, 258–9]

VANDERVELDE'S RIVAL, 1801

Mr. White, of Brownlow Street, possesses a picture exhibited by Turner in 1801, when he was working hard to rival Vandervelde, and to become a great marine painter, with all the ardour and sensitive ambition of the man. The picture is called *Dutch Boat in a Gale; Fishermen putting Fish on Board.** His greatest works at this time were all marine. The Duke of Bridgewater had just bought a large Vandervelde, the *Rising of a Storm*,† and the praise of this picture roused Turner, as the cackle about Claude led him afterwards to begin the *Liber*, and to paint the Carthaginian pictures.‡ The Dutch picture contained a packet, three boats, three ships, a hard, flat, inky sky, and sails in sunshine to contrast. Turner was determined to be larger, more boisterous and more real. He gives us a misty sky, heavy, louring clouds, a real muddy sea, one enormous line of wave, and a beam of light pointing out a distant vessel. The ships are the heavy one-masted Dutch galliots once common on the Thames. The three Dutch men-of-war signal with their colours to the distant coast.[1, 262–3]

* National Gallery, London † Toledo Museum, Toledo, OH ‡ *Dido building Carthage*, 1815, (National Gallery, London) and *Decline of the Carthaginian Empire* (Tate, London), 1817

Overleaf: Dutch Boat in a Gale; Fishermen Putting Fish on Board ('The Bridgewater Seapiece'), 1801

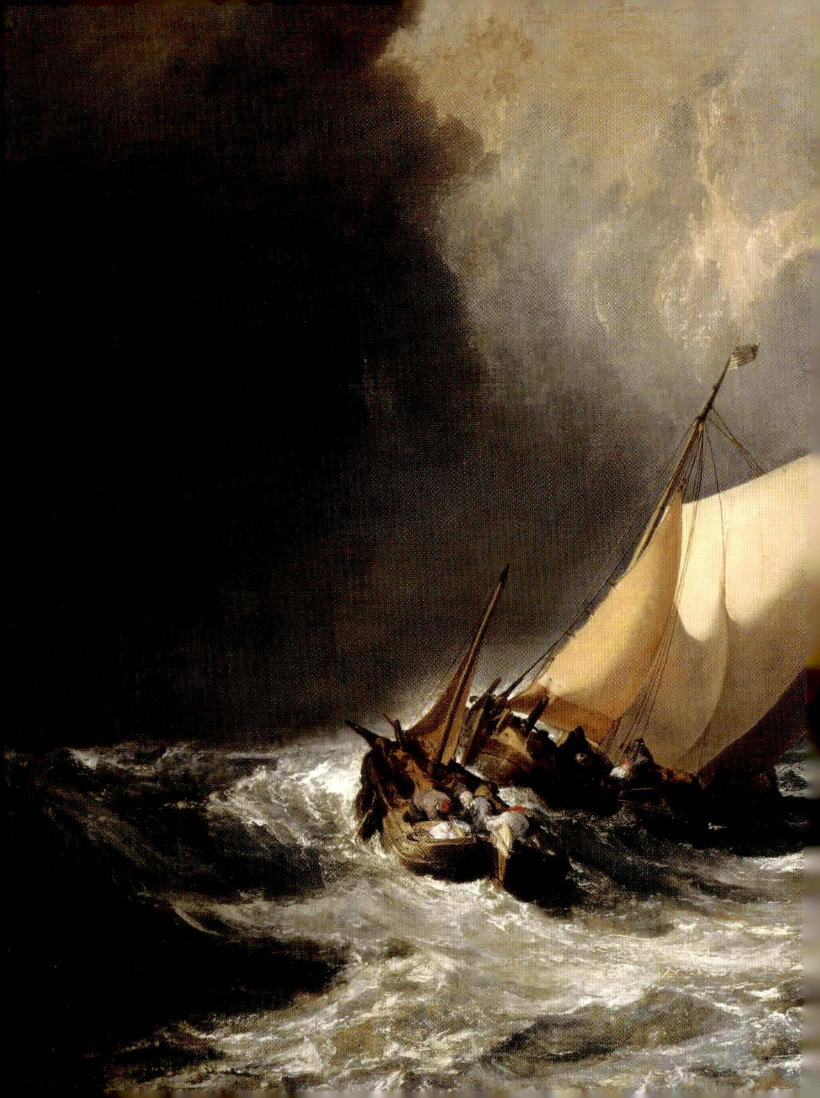

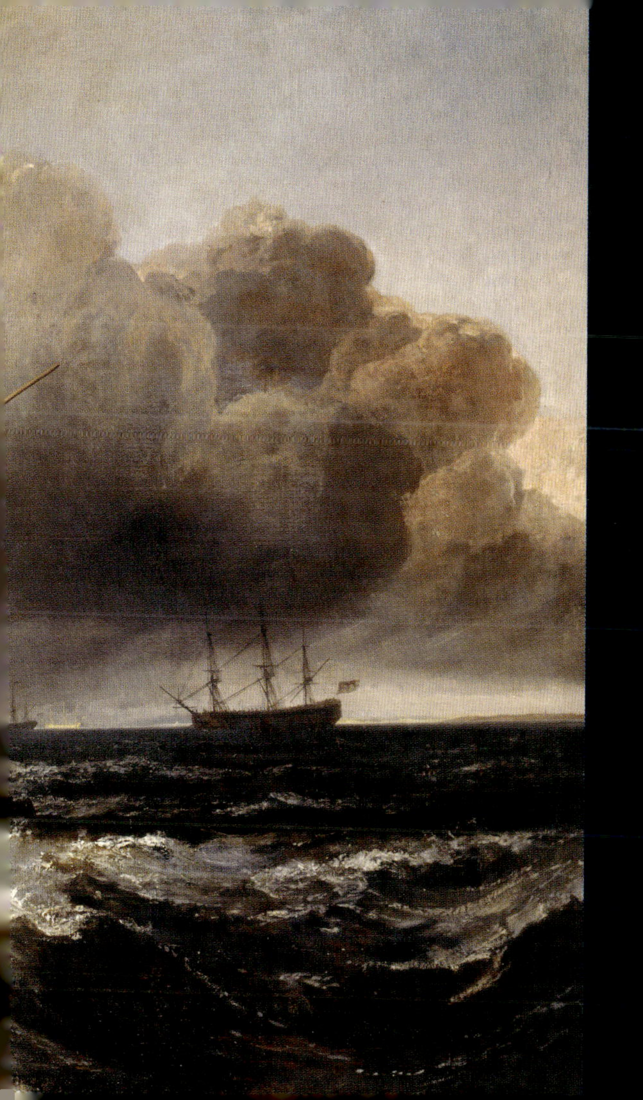

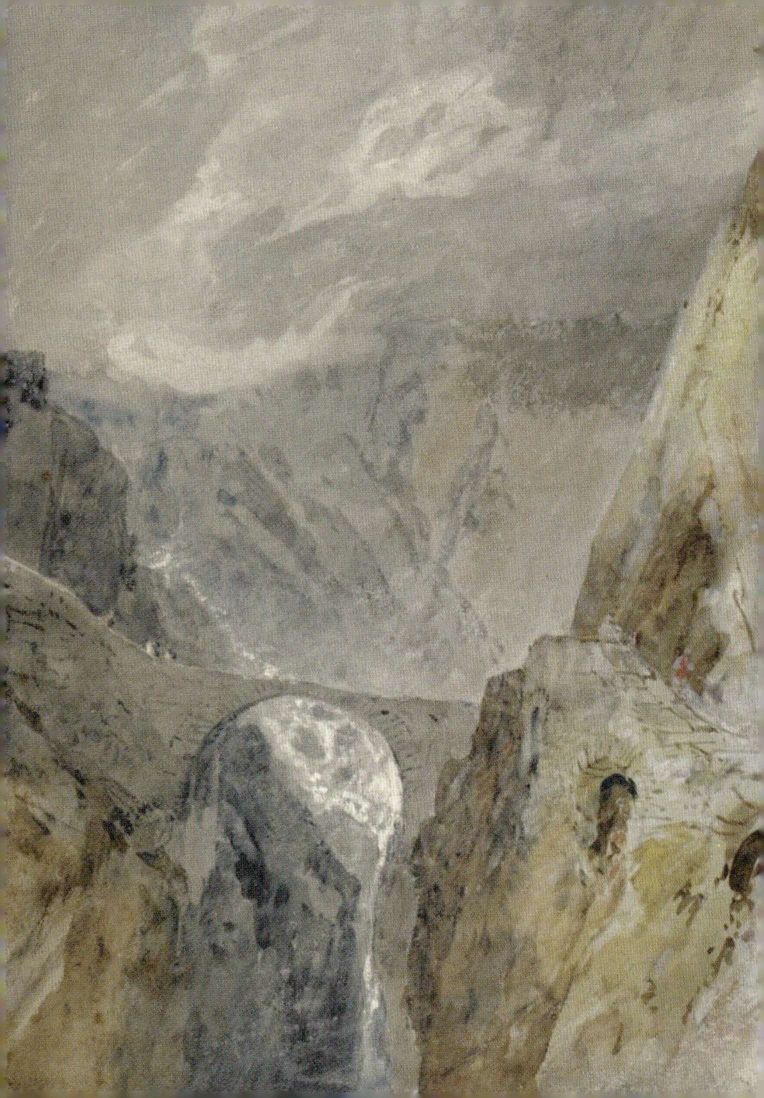

THE FIRST FOREIGN TOUR

Mr. [Ralph] Wornum, [Keeper of the National Gallery] an authority on the matter of dates, and dates alone, thinks Turner's first Continental tour was in 1801.* He says, the aforenamed Mr. Newby Lowson, an amateur, accompanied the painter on this, or a subsequent journey. Turner suffered his company only on condition that he never sketched any view he himself chose. Turner did not show his companion a single sketch.[(I, 223)]

In his first tour Turner seems to have had an eye for glaciers and fallen trees; but Mont Blanc and Grenoble were his favourite resting-places. He has a grand version of the Chartreuse, of the ascent to Courmayeur, and of the valley of the Isère. Grenoble he assails from every side with special predilection, determining, as it were, to engrave it in his mind.[(II, 351)]

When I think of Turner abroad, I remember my own travelling, and seem to see him wherever I turn, wherever I have myself been. I see him on the Cypressed Hill, looking down from San Miniato on the red-tiled dome

* Actually 1802, when visiting Europe was briefly possible after the Peace of Amiens.

Opposite: The Devil's Bridge and Schöllenen Gorge, 1802

Overleaf: Châteaux de St Michael, Bonneville, Savoy, 1803

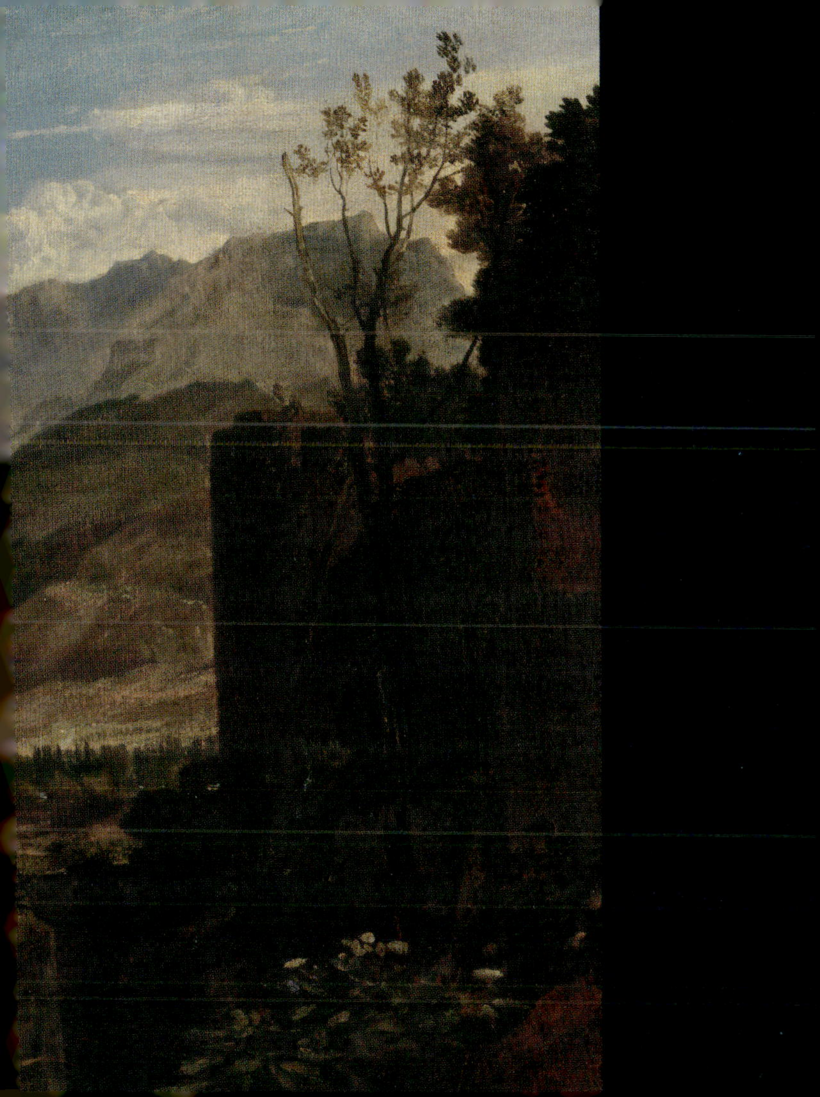

of Florence, on the Arno, and among the sapling trees of the Cascini. I see him at Naples, where, in the calm sunshine, Vesuvius feathers up its quiet plume of pure white smoke. I see him at Rome under the shadow of the massy double arches of the Coliseum. I see him on the Montanvert, watching the keen icy Aiguille pierce the sunset. I see him on the blue Moselle, and, as the vessel floats on, dreaming of a still fairer river, and of still more radiant skies. I see him at Paris, in Père Lachaise, looking down on the little dome of the Invalides, blue in the distance. I see him where Schaffhausen thunders, and where St. Gothard glooms.[I, 222]

THE *SHIPWRECK*

In 1805 Turner painted his celebrated picture, never exhibited, the *Shipwreck*,* for Sir John Fleming Leicester, afterwards Lord de Tabley, which C. Turner, J. Burnet, and F. Fielding afterwards engraved. This great picture was exchanged by Sir John for the *Sun rising in a Mist*,† now in the National Gallery, Lady Leicester having lost a

* Turner first visited France, Belgium and Germany in 1817, Italy in 1819, and further explored these countries and also Switzerland, Luxembourg, Denmark, and Bohemia, in Continental trips most years between 1821 and 1835, and every year between 1838 and 1844.

* Tate, London (see pp. 74–75) † National Gallery, London (see p. 86–7)

favourite nephew at sea, and being unable to bear the associations the scene called up. The painter has represented a large Indiaman becoming a wreck, while fishing-boats endeavour to rescue the crew. The wreck is labouring in a frightful sea. In the foreground are three boats, not by any means out of danger, and crowded with frightened, huddled groups of men and women. Some of the passengers are dropping from the bowsprit into the boat; the boat, in danger, is partly hidden by a wave. The broken rudder floats by on the dark and dirty water, which is opaque and cordy, and of a uniform grey, as if seen from a distance through rain and mist. The figures are admirably composed, and the objection of nobody looking wet is of no great weight, since coarse woollen sea-cloths have not a refractive surface, wet or dry. No marine painter ever painted with so sailor-like a mind as Turner.(I, 266–7)

TURNER'S *LIBER STUDIORUM*

From Mrs. Wheeler, the daughter of one of Turner's best friends, Mr. [William Frederick] Wells, the artist, I have received the following interesting record of their friendship:—

I had a life-long acquaintance with the late Mr.

Overleaf: The Shipwreck, 1805

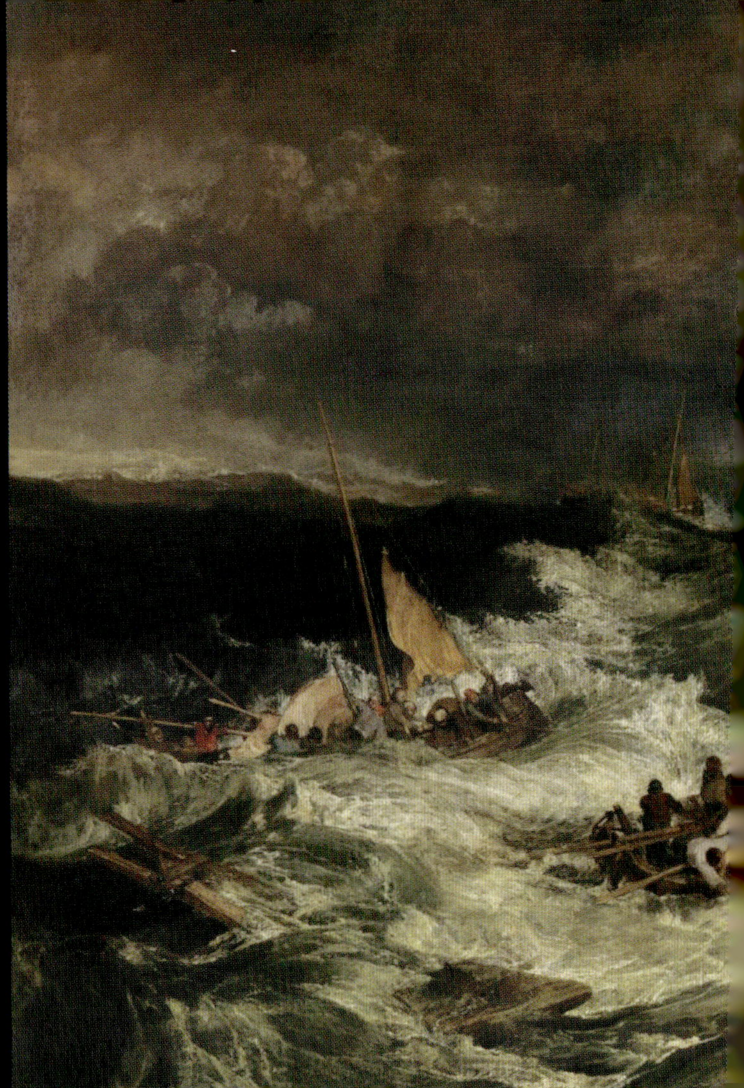

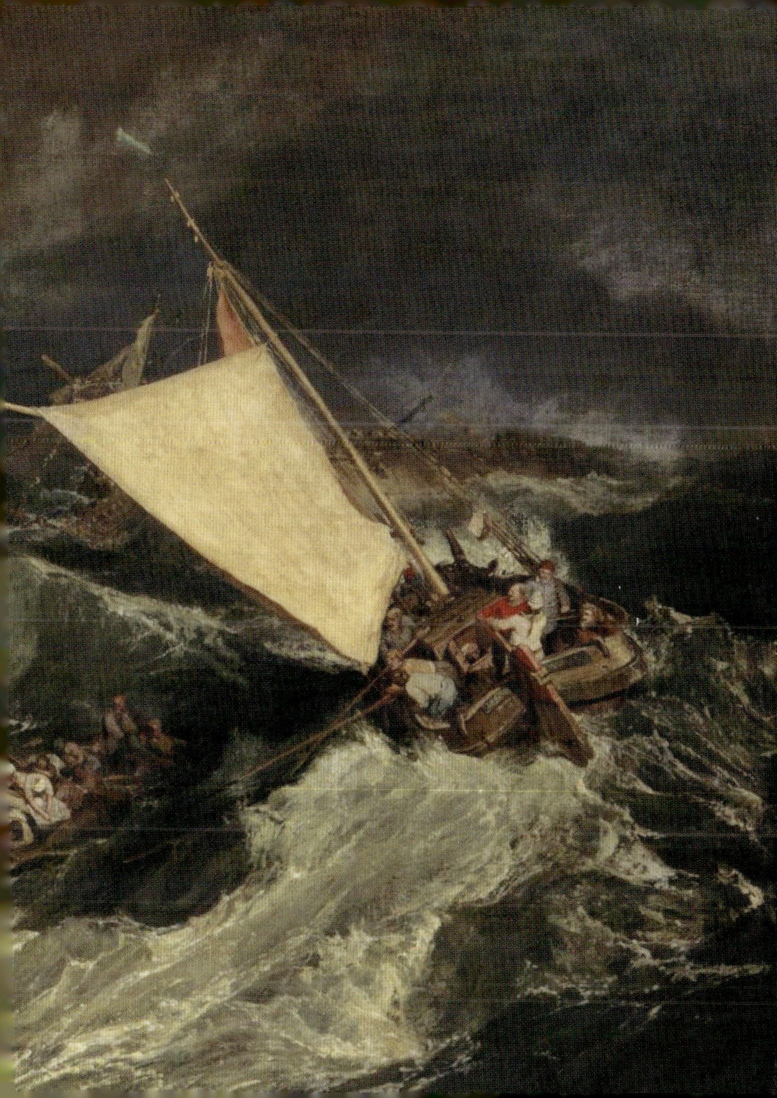

Turner, my father being one of his earliest and most esteemed friends.(II, 53)

Turner's celebrated publication, the *Liber Studiorum*,* entirely owes its existence to my father's persuasion, and the drawings for the first number were made in our cottage at Knockholt. He had for a long time urged upon Turner the expediency of making a selection from his own works for publication, telling him that it would surely be done after his death, and perhaps in a way that might not do him that justice which he could ensure for himself. After long and continued persuasion. Turner at length gave way; and one day, when he was staying with us in Kent (he always spent a part of the autumn at our cottage), he said, 'Well, Gaffer, I see there will be no peace till I comply; so give me a piece of paper. There, now, rule the size for me, and tell me what I am to do.' My father said, 'Well, divide your subject into classes—say. Pastoral, Marine, Elegant Pastoral, and so forth—which was accordingly done. The first drawings were then and there made, and arranged for publication. This was in the autumn of 1806.(II, 55)

* The *Liber* eventually included 71 mezzotints made after sepia watercolours prepared by Turner, and was published between 1807 and 1819.

CLAUDE AND THE *LIBER*

Turner deeply felt the injustice of Sir George Beaumont's prejudices, as well as the influence he had in picture society to direct all taste and to concentrate it on Claude; the painful knowledge of these facts gave rise, no doubt, to Turner's bequeathing two of his best pictures to the nation, on condition that they were placed side by side with two of Claude's best pictures, in order that posterity might do him that justice that either ignorance or something worse denied him while living;* in the same spirit, and in defence of himself as an artist, did Turner commence his wonderful, beautiful, and highly estimated work of the *Liber Studiorum*, as compared with the *Liber Veritatis* of Claude.[I, 270]

Turner had not much business at the time, and thought that he could profitably employ his time by rivalling Claude. He had intended to publish one hundred numbers; but no more than seventy ever appeared, for during the time that this seventy took to publish, Turner had become more successful, and he did not care then to spend his time in speculation.

For the earlier numbers he employed Mr. Lewis, the

* *Dido Building Carthage* and *Sun Rising in a Mist*

engraver, to whom he first paid five guineas a mezzotint, and then eight. This was totally inadequate for the time and trouble spent on them, and the result of this hard bargain was a quarrel that lasted fifteen years. But eventually Turner had to pay Mr. Charles Turner from eight to ten guineas, and I believe the price to other engravers rose at last as high as twelve guineas. Yet even Turner could never have thought that a copy of the *Liber* would one day sell for £3000, or the engraver believe that proofs which he had actually used to light the fire would sell for eight or ten guineas, or that he would be offered twenty-five guineas for any residue he could find of them.[I, 270–1]

Turner's 'book' was intended to show his command of the whole compass of landscape art, and the boundless and matchless richness of his stores both of fact and invention. They showed his fearlessness of plagiarism, and were so many bold challenges to all his contemporaries.[I, 271]

Turner's knowledge of engravers' effects was so marvellous that he has been known, when dissatisfied with a plate, to sit down and change a sunrise into a moonrise. It was no unusual thing for him, when a plate of the *Liber* began to wear, to take it and reverse its whole effect, making all that was before light now dark, and all that was before dark now light. Indeed, the concentrativeness of his mind, and his knowledge of light and shade, were Turner's greatest characteristics. To reverse the scale of chiaroscuro in a plate at five minutes' notice is as difficult as it would be for a musician to change the key of a sonata of Beethoven and play it at once correctly at sight after having made the change. He covered the margins of proofs with advice and directions to his engravers.(I, 272)

The publication of the *Liber* stopped at the fourteenth number, making in all (including the frontispiece, which Turner somewhat ostentatiously gave to his subscribers) seventy-one plates. The great work, strange to say, never paid, and it stopped as soon as Turner began the *England and Wales*,* and got other more profitable engagements. The ten plates intended for the fifteenth and sixteenth numbers of the work were more or less prepared for publication, and other plates were in various stages of progress.(I, 272–3)

The *Liber* was not successful in the business sense of the term. But the price that a fine and perfect copy will fetch at the present time would seem almost fabulous. Some time before Mr. Charles Turner's death, Messrs. Colnaghi bought all his *Liber* proofs and trials of effect for a large sum. When the money (£1500 I believe) was paid, the old engraver wrung his hands, and, with tears in his eyes, exclaimed: 'Why, good God, I have been burning banknotes all my life.' ...

* *Picturesque Views of England and Wales*, 91 engravings published between 1827 and 1838.

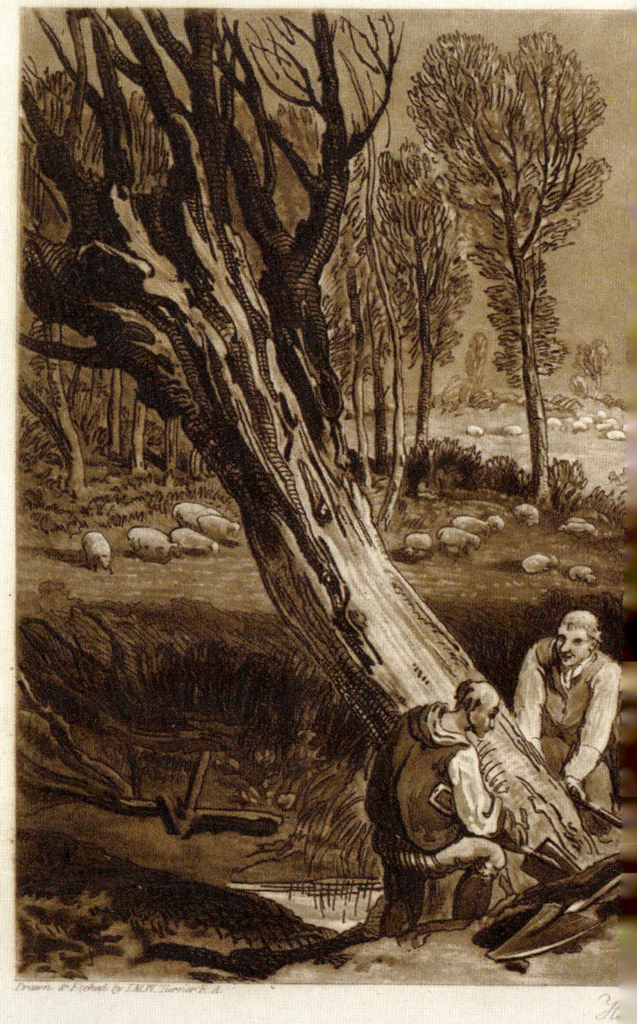

Drawn & Etched by I.M.W. Turner R.A.

Published M

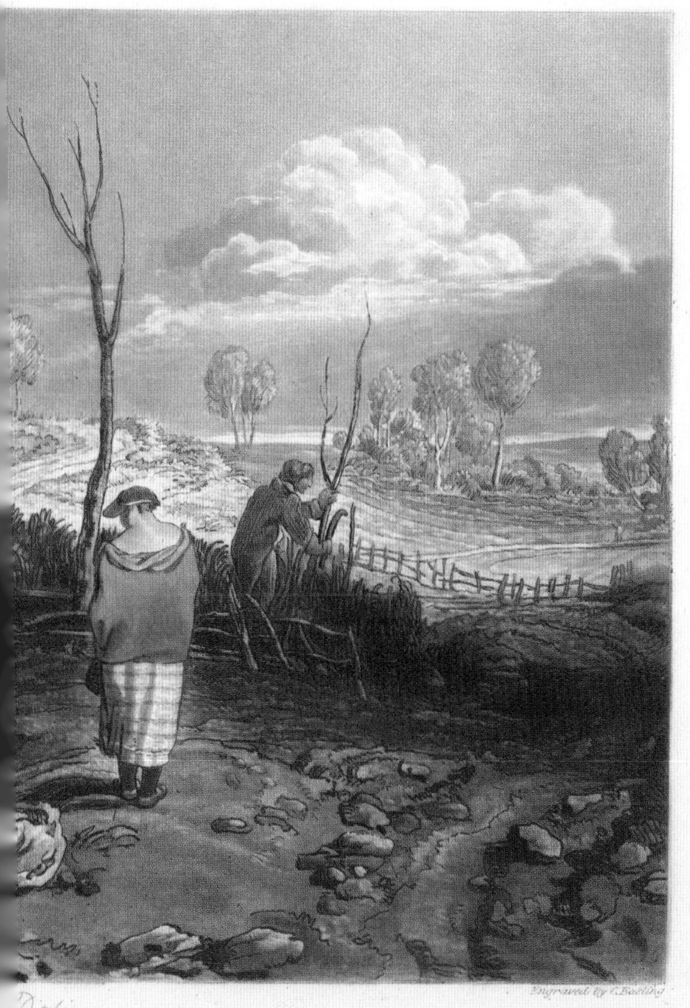

Engraved by C. Easling

Ditching

Queen Ann Street West

Mr. Ruskin, who dwells much and truly on the hopelessness and sadness of Turner's mind, says that sunset and twilight, and on ruins too, were his favourite effects. Speaking of the *Liber*, he shows that a 'feeling of decay and humiliation gives solemnity to all its simplest subjects, even to his view of daily labour. In the pastoral by the brook-side, the child is in rags and lame. In the *Hedging and Ditching*, the labourer is mean and sickly, the woman slatternly. The *Water-mill* is a ruin; the *Peat-bog* dreary.' (1, 286–7)

JOHN DILLON ON THE *LIBER*

Mr. Dillon, one of the great Turner collectors, says beautifully of his genius:—

> The premature discontinuance [of the *Liber]* would appear to have left incomplete the plan he had formed of formally arranging and expressly illustrating the varied objects of art under these or other heads; but the intellect which suggested the division, and the grasp of mind which sought to unite or combine them into a system, continued to direct all his after-labours, and to connect them into one harmonious whole. His mind was a generalizing

Previous pages: 'Hedging and Ditching', part X, plate 47 from 'the Liber Studiorum, 1812

> mind. Whatever his subject, there is always in him a 'touch of nature,' or a word of truth, which, recalling the past or revealing the future, connects the part with the whole, leads us from art to nature, and conducts us from the individual landscape to the universe. Thus, for example, it is not *Coniston Fells* only which we see; it is morning amongst the Fells.* It is not *Calais Sands*,† but the far-stretched shores of the ocean. It is not *Rome*, ancient or modern,§ or the *Fighting Temeraire tugged to her last berth to be broken up*;‡ it is not of these only we are reminded, but of the fate and fall of nations.(II, 331–2)

APPRECIATIONS OF TURNER'S EARLY PAINTINGS

I here condense a few of Mr. [John] Burnet's ([Sir David] Wilkie's engraver) excellent remarks on Turner's genius; they are as remarkable for their severe common sense as for the study, learning, and insight they display.

> Objects with distinct outline have a tendency to advance. [Richard] Wilson's idea was, that no foreground ought to be painted nearer than thirty feet,

* Tate, London † Bury Art Gallery, Bury St Edmunds § *Ancient Rome: Agrippina Landing with the Ashes of Germanicus* (Tate, London); and *Modern Rome – Campo Vaccino* (Getty Museum, Los Angeles, CA) ‡ National Gallery, London

for this reason the plants in his foreground are broad and blunt; where Turner makes foreground objects sharp and clear they are generally too small to interfere with the general breadth of his light and shade.

A multiplicity of objects prevents repose and breadth of shadow. The later works of Turner were treated in a lighter key to avoid spottiness. In the composition of skies, he is more original than any other painter. If the scene is bald, he breaks his skies into beautiful forms. If the piece is multitudinous, he used the sky for repose; he used the skies too for contrast of cool or warm colour. Objectionable lines he loses in the darks of his clouds; agreeable or characteristic lines he brigs into notice by opposition of light.

The skies are admirable, too, for perspective; the clouds duly diminish in size towards the horizon.

Turner's figures are not true as Raphael's, or correct as Paul Potter's, but 'they have a broad general look of nature.' We must not overlook the truth of character and bluff forms of Turner's fishermen and English sailors; they are true transcripts of the men they represent—they are portraits. Keeping the foreground light and warm makes the distance retire. Turner (unlike Wilson) does this.

Turner's earlier pictures are heavy; these he

gradually relieved by scumbling; nor even in his later works did he adopt rich glazings, but perfected his effects by washes of delicate opaque colours, that counteracted heaviness, but likewise destroyed richness and depth; this habit grew upon him till his lighter tints at last acquired a milky whiteness. The pictures of Claude, put beside those of Turner, look dirty and dingy. He never seems to have imitated Hobbema or Ruisdael, but to have extracted the essence of their pictures. The landscapes of Rubens and Rembrandt contain many of his principles.

Space seems to have been the guiding principle with Turner, while the pictures of many artists stretch merely from left to right of the canvas. His works lead the eye from the foreground to the distance; the light key of colour of the modern school owes its origin to Turner. Wilson, Gainsborough, and the dark Dutch school were henceforward laid on the shelf.

His light tints, the result of pearly scumblings, make his light pictures as luminous as his water-colour drawings. No one but Turner has represented the tremulous, dewy mist stealing along the ground in fading sunset shadows.[II, 197–8]

Overleaf: Sun Rising in a Mist (now called Sun Rising through Vapour: Fishermen Cleaning and Selling Fish), 1807

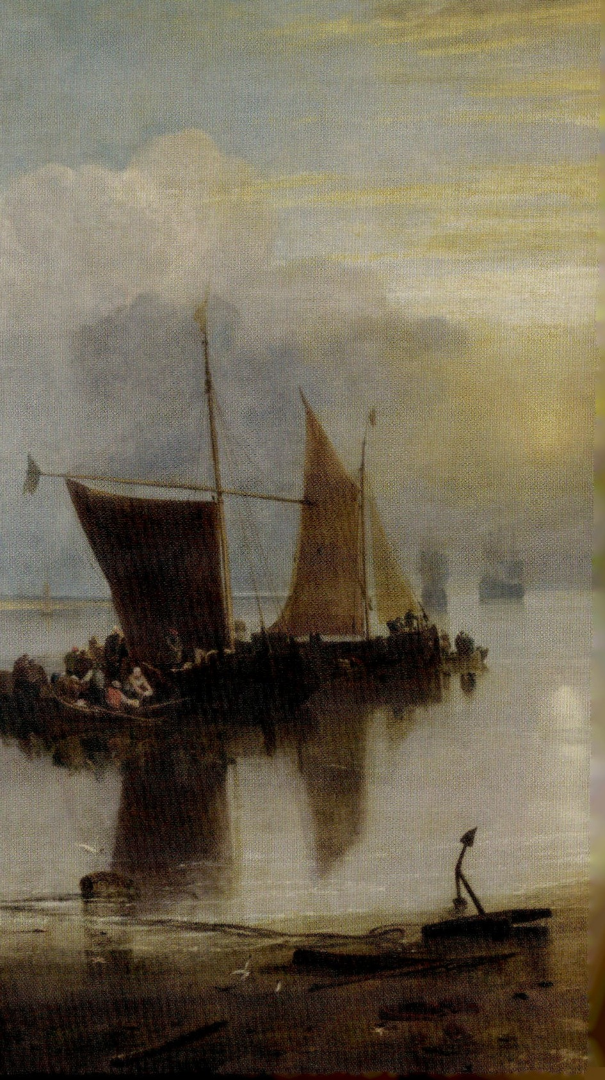

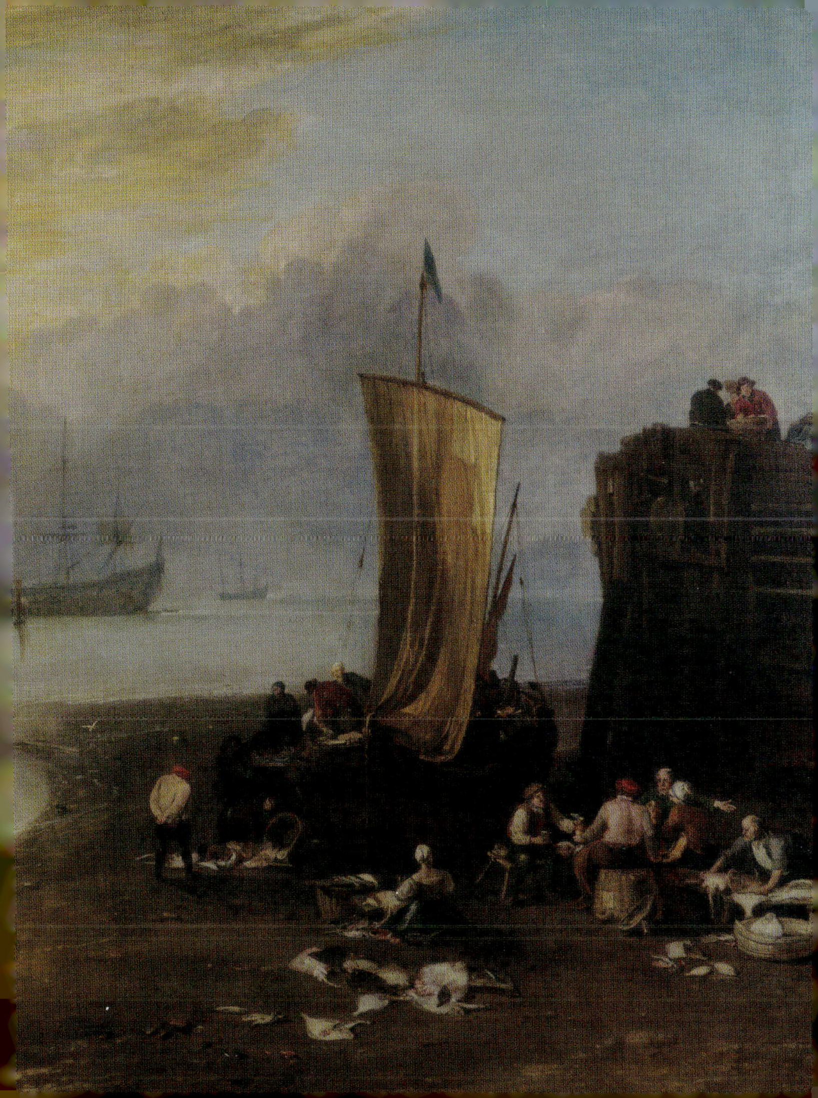

TEACHING PERSPECTIVE

When Turner lectured on perspective he was often at a loss to find words to express the ideas he wished to communicate. To aid his memory, he would now and then copy out passages, which, when referred to, he could not clearly read. Sometimes he would not make his appearance at all, and the disappointed students were sent away with the excuse that he was either ill or came from home without his lecture. But when the spirit did stir within him, and he could find utterance to his thoughts, he soared as high above the common order of lecturers as he did in the regions of art. His language was often elegant, his ideas original and most attractive.

Turner's want of expression rendered him almost useless as a Professor of Perspective, though he took great pains to prepare the most learned diagrams. He confessed that he knew much more of the art than he could explain. His sketch-books contain many drawings evidently made in preparation for these lectures. On one memorable occasion the hour had come for his lecture. The Professor arrived—the buzz of the students subsided. The Professor mounts his desk—every eye is fixed on him and on his black board. But the Professor is uneasy—he is perturbed. He dives now into one pocket—now into the other—no!

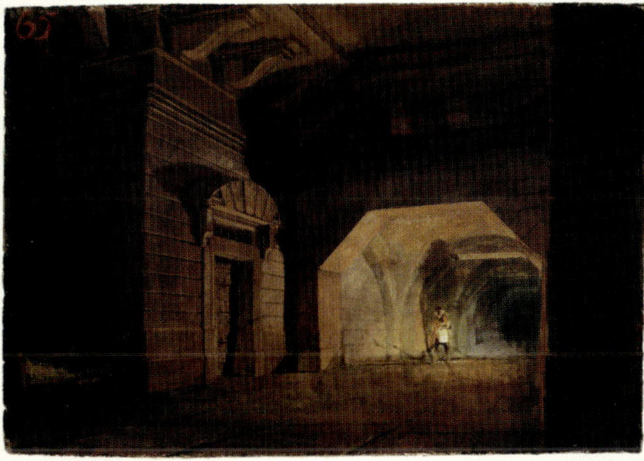

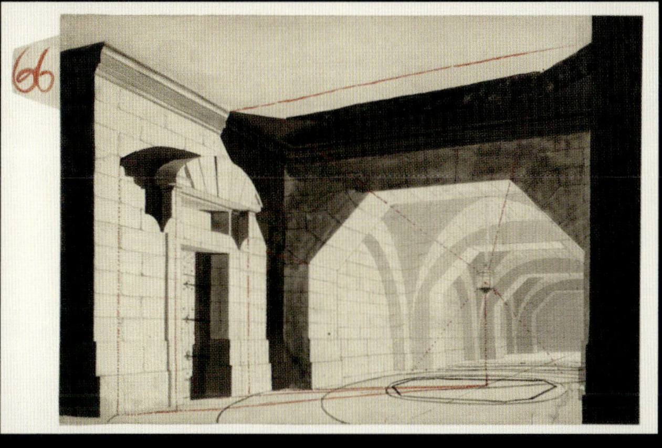

Diagrams used by Turner in his perspective lectures

Now he begins, but what he says is, 'Gentlemen, I've been and left my lecture in the hackney-coach.' I have no doubt the Professor would rather have painted five epical pictures than have had to deliver on lecture on Perspective.'(II, 107–8)

We also see, from the treasure-chests [containing the works on paper of the Turner Bequest], how conscientious and anxious Turner was about his perspective lectures; for here is a huge portfolio full of careful diagrams, massed-out shadows and reflected lights, huge perspective elevations of the dome of St. Peter's, the interchanged reflections of two glass balls, measured moonlight falling on the pillar of Trajan, the chiaroscuro of the jailer's lantern moving through the dark passages of Newgate, and studies of light and shade on hollow glass balls first empty and then half-filled. The exquisite knowledge and care of these diagrams is very conspicuous.(I, 325)

TURNER AND POETRY

Turner was a dumb poet; his brush was a lightning conductor, but his pen a torpedo.* Perhaps no one ever more vigorously wrestled for a blessing with the Angel of Poetry; perhaps no unlucky bard got more unlucky throws and more vexatious falls. He all his life, as his sketch-books prove, seems to have beguiled his time by efforts at verse,

* That is, it gives an electric shock that causes numbness.

generally utterly wanting in rhyme, and always lacking and stammering in sense. True rhythm, harmony, music, variety, everything is wanting; though there is sometimes a grand sounding line, sometimes a happy epithet offers a sustained dull clock-beam cadence imitative of Pope, showing that in Turner's brain the organ of 'Tune' was not altogether undeveloped.[II, 16]

There is hardly much hope for a poet who cannot even spell correctly. Turner felt poetry and painted poetry, but he could not write it. Persevering and yet indolent, he never took the trouble to learn the commonest laws of metre or rhythm. This desire to write verse was one of the *Fallacies of Hope*—a poem that, if it ever did exist, was not found among his sketches or papers after his death.[II, 33]

WALTER FAWKES (1769–1825)

One of Turner's oldest and dearest friends was [Walter] Fawkes, Esq., of Farnley Hall, near Otley, in Yorkshire. With this kind and hospitable squire Turner became acquainted about 1802, on one of his early topographical tours in Yorkshire, either to visit Richmond for Whittaker, or to sketch for Lord Harewood, who lives not far from Farnley.[II, 84]

Overleaf: Farnley Hall from the Junction of the Wharfe and the Washburn, with Fisherman, 1818

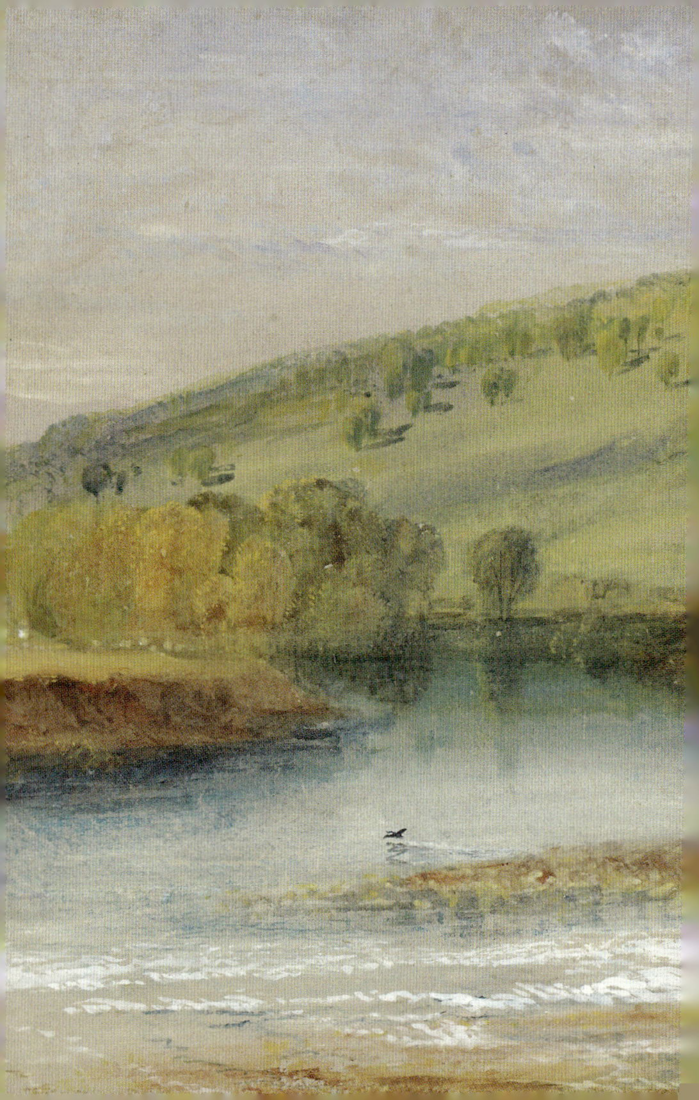

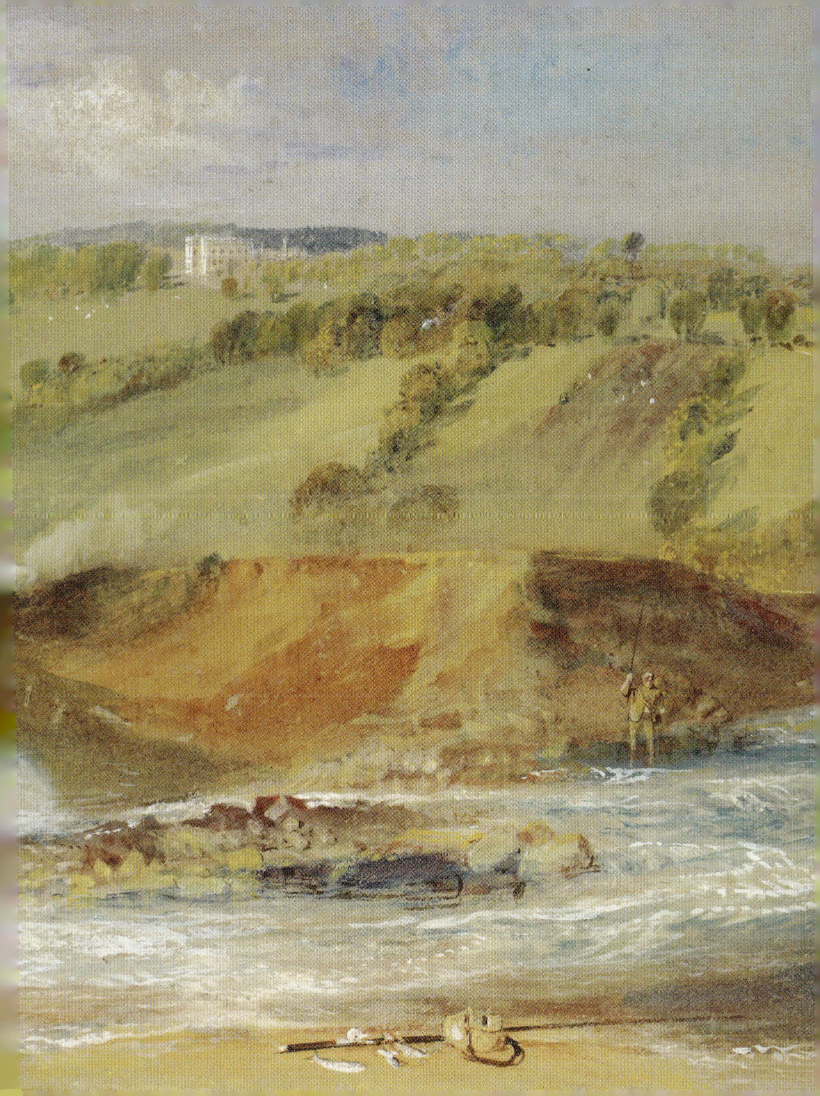

Farnley Hall looks down on the Wharfe, the river that flows beneath the walls of Bolton Abbey, one of Turner's favourite scenes. Those rounded scaurs that he all his life delighted in, and to some semblance of which he even moulded the eternal Alps, stretch in a misty and sun-barred line opposite the peacock-guarded terraces of the fine old Carolean hall.

At Farnley he delighted to be; there he shot and fished, and was as merry and playful as a child. There is still extant an exquisite water-colour drawing by him of a grouse that he himself shot and then immortalized.* There is also a drawing by him of Mr. Fawkes' tent on the moors, some six miles off; the servant is drawing corks, and the luncheon is being prepared.† It was on one of these occasions that, returning from shooting, nothing would satisfy Turner but driving the present Mr. Fawkes home a rough way, partly through fields, and in a tandem. Need I say that this precarious vehicle was soon capsized, amid shouts of good-humoured laughter? and henceforward, for that reason. Turner was known at Farnley by the nickname of 'Over-Turner'. A caricature of him by Mr. Fawkes still exists at Farnley.§ It is thought by old friends very like. It shows us a little Jewish-nosed man in an ill-cut brown

* Indianapolis Museum of Art, Indianapolis, IN † Private collection
§ Now Indianapolis Museum of Art, Indianapolis, IN

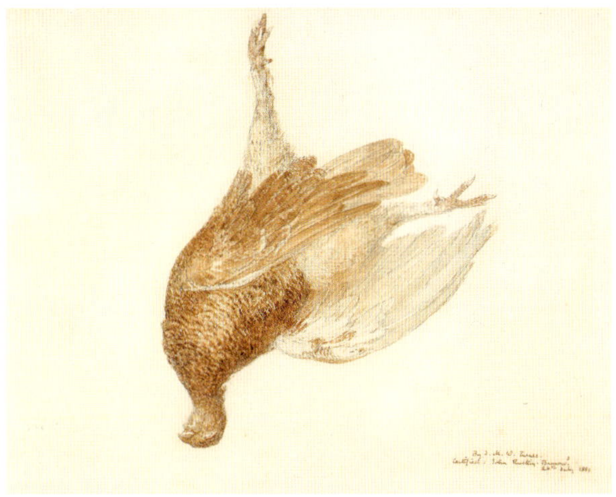

Dead Grouse, c. 1818

tail-coat, striped waistcoat, and enormous frilled shirt; his feet and hands are notably small. He sketches on a small piece of paper held down almost level with his waist.[II, 85–6]

The Farnley portfolios abound with his sketches of the house and estate, all rapidly but beautifully wrought; some are rough, some are *chef-d'œuvres*, particularly a brook-side with wood-flowers, and a water-scene. He drew the oak-panelled study and the white drawing-room, the Cromwell relics, and the staircase; the porches (one designed by himself), and the conservatory: the latter a beautiful fairy-like drawing of a greenhouse studded with grapes, hung with gay Chinese lanterns, crossed with errant sunbeams, and wonderfully elaborate in execution.*

The Farnley collection also includes a matchless series of drawings, forming a complete Rhenish tour. There are, I think, fifty-three [actually only 50]; they were done at the prodigious rate of three a day, and are miracles of skill, genius, and industry.†

On his return from this particular tour Turner landed at Hull, and came straight to Farnley. Before he had even taken off his great-coat he produced these drawings, rolled up slovenly and anyhow, from his breast-pocket. Mr. Fawkes, for some £500, bought them all, much, I have no doubt, to Turner's delight, for he could not bear that any series of his should be broken. He then said that Mr. Fawkes should have no expense in mounting them, and he stuck them rudely on cardboard with wafers, to the infinite detriment of the drawings, as it was found when they came to be re-mounted.

These Rhenish drawings are most exquisite for sad tenderness, for purity, twilight poetry, truth, and perfection

* Mostly in one private collection † Now dispersed, with the largest group at the British Museum, London

of harmony. They are to the eye what the finest verses of Tennyson are to the ear. They do what so few things on earth do: completely satisfy the mind. Few of them are gorgeous in colour; most are in a minor key, somewhat subdued and regretful, as if the present Rhine were not quite the Rhine of his earlier days. There is one, I remember, I christened *The Primrose*, from the pale, tender yellow atmosphere that wraps the whole scene.* Perhaps one of the most matchless is the saddest of all: *Twilight in the Lorelei*, all grey and dim, but just a speck of light here and there from boats on the river.† (II, 86–7)

Turner was so sensitive that he could never make up his mind to visit Farnley after his old friend's death; but when Mr. [Hawksworth] Fawkes went to London on one occasion, he took the Rhine drawings to show Turner. When they came to the grey *Lorelei*, tears sprang out of the old man's eyes, and glancing his hand over the faint light in the sky and water, as if he were working, he groaned, 'But Hawkey—but Hawkey!' as much as to say:

> When, ah! woeful *when*,
> How far unlike the now and then.§

* Private collection † Seven of the Fawkes Rhenish views include the cliff of the Lorelei § Lines from S. T. Coleridge, 'Youth and Age'

Overleaf: Lorelei (now known as Lurleiberg), 1817

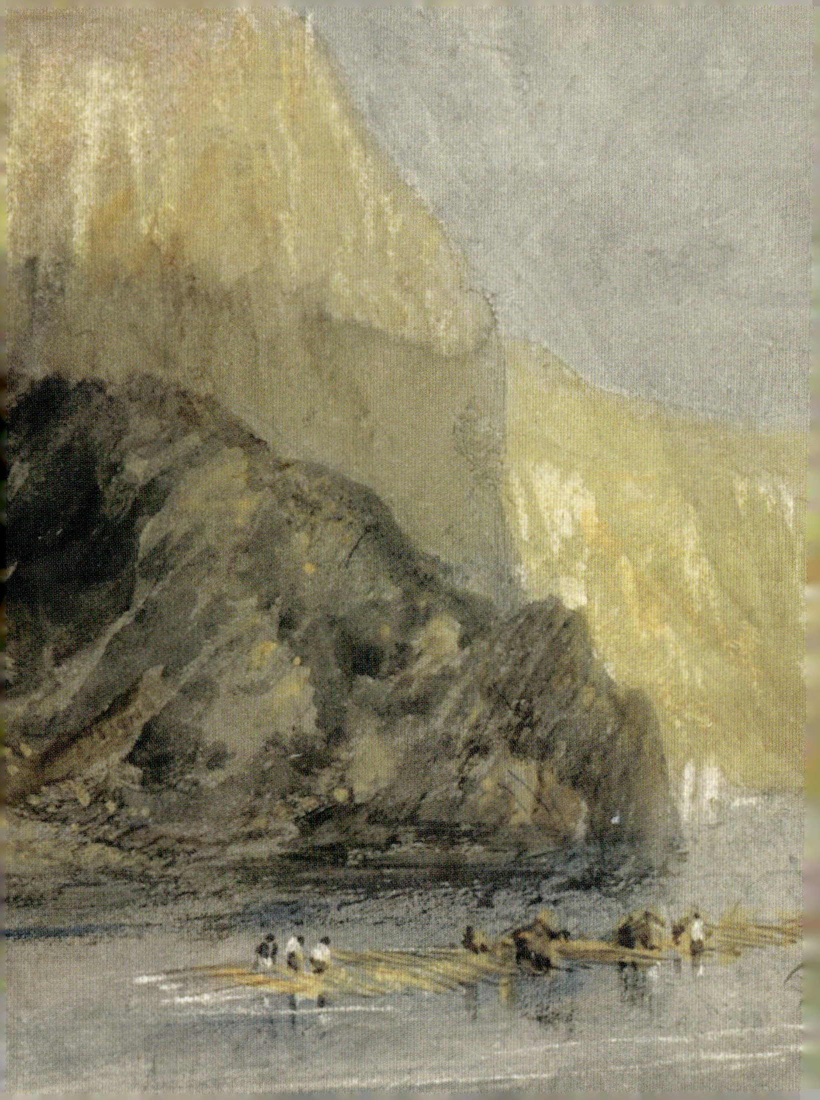

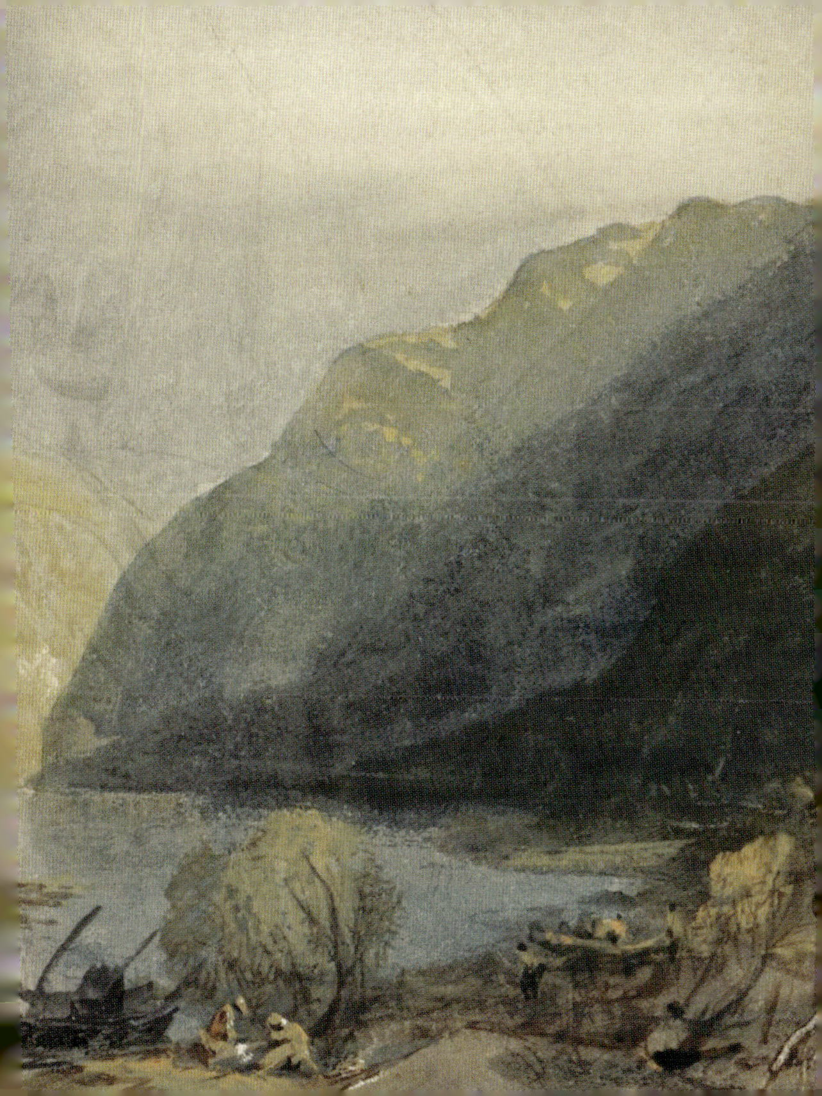

One stormy day at Farnley, (says Mr. Fawkes), Turner called to me loudly from the doorway, 'Hawkey—Hawkey!—come here—come here! Look at this thunder-storm! Isn't it grand?—isn't it wonderful?—isn't it sublime?'

All this time he was making notes of its form and colour on the back of a letter. I proposed some better drawing-block, but he said it did very well. He was absorbed—he was entranced. There was the storm rolling and sweeping and shafting out its lightning over the Yorkshire hills. Presently the storm passed, and he finished. 'There,' said he, 'Hawkey; in two years you will see this again, and call it *Hannibal Crossing the Alps.*'*[(II, 87–8)]

DEVON AND PLEIN AIR PAINTING (1811–14)

Mr. Cyrus Redding met Turner, in 1812, on one of his Devonshire tours. He remembers that his sketches were not larger than sheets of letter-paper. He describes him as rough, reserved, and austere, and with a singular paucity of language.[(I, 200)]

For the following interesting communication relative to probably the same tour, I am indebted to Sir Charles Eastlake, President of the Royal Academy.

* Tate, London, see pp. 106-7

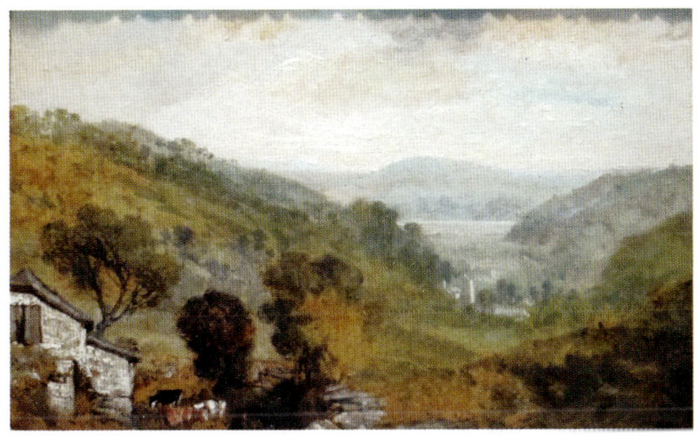

View in Devonshire, c. 1813

Turner visited Plymouth (my native town) while I was staying there in the summer of 1813, or perhaps 1814, painting portraits. As he wished to see the scenery of the river Tamar, I accompanied him, together with Mr. Ambrose Johns, of Plymouth (a landscape-painter of great merit, lately deceased at a great age), to a cottage near Calstock, the residence of my aunt, Miss Pearce, where we all stayed for a few days. From that point as a centre, Turner made various excursions, and the result of one of his rambles was a sketch of the scene which afterwards grew

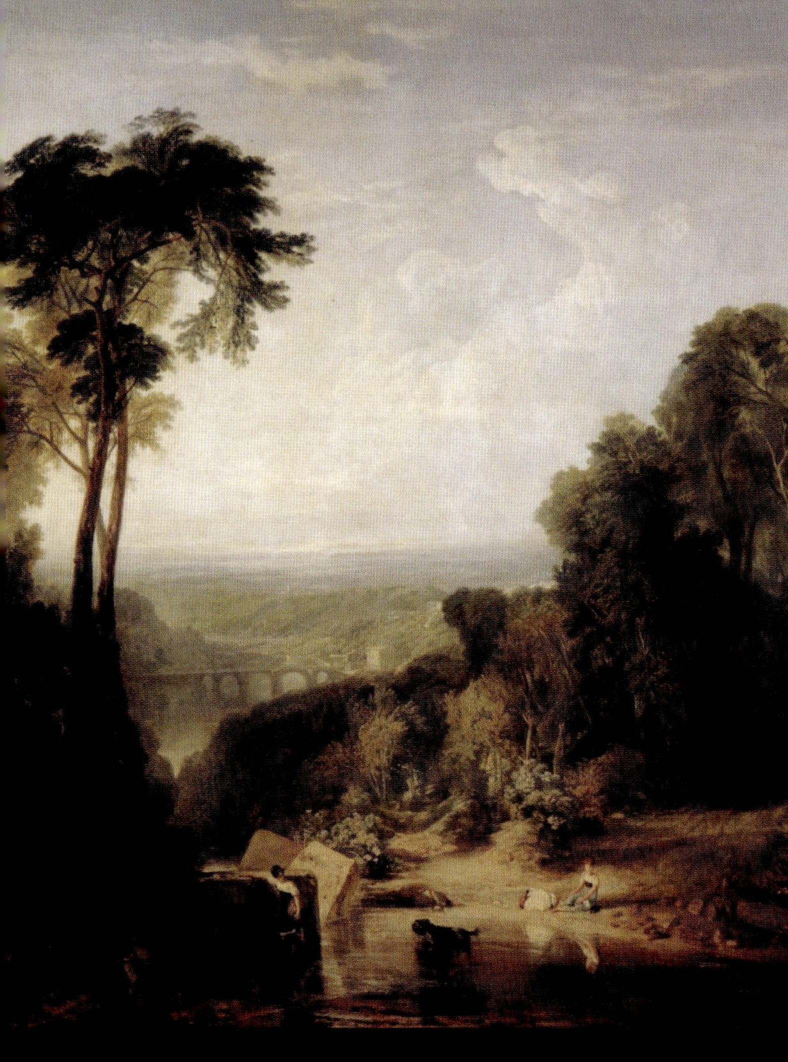

into the celebrated picture of *Crossing the Brook*.* The bridge in that picture is Calstock Bridge; some mining works are indicated in the middle distance. The extreme distance extends to the mouth of the Tamar, the harbour of Hamoaze, the hills of Mount Edgcumbe, and those on the opposite side of Plymouth Sound. The whole scene is extremely faithful.[I, 219]

Turner made his sketches in pencil and by stealth. His companions, observing his peculiarity, were careful not to intrude upon him. After he returned to Plymouth, in the neighbourhood of which he remained some weeks, Mr. Johns fitted up a small portable painting-box, containing some prepared paper for oil sketches, as well as the other necessary materials. When Turner halted at a scene and seemed inclined to sketch it, Johns produced the inviting box, and the great artist, finding everything ready to his hand, immediately began to work. As he sometimes wanted assistance in the use of the box, the presence of Johns was indispensable, and after a few days he made his oil sketches freely in our presence. Johns accompanied him always; I was only with them occasionally. Turner seemed pleased

* Tate, London

Opposite: Crossing the Brook, 1815

when the rapidity with which those sketches were done was talked of; for, departing from his habitual reserve in the instance of his pencil sketches, he made no difficulty of showing them. On one occasion, when, on his return after a sketching ramble, to a country residence belonging to my father, near Plympton, the day's work was shown, he himself remarked that one of the sketches (and perhaps the best) was done in less than half an hour.

When he left Plymouth, he carried off all the results. We had reckoned that Johns, who had provided all the materials, and had waited upon him devotedly, would at least have had a present of one or two of the sketches. This was not the case; but long afterwards, the great painter sent Johns in a letter a small oil sketch, not painted from nature, as a return for his kindness and assistance. On my inquiring afterwards what had become of those sketches, Turner replied that they were worthless, in consequence, as he supposed, of some defect in the preparation of the paper; all the grey tints, he observed, had nearly disappeared. Although I did not implicitly rely on that statement, I do not remember to have seen any of them afterwards.* (I, 219–221)

* The sketches are now dispersed, with many in the Tate, London.

PICTURES OF NOTHING: TURNER AND THE CRITICS

[William] Hazlitt, in his *Round Table*, in an [1814] essay on 'Imitation and Pedantry,' condemns the vagueness of Turner's later [presumably meaning latest] pictures, while thus praising his general breadth of genius:—

> We here allude particularly to Turner, the ablest landscape-painter now living, whose pictures are, however, too much abstractions of ærial perspective, and representations not so properly of the objects of nature as of the medium through which they are seen. They are the triumph of the knowledge of the artist, and of the power of the pencil over the barrenness of the subject. They are pictures of the elements of air, earth, and water. The artist delights to go back to the first chaos of the world, and to that state of things when the waters were separated from the dry land, and light from darkness, but as yet no living thing, nor tree bearing fruit, was seen upon the face of the earth. All is 'without form and void'. Someone said of his landscapes, that they were 'pictures of nothing and very like'. (II, 190–1)

Overleaf: Snow Storm, Hannibal and his Army Crossing the Alps 1812

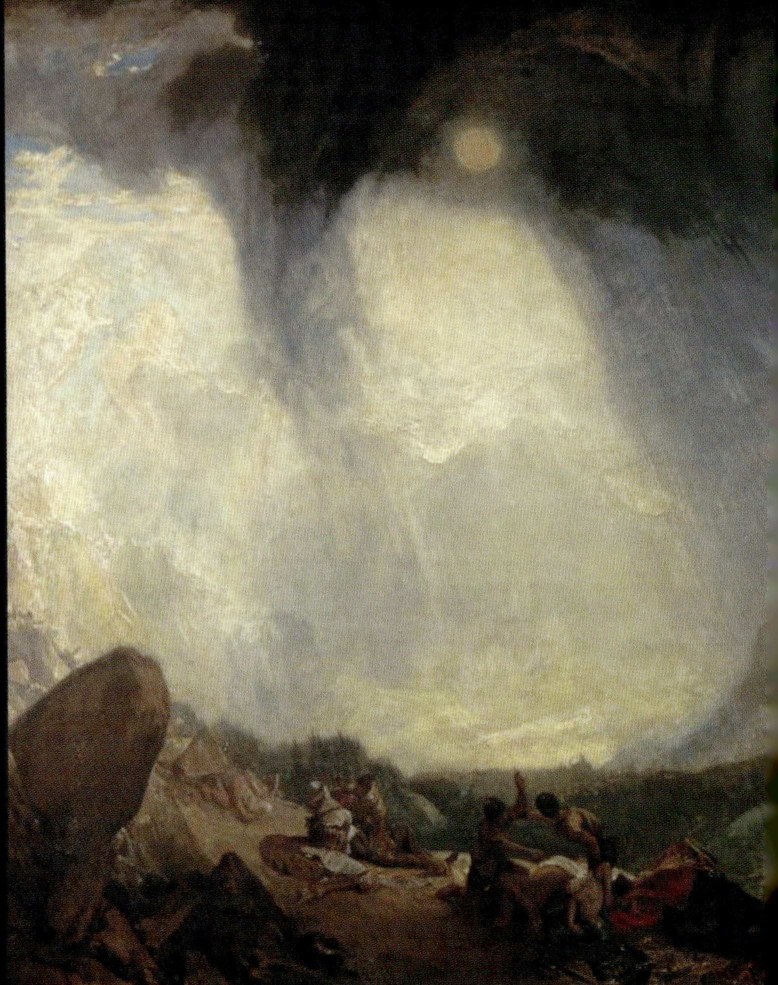

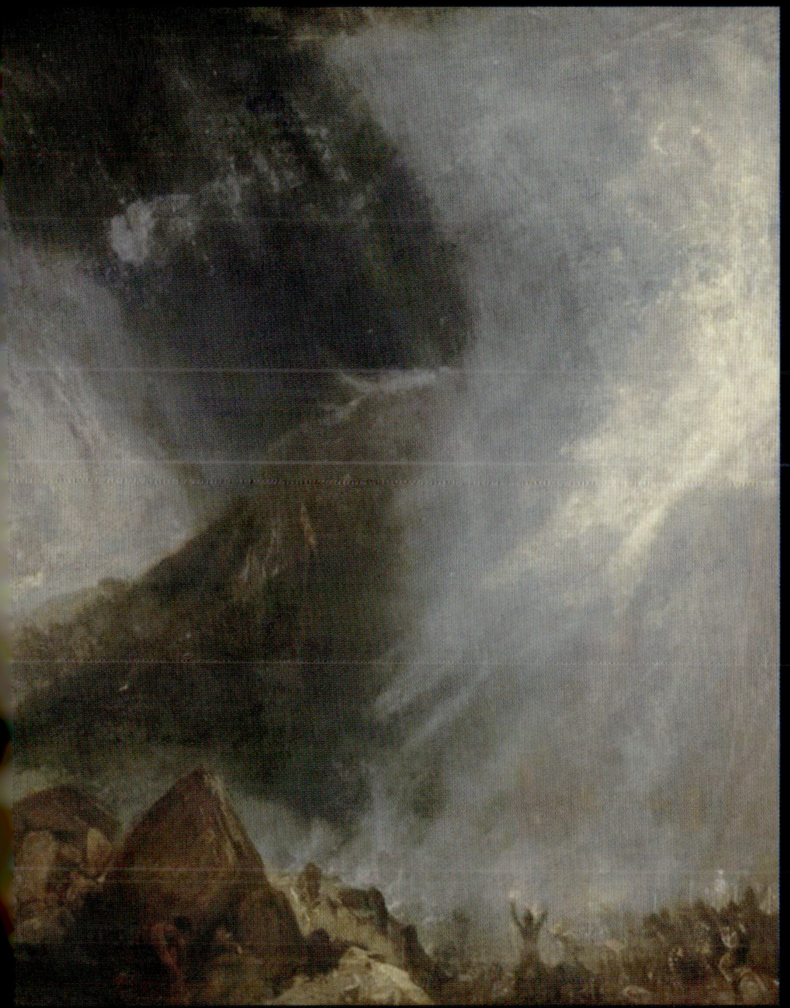

[Trimmer reported that the portraitist, Henry Howard]

> though below Turner as an artist, was his superior in education; and although doing ample homage to his genius, he often got into warm professional disputes with him. But Turner was mostly in the right. They once, I remember, had a very hot dispute, and for the time being lost temper. Howard maintained they should paint for the public; Turner, that public opinion was not worth a rush, and that one should paint only for judges. But according to all artists, no one but an artist can judge of the difficulties of painting, and consequently of the merits of a picture.(I, 172)

SANDYCOMBE LODGE

Turner, always fond of architecture from the time he had worked as a draughtsman for architects, several times essayed the arduous task of designing a house—a task which seems to me by no means beyond the intellect of an intelligent man, especially if he have an artistic taste. He designed his own house, Solus Lodge, at Twickenham; he designed his own doorway in Queen Anne Street; and he made designs for his friend Fawkes's house at Farnley, in Yorkshire. The name of this Solus Lodge—so called,

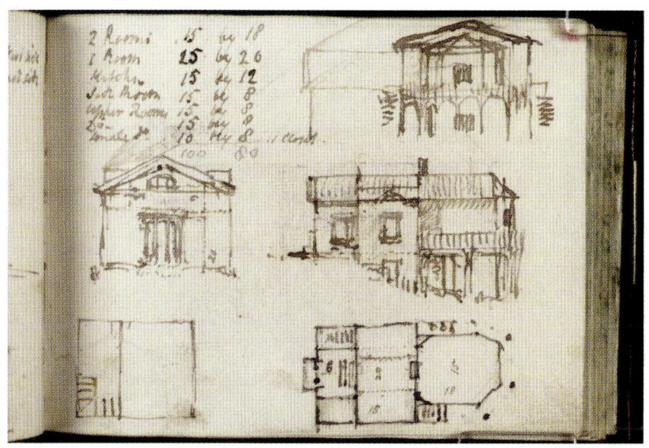

Page from a sketchbook of possible designs for Sandycombe Lodge, c. 1809–11

I suppose, to express his love of, or wish for, solitude—Turner afterwards changed into Sandycombe Lodge, which has a sort of Devonshire flavour about it, to my mind. Here he once received some Academicians, including Mr. Mulready, to tea; and here he once feasted Mr. Pye, his celebrated engraver and the great opponent of Academic abuses, with a bit of strong cheese and a pint of stale porter. It was here, too, he used to protect from the birds'-nesting boys the blackbirds who sang and cheered him after his day's work; and it was here, in his rude tangle of a garden, that he grew water-plants to introduce into his foregrounds. To be near Reynolds's old house at Richmond is said to have been one of Turner's chief reasons for building Solus Lodge. More probably it arose from his wish to be undisturbed, to study the Thames, and to be near his old schoolboy home at Brentford.[1, 165–7]

> About this time (says Mr. Trimmer), Turner removed to Twickenham, where he purchased Sandycombe Lodge, near Richmond Bridge. It was an unpretending little place, and the rooms were small. There were several models of ships in glass cases, to which Turner had painted a sea and background. They much resembled the large vessels in his sea pieces. Richmond scenery greatly influenced his style. The Scotch firs (or stone-pine) around are in most of his large classical subjects, and Richmond landscape is decidedly the basis of *The Rise of Carthage*.[1, 167]
>
> At the end of his garden was a square pond—I rather think he dug it himself—into which he put the fish he caught. The surface was covered with waterlilies. I have been out fishing with him on the Old Brent, with a can to catch trout for this preserve; but the fish always disappeared; at last he discovered that a jack was in the pond: and Turner would have it that it had been put in to annoy him.[1, 168]

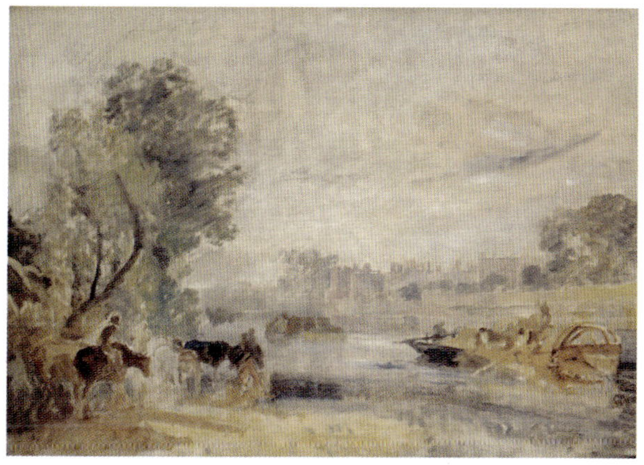

Hampton Court from the Thames, c. 1806–7

He had a boat at Richmond, but we never went further than the water's edge, as my father had insured his life; but I have seen him start on his sketching expeditions. From his boat he painted on a large canvas direct from nature. Till you have seen these sketches, you know nothing of Turner's powers. There are about two score of these large subjects, rolled up, and now national property. In my judgment these are among his very finest productions: no retouching, everything firmly in its place.

If the subject had been photographed, there would have been greater exactitude, but Turner's would have carried the bell in elevation of sentiment and mind. This is the perfection of the art; but Turner's mind was so comprehensive that he could not carry out the detail, though he was far from despising it, and I was told by Howard he would spend hours sketching a stone. Probably these are thrown aside as worthless, and not popular, but what studies for young painters![(I, 169)]

THE YORKSHIRE FROST

Besides his boat (continued Trimmer) he had a gig and an old horse: an old crop-eared bay horse, or rather a cross between a horse and a pony. In this gig he used to drive out sketching, and take my father and myself with him. His sketching apparatus was under the seat.

He has immortalised his old crop-ear in his *Frosty Morning*, which is now exhibited.* There are two horses, but they are both taken from Crop-ear, Turner could not paint a horse; still, he has been very happy in catching the stiffness of old Crop-ear's fore-legs.

* Tate, London

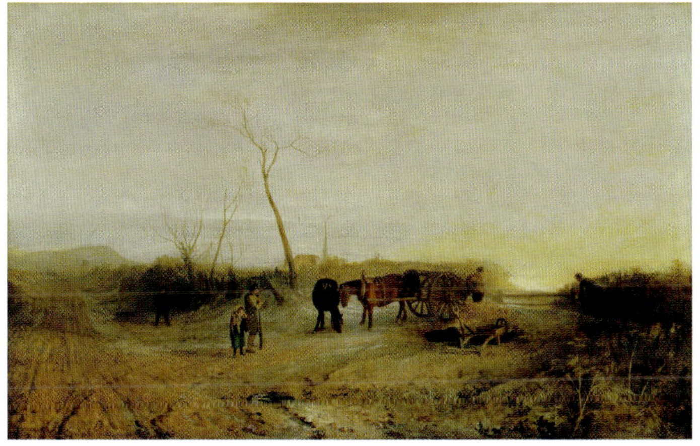

Frosty Morning, 1813

The *Frost Piece* was one of his favourites. Once he talked of giving it to my father, who greatly prized it. He said he was travelling by coach in Yorkshire, and sketched it en route. There is a stage-coach in the distance that he was on at the time. My father told me that when at Somerset House it was much brighter, and made a great sensation. It was over the fireplace in his gallery. The girl with the hare over her shoulders, I have heard my father say reminded him of a young girl whom he occasionally saw at

> Queen Anne Street, and whom, from her resemblance to Turner, he thought a relation.* The same female figure appears in his *Crossing the Brook.* (II, 170–1)

CARTHAGE AND CLAUDE

1815 was a wonderful year with Turner, for in that same year he exhibited the *Crossing the Brook* and *Dido building Carthage.*† In this picture Turner wished to show the rise of a maritime empire that he considered typical of England, France and Rome being no doubt also analogous in his mind. Seldom or never accurate to exact fact, Turner, contrary to truth, has made the city on a river, and has placed a bridge in front, and a vast alps of Claudesque architecture, porticoes, and vestibules half completed on either side. Dido, surrounded by her people, stands on the left, watching the work. The luminous sun is in the centre, fusing everything to one golden focus of brightness. There, too, are the inevitable stone pines, and with fine poetry (justly eulogized by Ruskin) Turner has made some lean, sinewy, dark, long-limbed Carthaginian boys launching boats, emblematic of the future sea-power of Carthage. The whole is a splendid dream. Turner was justly proud of it when he determined to leave it to the

* Presumably Evelina, but unsubstantiated † National Gallery, London

nation on condition of its being hung yard-arm and yard-arm with Claude. Unfortunately, the atmosphere is fast decaying and becoming hot and turbid, so that the purity of Claude now injures it by contrast.

Turner seems to have considered the decline of Carthage a moral example to England; for it arose from the decline of her agriculture, the increase of her luxury, and her besotted blindness, till too late, to the insatiable ambition of Rome. Carthage fell at last, 146 BC, after a century and a half of war, the very year Mummius destroyed Corinth.

Besides the vigour and grasp of the picture, it displays some learning, for Turner has not forgotten Sichæus's tomb or the Byrsa. The architecture, of course, is full of pardonable anachronism. The architecture of Carthage must have been Oriental.

Turner, in his angry pride, would never part with this picture, when he found it did not sell at the Academy. Chantrey once tried to buy it, but was startled by finding each time its price rose higher: £500,— £1000,— £2000.

'Why what in the world, Turner, are you going to do with the picture?'

'Be buried in it, to be sure,' growled Turner.(I, 298–300)

Overleaf: Dido Building Carthage, or The Rise of the Carthaginian Empire, 1815

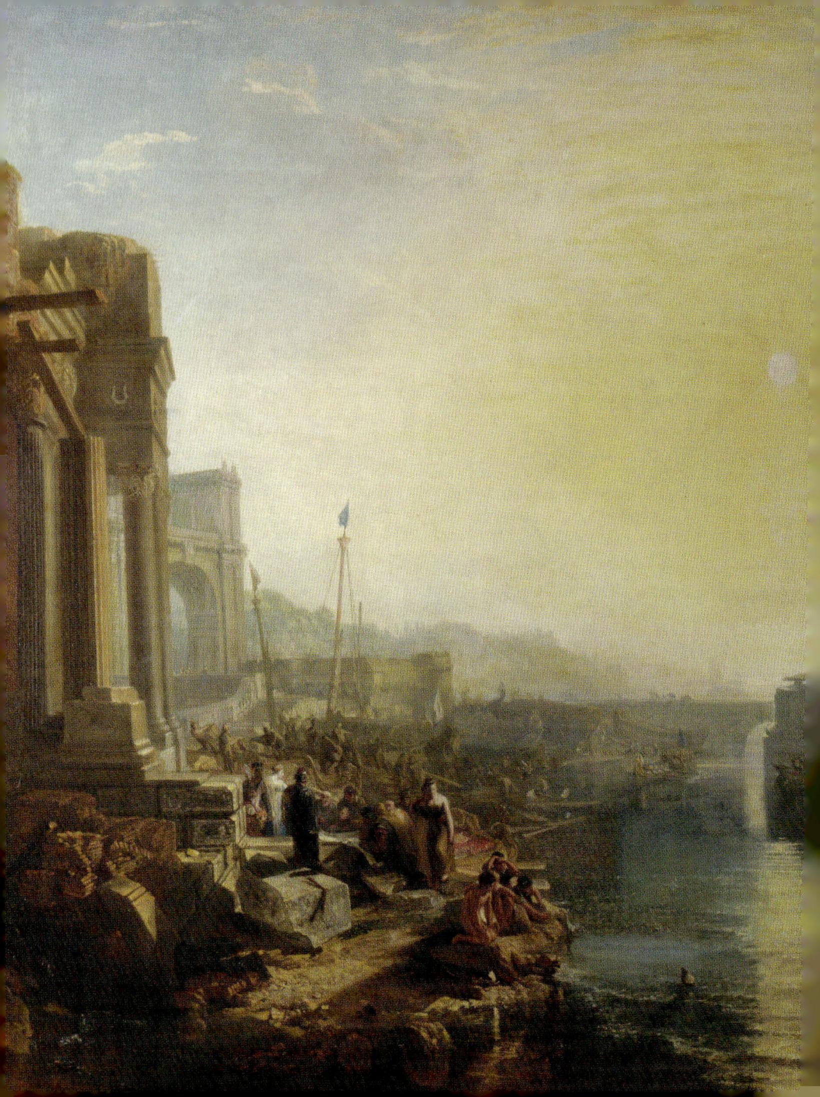

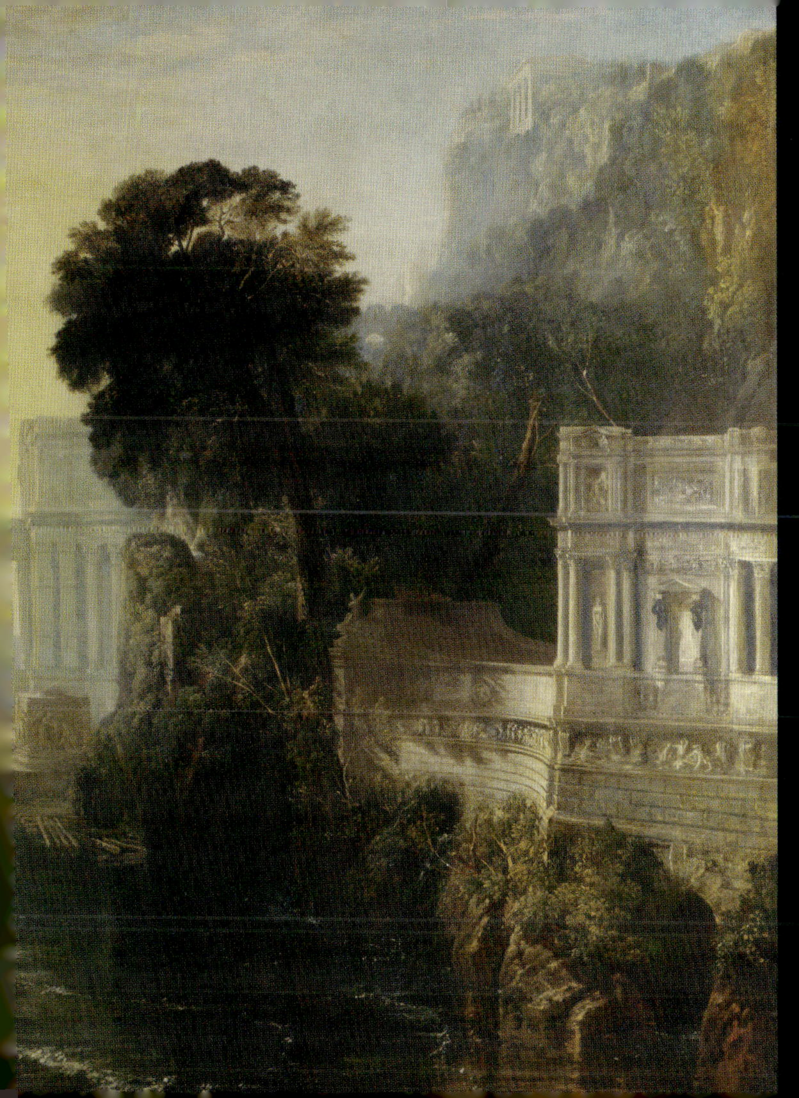

In 1817 Turner returned full charge against Claude, and exhibited his *Decline of the Carthaginian Empire; Hostages leaving Carthage for Rome*.* The perspective is bad, the sky, once fine, is now foxy, and the temples are rather leathery. The critics were severe against this picture, and even Mr. Ruskin condemns it. But Turner declared he preferred it to its predecessor. When Turner wished to impress one with a sense of foreboding danger, grief, or terror, he generally introduced a sunset. His motto here shows that he had, of course, a meaning in this sunset. He says with rude sublimity:

> While o' er the western wave th' ensanguined sun,
> In gathering haze a stormy signal spread,
> And set portentous.[1, 300]

> Mr. Ruskin, I know, (writes C. R. Leslie), will agree with me in considering it unfortunate for Turner that his picture of *Dido building Carthage* is placed in the National Gallery beside Claude's *Embarkation of the Queen of Sheba*; for his notice of the two pictures of Carthage is among the few instances in which he admits a fault in Turner. 'The foreground,' he says, of the *Building of Carthage*, and the greater part of the architecture of the *Fall* are equally heavy, and evidently paint, if we compare them with genuine passages of Claude's sunshine.' For my own part,

* Tate, London

when I look at the *Building of Carthage*, I feel as if I were in a theatre decorated with the most splendid of drop-scenes; but when I stand before Claude's *Embarkation*, I am in the open air enjoying the sea breeze and listening to the plash of the waves on the beach. Yet this does not convince me that Claude was a greater man than Turner, because it is a comparison of one of the most artificial pictures of the English painter with one of the most natural works of the Frenchman; and I only make the comparison to show that Claude is not to be deposed, to place on his throne one who wants it not, because he has raised himself to a throne unoccupied before, and from which his sway is extended over a wider dominion, though, for that very reason, with less absolute power in every corner of it. Claude could not paint a storm; Turner's sea storms are the finest ever painted; and though Claude is best seen in tranquil sunshine, yet there are many beautiful and brilliant mid-day appearances, of perfect stillness, that were never seen on canvas, till Turner gave them with a power precluding all imitation; and I can well believe, with Mr. Ruskin, in the truth of his Venetian scenes, those splendid palaces and churches under the brightest skies and reflected in the clearest waters. Others may have painted with more truth

> many of the lesser facts; but he alone has given the great facts that are the prevailing associations with Venice. I have never seen Switzerland; but I have known those who have gone there sceptics, with respect to Turner's excellence, and returned worshippers; and I know enough of lake scenery to feel how great a painter he is of mountains and lakes, with all their changes of sunshine, cloud, and mist. Such are the things which are the real praise of this wonderful painter of light, and space, and air.(II, 204–5)

THE OLD MASTERS

Turner never imitated Salvator Rosa—because he had rocks and torrents of his own to go and copy and recompose from—he imitated Morland, Wilson, Reynolds, and Loutherbourg, but never West or Fuseli. Tintoretto and Paul Veronese were of service to him, says Mr. Ruskin, but how I do not know. Titian Turner competed with in his *Venus and Adonis*,* Turner has been heard to rebuke a young man at a party for foolishly running down Titian; and the putting in of the beech-leaves in the upper right-hand corner of *Peter Martyr*† he has been known to mention with 'singular delight.' One day, at the British Institution, as he was looking with admiration at a

* Private collection † Destroyed

glowing Cuyp,* Turner said to a friend, 'They would have called that too warm if I had done it.'(II, 326–7)

CUYP AND TURNER

No one now will accuse Turner of gaudiness of colour when they have once studied the burning crimsons and purple of a summer sunset or the luminous folds of a white cloud with the sun on it. Turner used pure colour only in minute touches, and knew that all paint was clay compared with light and flame. Once, to give verdure with sunshine on it, he used pure yellow in this way, in his determination to express its relative intensity of light.

Turner never gives detail on near objects in cold sky blue; he uses it only where Nature uses it, and brings in his warm colour directly detail and surface become visible by light. His works are distinguished by the intensity of light he sheds through every hue, as he never lowered his middle tint to give greater value to his high light, as the old masters did. It is this unusual brilliancy that makes his pictures sometimes appear to ignorant critics glaring and dazzling. No one is more cautious and sparing in the use of pure colour than Turner. He attains his brilliancy by his

* Probably *A Hilly Landscape with Figures* (*c.* 1665), National Gallery, London

Overleaf: Dort, or Dordrecht: The Dort Packet-Boat from Rotterdam Becalmed, 1818. A homage to Cuyp's The Maas at Dordrecht (1645–50)

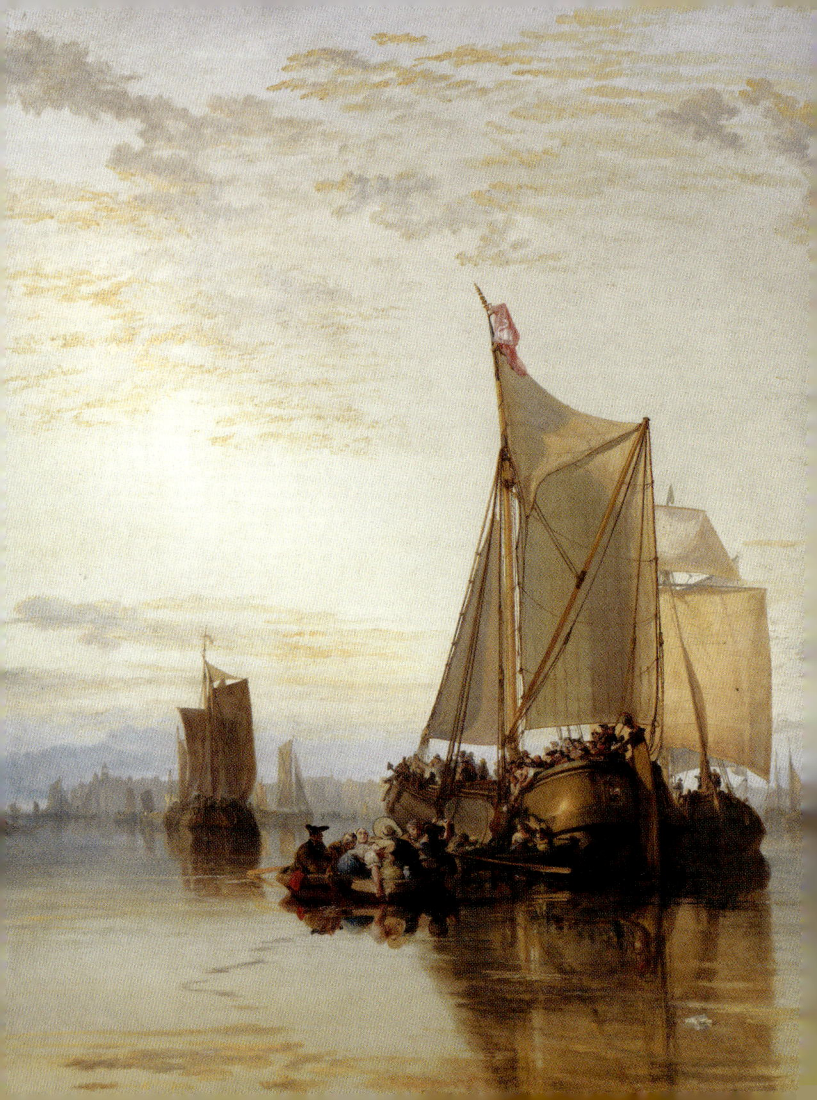

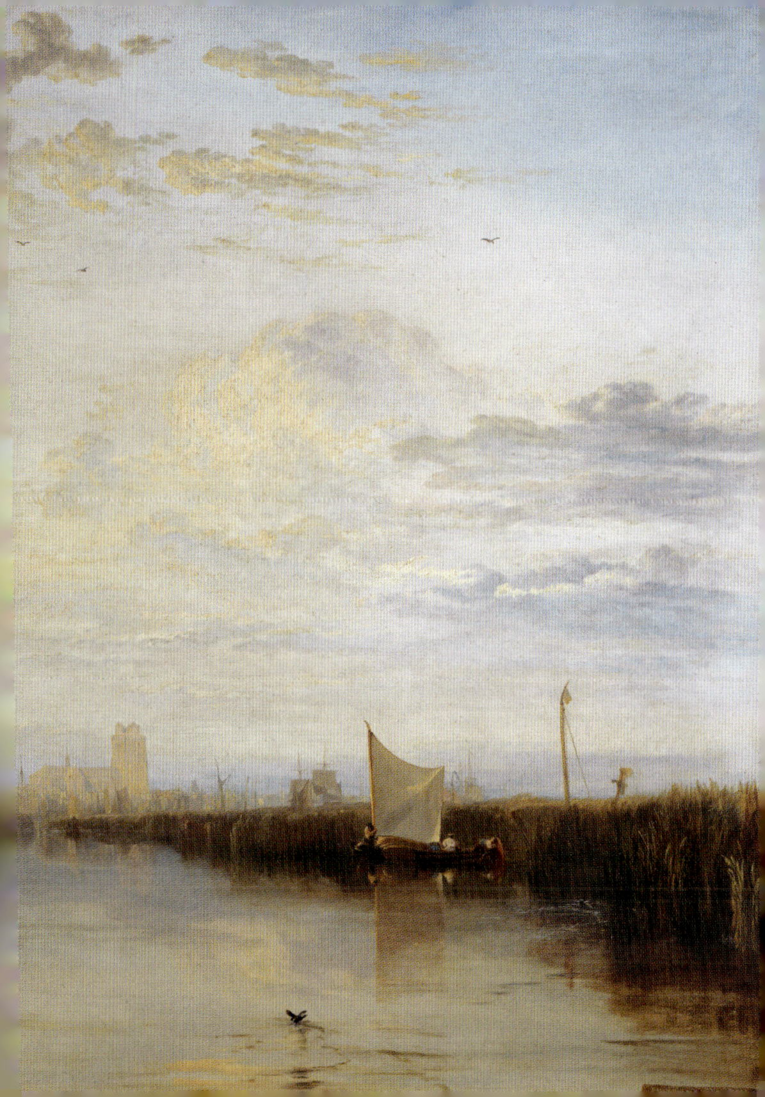

variety and subtlety of semitones. He stipples his grounds, not his shadows, with one broad yet sharp touch.

Mr. Ruskin says that there is no instance in the works of Turner of anything so faithful and imitative of sunshine as the best parts of Cuyp; but at the same time there is not such solecism in them.

Cuyp gives us only a narrow view of Nature, and is too intent on the truth of his omnipresent sunshine to think of any other truth. Cuyp is trying for tone, not colour; he is giving us a monochrome in gold colour. But Turner wants colour, and he must give us both cold and warm colour. He must have his contrast and balance, his *forte* and *piano*. He shows us the sunset in the west, and he shows us the colour dying off cold to the east. As instances of this sacrifice of tone to colour, Mr. Ruskin adduces the blue and white stripes on the drifting flag in the *Slave Ship*,* and the white part of the dress of the *Napoleon*,† which, though valuable for colour, are discords in tone.

The best proof of the grammatical accuracy of the tones of Turner, is the perfect and unchanging influence of all his pictures at any distance. Some of his pictures seem to me too artificially balanced with hot and cold colour; yet Turner did what no one had attempted before, he gave us reverse tones in one picture.[(II, 327–9)]

* Museum of Fine Arts, Boston MA (see p. 212) † *War – The Exile and the Rock Limpet*, 1842, Tate, London

WORK FOR THE ENGRAVERS

The first published work that introduced Turner's name to his world-wide fame, was the *Southern Coast*, begun in 1814, and got up with great difficulty and labour by the distinguished engraver of many of its beautiful plates, W. B. Cooke.* The first of these drawings were made for £7. 10*s*. each, some of which have been since sold for 100 guineas, and, I believe, even for 200 guineas.[(I, 295)]

We have already shown that Turner was a bitterly disappointed man. He had been cruelly frustrated in love, and his nature was one that could not forget. In art, too, he had had hard struggles. His oil pictures did not sell at first; the engravings from his works were unlucky. The *Liber* was stopped because it was at first partially a failure. His plates to the *History of Richmondshire* were a great loss to the publishers.† Was it any wonder he first learnt to despise a public who could not understand his genius, and would have let him starve had he been less fertile in resources? Even his very drawing-lessons failed.[(I, 251)]

In 1824 appeared Turner's *Rivers of England*, published

* *Picturesque Views on the Southern Coast of England*, published 1814–26, contained 40 images by Turner. † *History of Richmondshire*, published 1819–23, as part of a never completed General History of the County of York, contained 20 images by Turner.

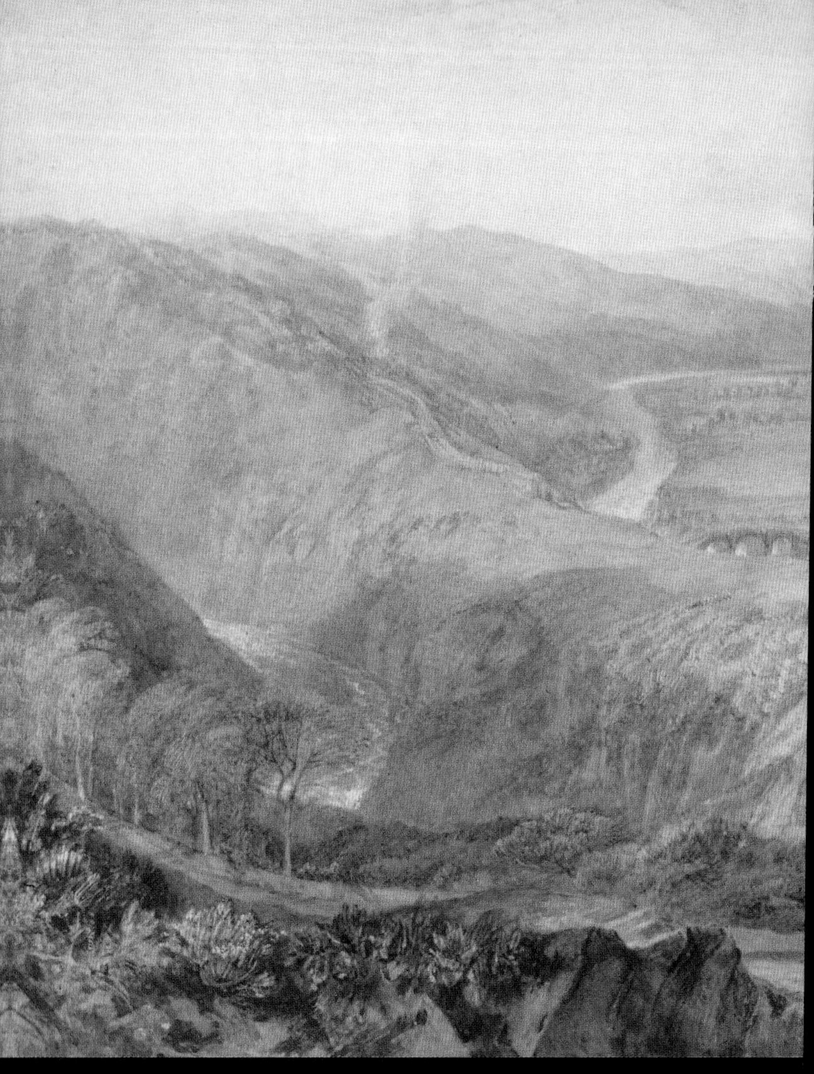

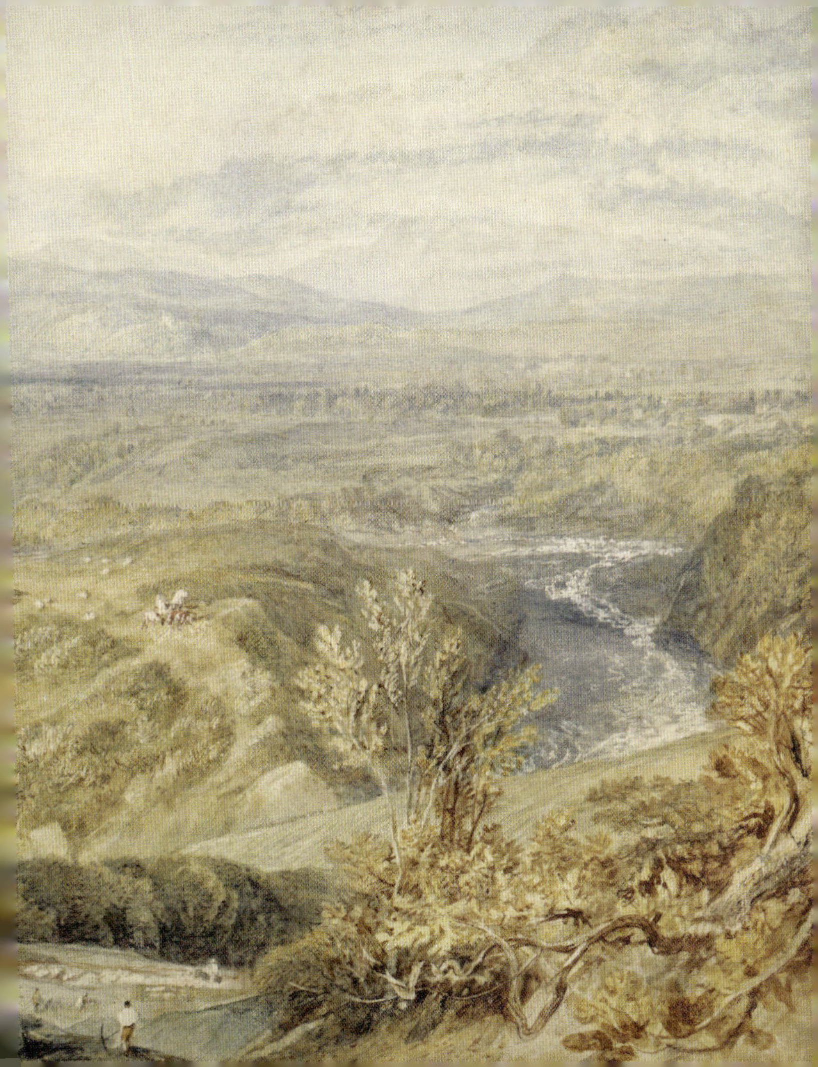

by W. B. Cooke, including the *Norham Castle*, which he always considered the turning-point of his success.* In 1827 he began his *England and Wales*, worn out, I believe, by the exactions and petty tyranny of W. B. Cooke. This series lasted eleven years. The alphabetic plan of the series indicated that desire for comprehensive unity that specially distinguished Turner's mind. When his later Venetian pictures were bought, he was always saying, 'What do people want with such scraps?' His desire in the *Liber* had been to epitomize all landscape ideals; his desire in the *England and Wales* was to epitomize all the beauties of his own country.[(1, 254)]

It was Mr. [H. A. J.] Munro's habit to visit Turner on Sunday afternoons, when the painter was more at leisure. They were once pleasantly chatting together—for they were sincere friends—when in bounced Mr. W. B. Cooke, like a bullying tailor come to look after a poor sweating journeyman. He wanted to know if those drawings of his were never to be finished. When the door presently closed behind him, the big salt tears came into Turner's eyes, and he murmured something about 'no holiday ever for me.'[(1, 409)]

* *Rivers of England*, published 1822–26, contained 16 images by Turner.

Previous pages: Crook of Lune, Looking towards Hornby Castle, 1816–18; one of the watercolours prepared for The History of Richmondshire

ITALY 1819

Of all Turner's sketch-books that I saw, I think none interested me more than one full of sketches made at Rome, and chiefly in the Vatican galleries. They show the intense delight the artist must have felt in the classic city where he found on every hand ample materials for the war he was ever carrying on with Claude. What he had so long only dreamt of, now he saw. He now could realize the visions of his schooldays, of those hours spent in academic and architectural study. His comprehensive mind filled itself with booty, his great memory stored itself with facts, his note-books are gorged with classical detail, with drawings of statues, bas-reliefs, and inscriptions, to be used hereafter in the foregrounds of classical pictures. That greedy accumulativeness that made Turner amass money, made him also, in its intellectual tendency, accumulate facts. He could not refrain from taking ten or twelve views of London Bridge; it was a pain to him to have to break his charitable store by giving away a shilling uselessly. Such are the inconsistencies of man.(I, 363–4)

Overleaf: an opening from Turner's Vatican Museum sketchbook: left-hand page, female figures from the Column with Reliefs of the Hours, and detail of a sarcophagus; right-hand page, sculptural fragments including a Danaë and a group of a Nymph and a Satyr, 1819

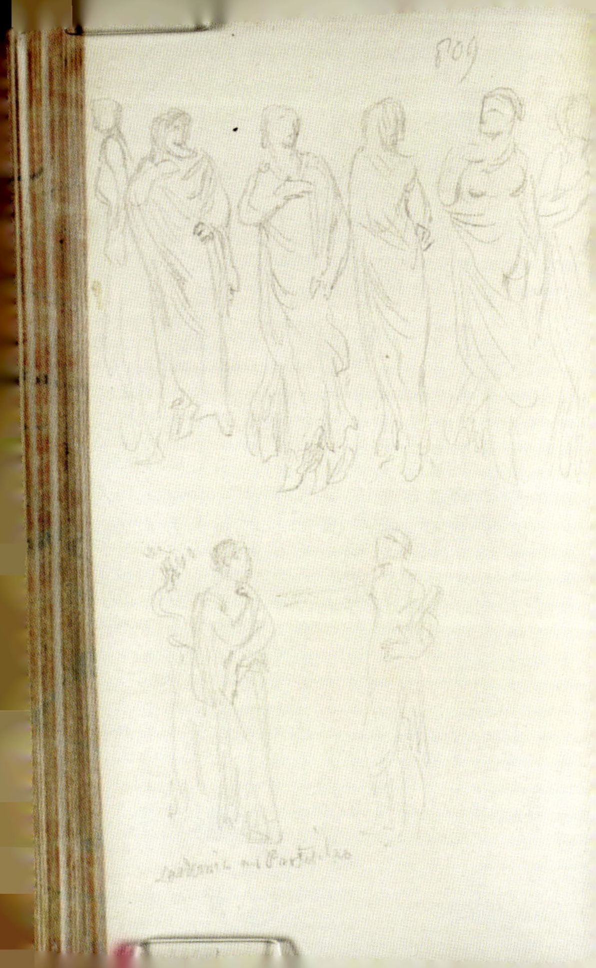
809

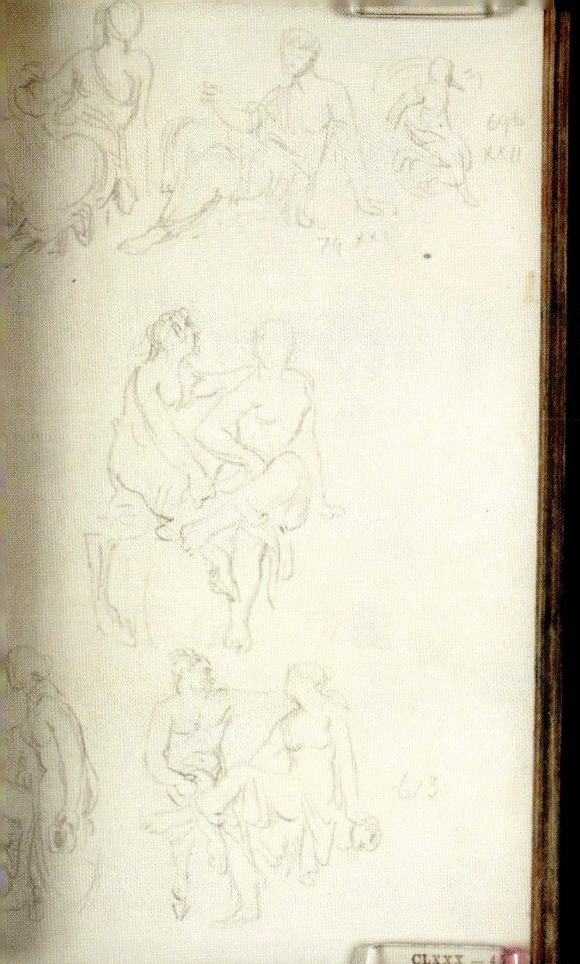
673

PLAGIARISM

Nothing angered Turner more than piracy. [Samuel] Owen, the water-colour painter, had been imitating him, on which he wrote him a very brisk note, requesting him in future to draw from his own resources, and not from his. He once saw someone making a memorandum of his pictures in Queen Anne Street gallery, whereupon Turner walked up to him and whisked him out forthwith, greatly to his surprise.(I, 177)

Turner hated plagiarism. At one of the councils a drawing of 'The Falls of Terni' came under notice. Turner declared fiercely that it was a copy of his own drawing.* 'Swear to it; sure of it; sure of it.' (No one could represent the dead, hopeless fall of a great body of water like Turner, [James Duffield] Harding, among others, imitated this very Terni. Mr. Munro, I think, has the drawing.) [Henry] Howard, the secretary, kindly willing to find excuse for the imitator, said—

'Perhaps, Mr. Turner, the artist only selected the same spot as you did. This would account for a resemblance that may after all be mere chance.'

'No, no, Howard,' said [Sir Francis] Chantrey; 'if the

* Blackburn Museum, Blackburn

artist had really been there, then you might be sure his drawing would not be like Turner's.'

He meant that Turner was not a mere copying machine; but a selector, reviser, a readjuster of Nature—elevating what was important, depressing what was detrimental or insignificant, throwing in effect, yet never forgetting the truth and likeness above all.[II, 256]

BAY OF BAIÆ

In 1823, Turner, still Claudesque, but in his own great way, exhibited his *Bay of Baiæ; with Apollo and the Sibyl.** Mr. Wornum calls this picture a great masterpiece, and Turner's first thoroughly original work. To the right is the castle of the bay, and on the opposite side Pozzuoli. The two figures to the left under the tall pines are Apollo and the Sibyl, whom he loved, and to whom he granted to live as many years as she held grains of sand in her hands; but who, asking also for perpetual youth, wasted away to an echo. This is the Baiæ that Horace said was the fairest bay in the whole world. It is close to Avernus, where Æneas consulted the Sibyl, and from whence Ulysses descended into hell.[I, 303]

* Tate, London

Overleaf: The Bay of Baiæ, with Apollo and the Sibyl, 1823

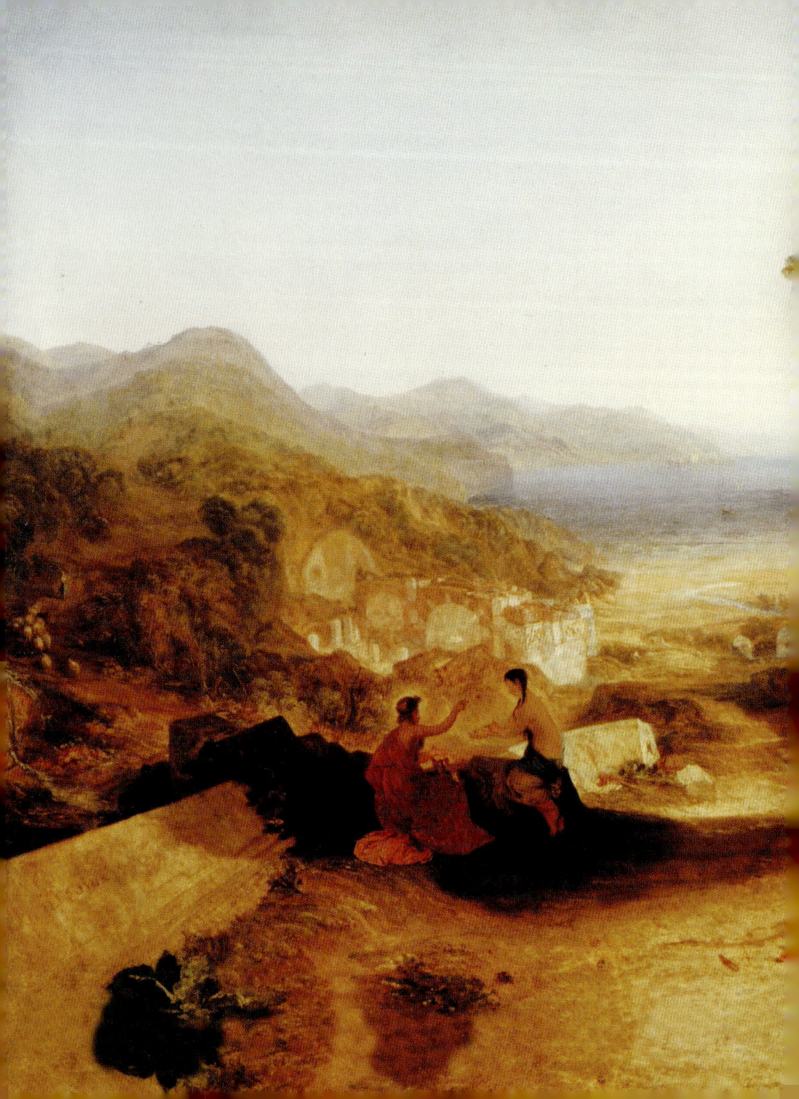

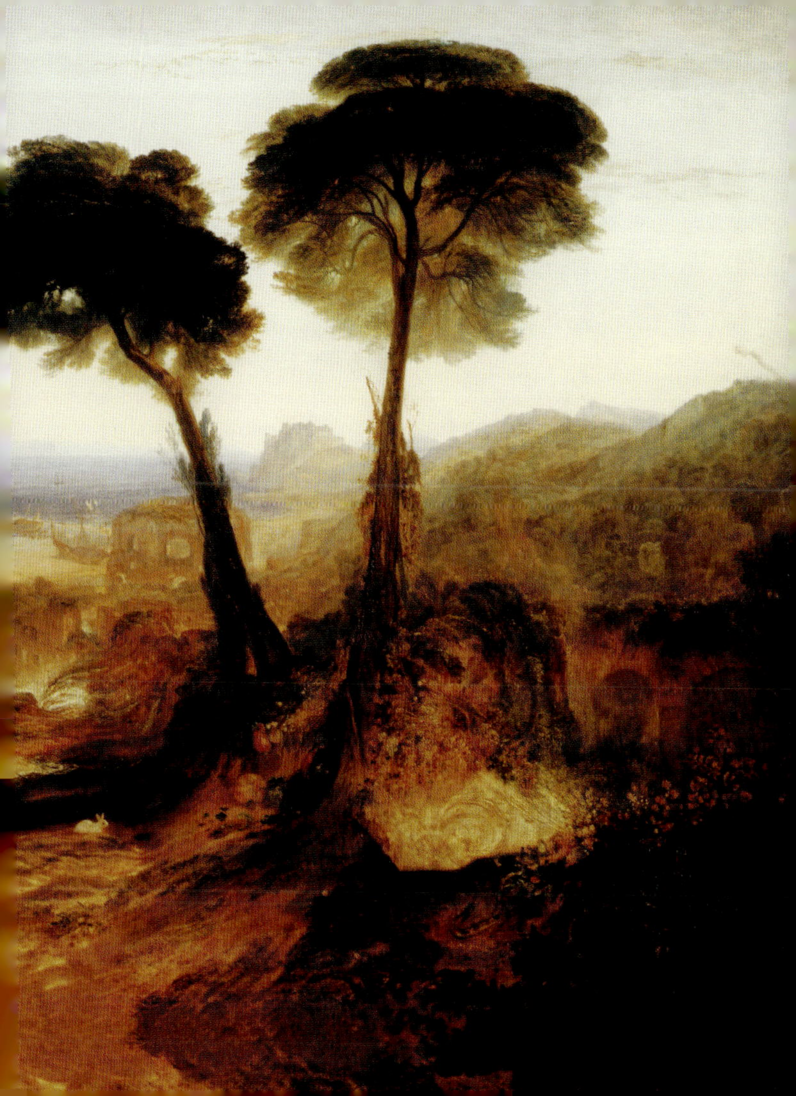

One day Mr. G. Jones, having discussed Turner's picture of the *Bay of Baiæ* with a traveller who had recently been there, was surprised to find that half the scene was Turner's sheer invention; upon which, in fun, Mr. Jones wrote on the frame, 'Splendida Mendax'.*

Turner saw it, and laughed. His friend told him that where he had planted some hills with vineyards, there was nothing in reality but a few dry sticks. Turner smiled, and said it was all there, and that all poets were liars. The inscription remained on the frame of the picture for years; Turner never removed it.(I, 228–9)

WORKING TO ORDER – SIGHTS UNSEEN

Turner was often unjustly accused of being extravagant in the price he demanded for his drawings; but the complaining purchaser forgot that he was buying something which in a few years would be worth perhaps double the money given for it. Mr. Cockerell, for instance, on his return from Greece, engaged Turner to execute him a drawing of a temple in Ægina from rough hints furnished him. It was a troublesome task, and probably uncongenial to the artist, whose mind it diverted from its own channels. He had to paint a country and people he had never seen. The

* Meaning 'splendidly false'. Corrected by George Jones in his copy of Thornbury's *Life* to 'splendide mendax'.

painter set to work, and executed his task with a patience and care worthy of one who had to win his spurs: he produced in the given time a beautiful and elaborate water-colour drawing fit for the engraver, and highly finished enough to afterwards adorn a gallery. But he demanded for it thirty-five guineas, which Mr. Cockerell thought an exorbitant demand from an old friend. Some years after, Mr. Cockerell sold the drawing for fifty guineas, and it is now in the possession of Mr. Munro—most probably worth, if it were sold, at least some sixty guineas.*(I, 390)

VARNISHING DAYS (I): THE BLACK CLOUD

When Turner's picture of *Cologne*† was exhibited, in the year 1826, it was hung between two portraits by Sir Thomas Lawrence, of Lady Wallscourt and Lady Robert Manners.

The sky of Turner's picture was exceedingly bright, and it had a most injurious effect on the colour of the two portraits. Lawrence naturally felt mortified, and complained openly at the position of his pictures.

Artists were at that time permitted to retouch their pictures on the walls of the Academy. On the morning of the opening of the Exhibition, at the private view, a friend of Turner's who had seen the *Cologne* in all its splendour,

* Private collection † Frick Collection, New York, NY (see overleaf)

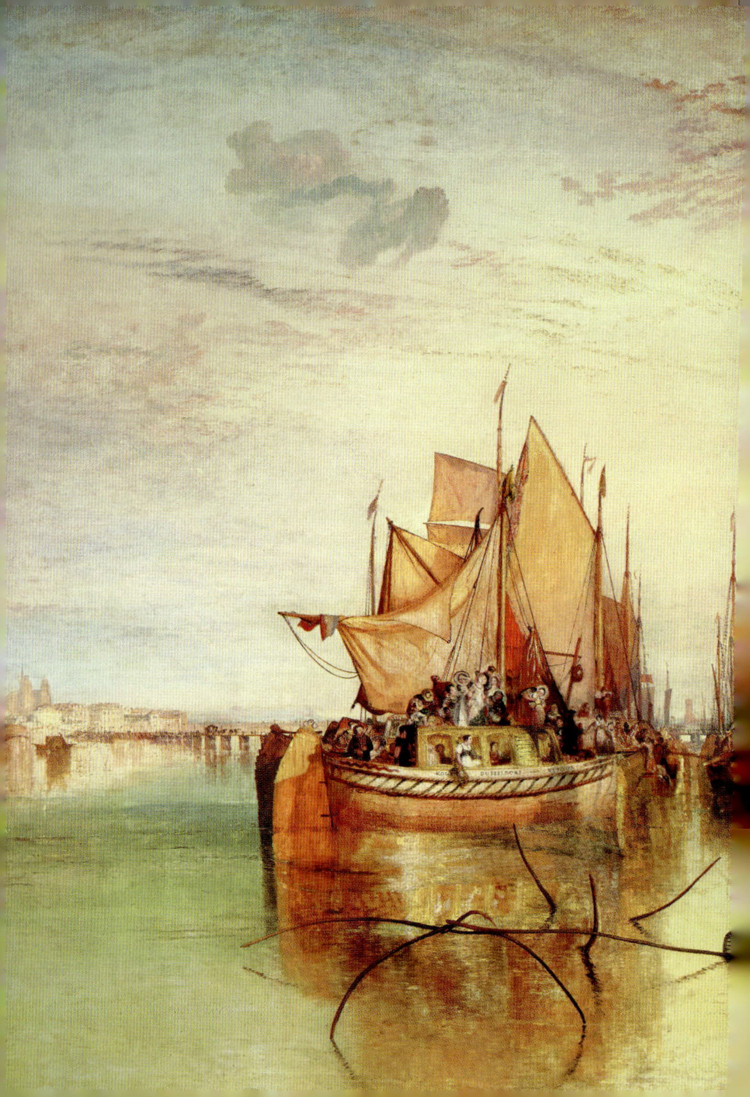

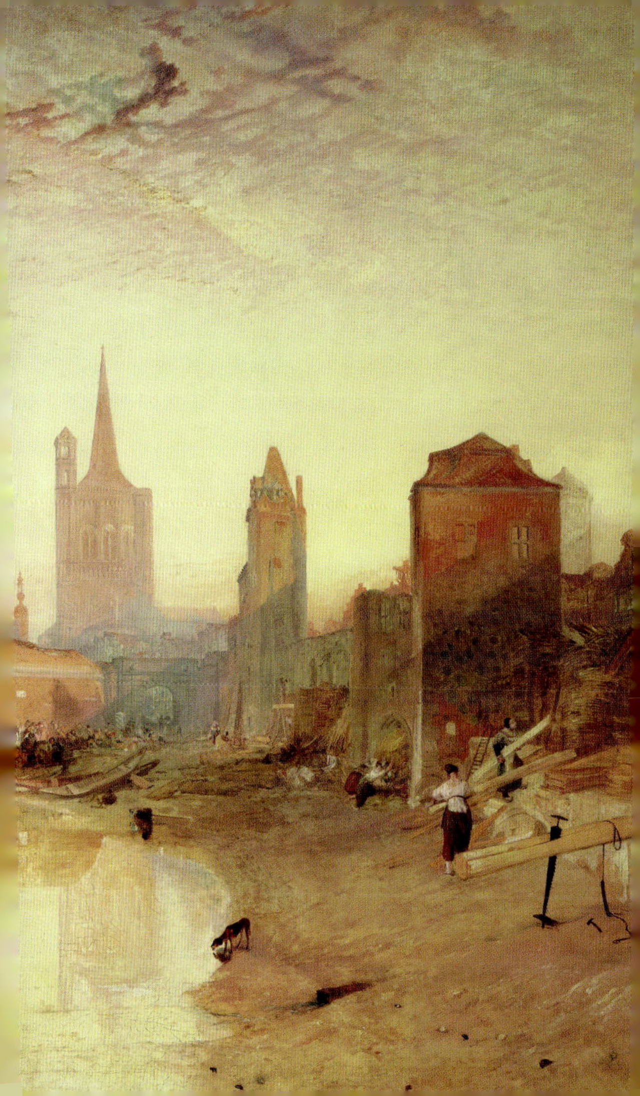

led a group of expectant critics up to the picture. He started back from it in consternation. The golden sky had changed to a dun colour. He ran up to Turner, who was in another part of the room—'Turner, Turner, what have you been doing to your picture?' 'Oh!' muttered Turner, in a low voice; 'poor Lawrence was so unhappy! It's only lampblack. It'll all wash off after the Exhibition!' He had actually passed a wash of lampblack in water-colour over the sky, and utterly spoiled his picture for the time, and so left it through the Exhibition, lest it should hurt Lawrence's.[II,113–4]

Chantrey's jokes with Turner on varnishing days were innumerable. The former was as full of tricks and mischief as when, as a boy, he had carried the milk cans to market. Once, when there was a report that the great artist was using some water-colour to tone his picture of *Cologne*, Chantrey, either to try, or probably not believing the story, went to the picture, and wetting his finger, drew a great schoolboy cross on the sail of one of the vessels. To his horror, surprise, and bitter regret, he found that he had removed so many inches of glazing. Turner, however, was not even ruffled; he laughed heartily at the sculptor's temerity, and at once repaired the mischief.[II, 257]

Previous pages: Cologne, the Arrival of a Packet Boat in the Evening, 1826

FISHING

Turner was very fond of fishing; he seldom went to visit a country friend without binding up a rod with his pilgrim's staff.

He was an intensely persevering fisherman too, no bad weather could drive him from his post, no ill-luck tire out his imperturbable patience; and here, too, I see reflected his greatness: the body that bore the long day's rain contained the mind that had borne the long struggle to fame. The hand that bore for hours' without repining the unlucky rod, was the hand that went on for years painting great pictures, though they would not sell.

When Turner went to Petworth, he always spent much time in fishing. When he went to revisit the scenes of his childhood at Brentford, or walked over from his house at Twickenham, to visit his friend Trimmer, of Heston, he always appeared carrying his rod.

Perhaps it was being amid nature, after all, that made the melancholy monotony of this dull sport so delightful to Turner; all that wet day he perhaps was observing ripples and reflections, and eddies and gleams of green weed and silvery glances of sullen fish, that were all garnered up in that vast and tenacious memory, which no note-taking habits could weaken.(II, 133–4)

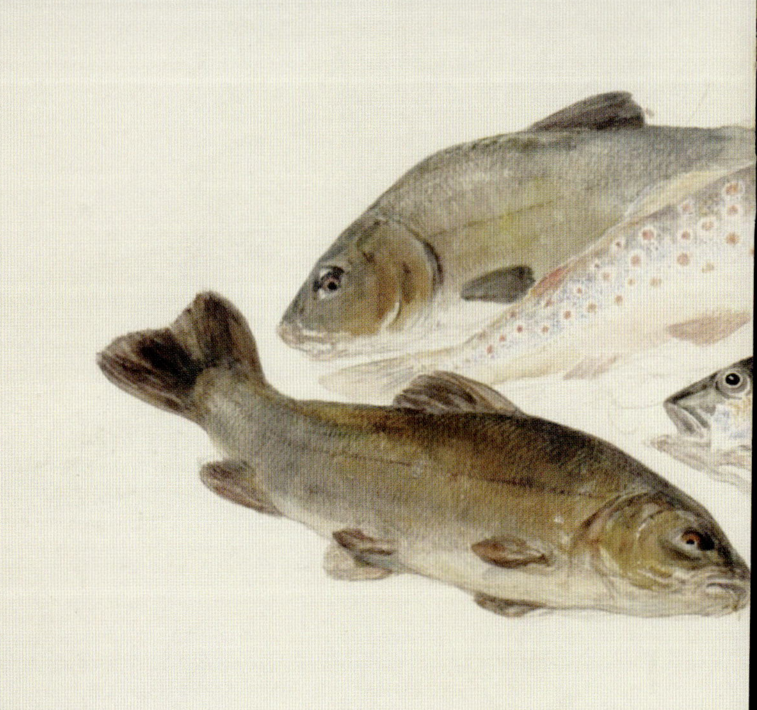

Study of Fish: Two Tench, a Trout and a Perch, c. 1822–4

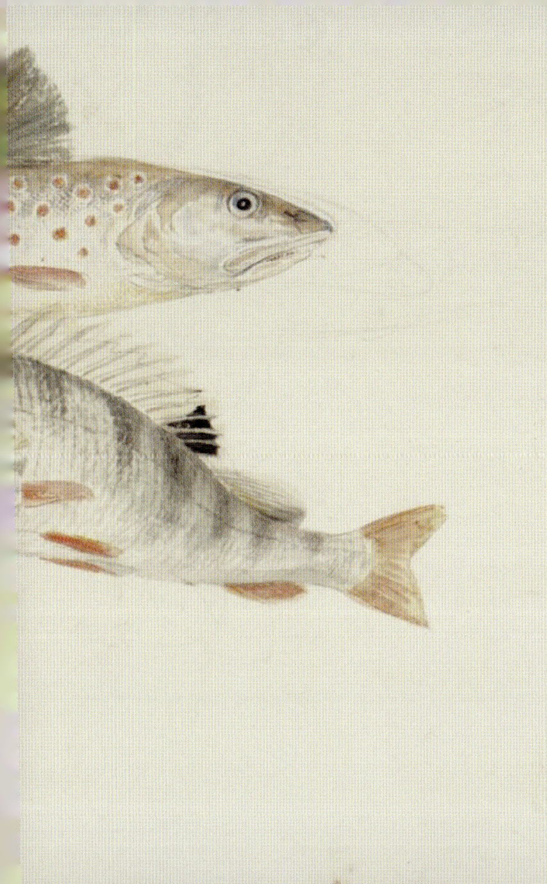

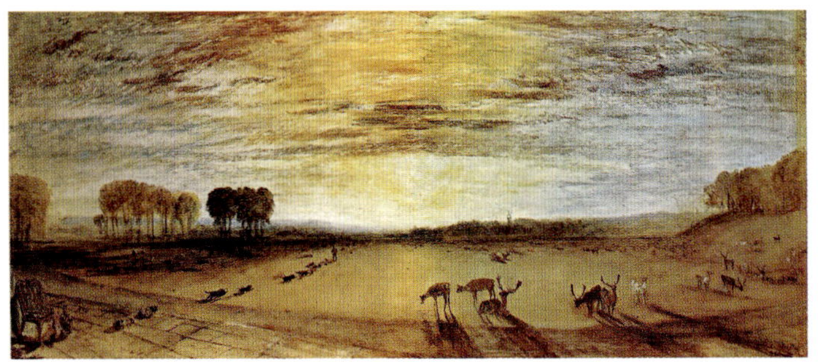

Study for Petworth Park: Tillington Church in the Distance, c. 1827–8

PETWORTH, SUSSEX

Turner was often at Lord Egremont's, and spent some of his happiest days there, fishing with Chantrey and his old friend, George Jones, R. A. The kind, rough, honest master of Petworth liked him, and the pair of eccentric men got on well together.(II, I)

In 1828 Turner painted his picture of *Petworth Park, Sussex*,* for the third earl; it was to decorate the Carved Chamber, sixty feet by twenty-four, of the old house of the Percys, and to fill the beautiful frames carved by Grinling Gibbons. This was the memorable year he painted the *Polyphemus*. In the foreground is the lake, and in the distance the tower of Tillington Church.

* One of a set of four landscapes still at Petworth House.

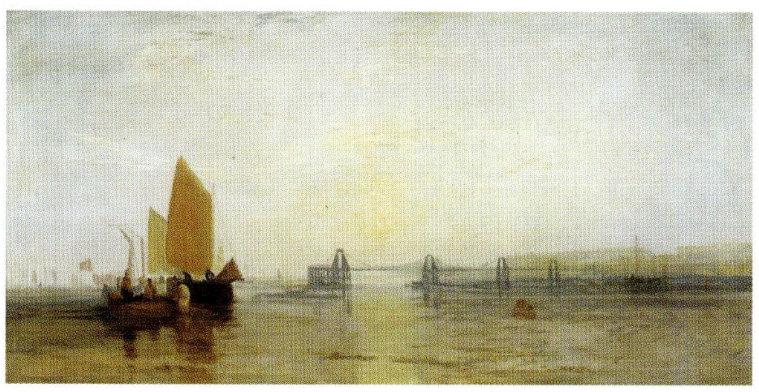

Study for The Chain Pier, Brighton, c. 1828

For Petworth he also painted the *Chain Pier of Brighton*,* then the landing-place for London and Dieppe steamers, and one of the wonders of Lord Egremont's county. It was commenced in 1822, and opened 1828 [in fact 1823]. Turner has sketched it at sunset, with the breakers coming in, and has ingeniously managed the perspective.(I, 306) Storey describes as follows:

> Fully to enjoy these pictures we must shut out all the surrounding objects with our hands, but whether or no, as we look at them, we soon forget everything else. As mere decorations they are perhaps inferior, but there is no need for me to say that Turner's pictures are deep mines of jewellery and thought,

* Petworth House

and to see them we must study them. Perhaps on this account the first glance at them is sometimes disappointing. The fourth picture, *Brighton Pier*, I cannot describe, for the sun of the others, still dazzling my eyes, prevents me from enjoying its cooler beauties.[II, 13]

FLOATING CARROTS

Turner was intensely obstinate. I think it was during a visit to Petworth that a discussion ensued between Lord Egremont and Turner as to whether carrots could float in water. I suppose Turner had introduced some in one of the Petworth pictures.

'Carrots don't swim.'

'They do.'

'They don't.'

'They do.'

Lord Egremont rings the bell, and calls for a bucket of water and some carrots. The water is brought, the carrots are thrown in. The obstinate painter is right; they do swim after all.[II, 160]

CHANTREY'S TRICK

Turner would rise early and get all his work done before the other guests were well about; then, like Scott, he could

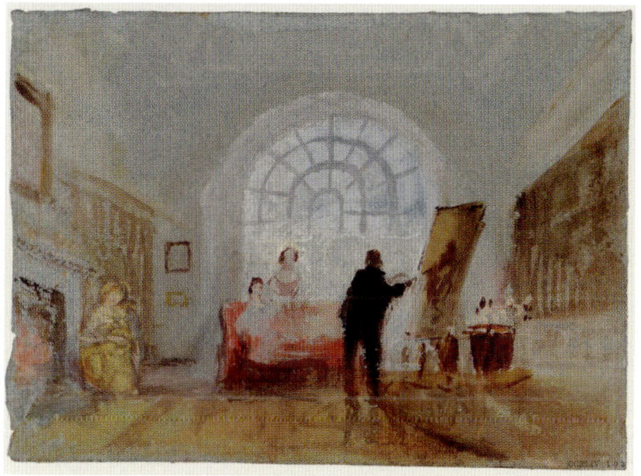

Petworth House: The Old Library
('The Artist and his Admirers'), 1827

idle the rest of the afternoon as he chose, to the astonishment of those who did not know his secret.

It was when Turner was painting a series of landscapes for the dining-room that Chantrey was there. The painter, reserved and loving quiet, and having secrets in his trade, worked always with his door locked, and no one but the master of the house was ever admitted.

Chantrey, disliking this secrecy, out of good-humoured mischief determined to play Turner a trick.

One day when all was still in the house, he paces down the corridor, imitating Lord Egremont's peculiar step and his cough. He arrives at the mysterious door and gives two distinct sharp raps, his lordship's signal for admittance. Instantly Turner shuffles up, the key turns, and Chantrey slips in before the angry recluse has time to rectify his mistake. This trick of Chantrey's became a standing joke at Petworth and at Academy meetings.[(II, 254–5)]

FRANCIS CHANTREY

The good-natured, jovial sculptor had a boundless admiration for Turner's genius. No one better at the time appreciated the mental scope of the artist. His lance was ever in the rest to tilt against Turner's maligners: hydras that seemed to sprout out fresh tongues the faster the club fell and the brand scarred.

Chantrey would never in his hearing, however, allow any one to disparage his friend's imagination. He would not endure sneers from those who could see faults, and yet would not see merits. The gorgeous colours he admired, though he did not altogether approve them; the breadth of air he would allow no one to gainsay. He felt as a sculptor, except occasionally in figures. He admired Turner's wonderful appreciation of forms, his perfect chiaroscuro, and the learning and grace with which he varied the lines of his compositions; his mountains, skies, water, trees, ships, buildings; he thought no one was more profound in the knowledge of this art than Turner.

Chantrey considered Turner as a poetic genius of the highest rank—in depicting light and atmosphere as the greatest of past or present painters, perhaps unsurpassable as a consummate arranger of lines in his landscape and architectural compositions. He knew thoroughly that his effects were not merely the result of observation and selection, but of long thought and treasured learning.(II, 253–4)

ROME 1828

[Sir Charles Eastlake relates that]

When Turner was in Rome, in 1828-29, he resided in the same house with me (12, Piazza Mignanelli, where Mr. Percy Williams now lives). He painted there the *View of Orvieto*, the *Regulus*, and the *Medea*.* Those pictures were exhibited in Rome in some rooms which Turner subsequently occupied at the Quattro Fontane. The foreign artists who went to see them could make nothing of them. Turner's economy and ingenuity were apparent in his mode of framing those pictures. He nailed a rope round the edges of each, and painted it with yellow ochre

* All Tate, London

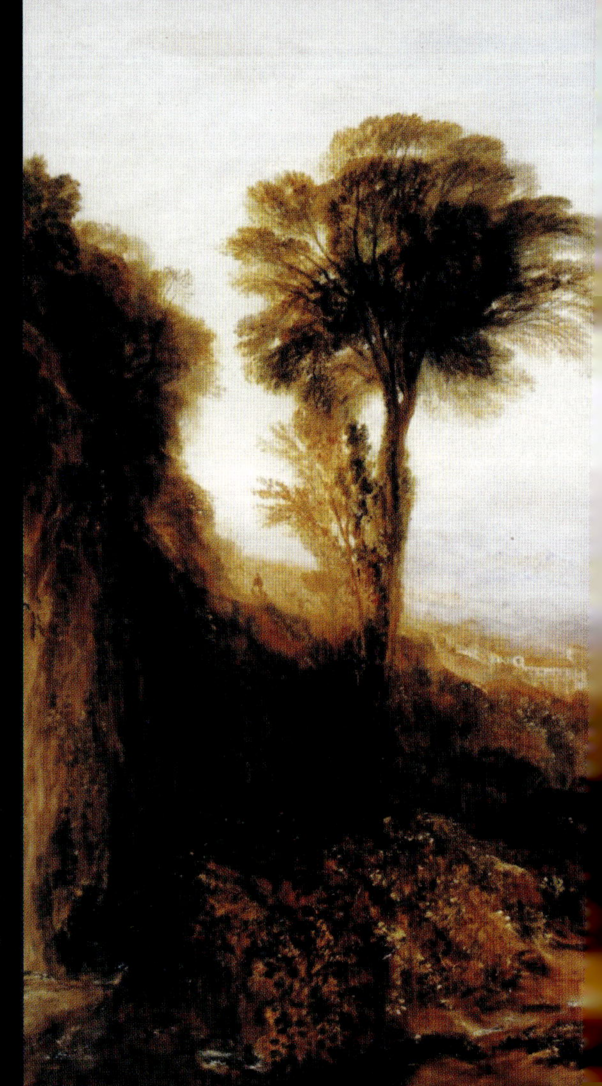

View of Orvieto,
Painted in Rome,
1828–30

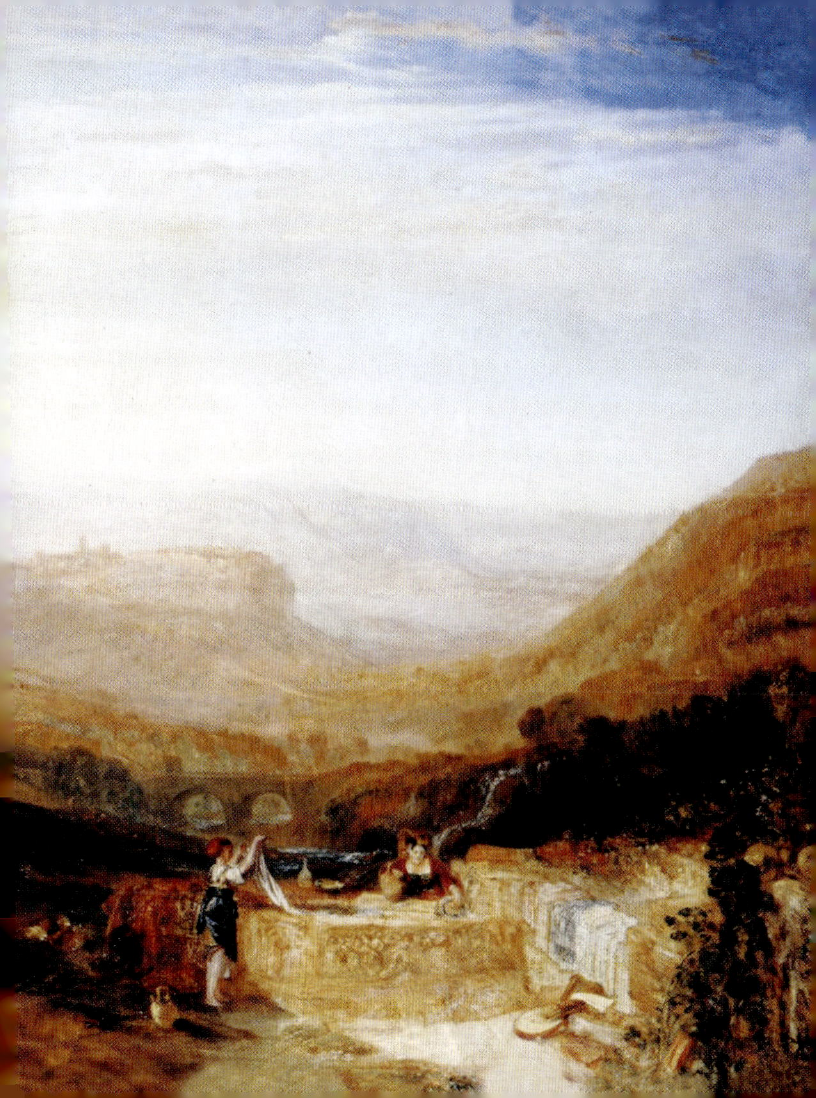

> in tempera. When those same works were packed to be sent to England, I advised him to have the cases covered with waxed cloth, as the pictures without it might be exposed to wet. Turner thanked me, and said the advice was important; 'for,' he added, 'if any wet gets to them, they will be destroyed.' This indicates his practice of preparing his pictures with a kind of tempera, a method which, before the surface was varnished, was not waterproof. The pictures referred to were in fact not finished; nor could any of his exhibited pictures be said to be finished till he had worked on them when they were on the walls of the Royal Academy.(I, 221)

Mr. [Edward Villiers] Rippingille, when he was at Rome, inquired about Turner; he says:

> No other country appears to have felt his kind of merit as it was felt at home, and in this we see the clue to Turner's great success and popularity. I do not find that in foreign countries Turner was at all esteemed. In a subsequent portion of his life Turner was in Rome, and there exhibited pictures which (no disgrace, I must say) won him no credit. At the time he was in the Eternal City, an English tradesman was living there, who made a great to do, and

> sold English mustard; and when his namesake came and exposed his wares, the Romans, who are a peculiar class of jokers, proclaimed that one sold mustard, and the other painted it. Some intelligent Romans, with whom I talked, wondered that the English could be so devoid of taste as to admire and tolerate such extravagant productions.(I, 227)

THE *POLYPHEMUS*

Why the painter selected this subject it is difficult to say. The picture* may have been merely the framework for a magnificent sunrise, or it may be that Turner desired to write his name on Homer's tomb, to 'share his triumph and partake his gale;' or it may be that something in the story of Ulysses interested one who was also a traveller—wily, silent when need be, and vigilant. He felt that here he was doing something timid Claude would not have dared to do, that would have half blinded sombre Poussin, and have been to Vandervelde a sheer impossibility. There was room here for imagination and for truth. He would associate all the hope and splendour and joy of the morning with thoughts of human bravery and freedom; and invest it all, according to honoured precedent with classic interest. It was a virgin subject.(I, 309–10)

* *Ulysses deriding Polyphemus*, 1829, National Gallery, London

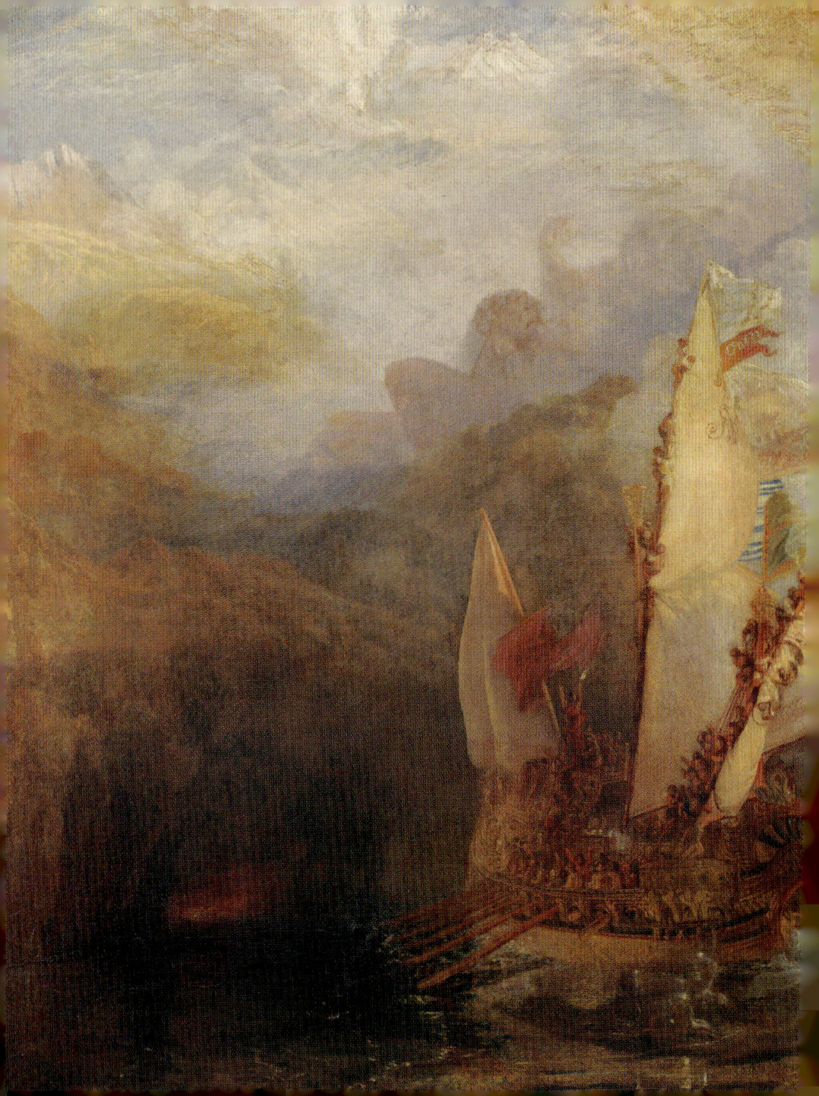

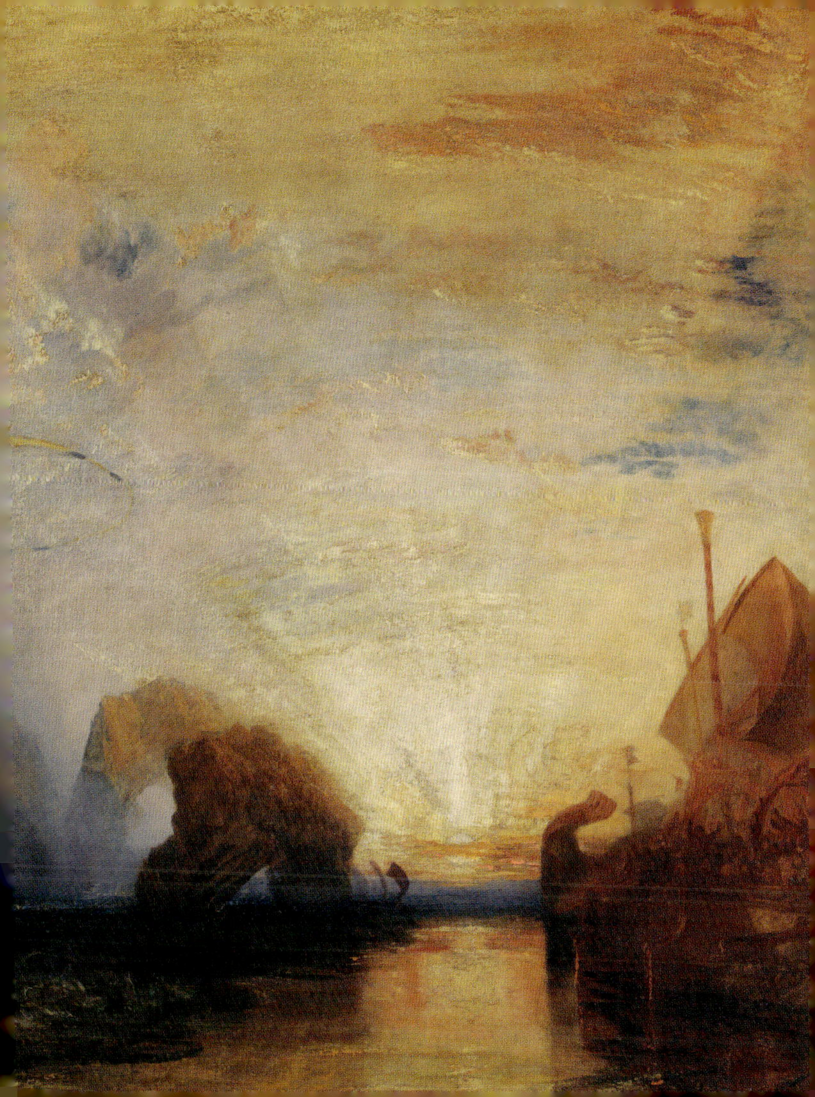

The painter has chosen the moment when Ulysses, the destroyer of Troy, vociferates his real name, and the Cyclops, with speaking trumpet voice, answers that such a man had indeed been prophesied as his destroyer. Then, in return to the rather cruel and bragging exultation of the Greek, the Cyclops, with hands uplifted to heaven, prays to his father Neptune to beleaguer Ulysses with misfortunes.

This is the moment of the picture. How it proves that genius is better than learning! Turner was no deep student of Homer; he knew him only through the formal prettinesses of Pope's translation; yet he paints him better than all the learned men, and commits no anachronism. Even when he invents, he seems to have an instinct for truth, for those pierced rocks are said to be characteristic of the island of Corcyra where the scene of the story is laid. Yet Turner was probably thinking of the Calf of Man or the Needles. Not that I am fond of the arched rock; we have had too much of it in theatrical scenery, and I always associate it with sham smugglers, corked eye-brows, and enormous horse-pistols.

The galley, too, of Ulysses, though perhaps an impossibility, is a grand impossibility, rather unwieldy and top-heavy, too: a sort of cross, in fact, between the Venetian fishing-boats and the Lord Mayor's barge, made

Previous pages: Ulysses Deriding Polyphemus, 1829

apparently of gold snuff-boxes, with gold pencil-cases for masts; but that is neither here nor there.

What vigour in that sun, that cometh forth like a bridegroom out of its chamber and rejoiceth like a strong man to run its course. What Orient splendour of colour, fanning out far beyond towards Ithaca and home.(I, 313–14)

For colour, for life and shade, for composition, this seems to me the most wonderful and admirable of Turner's idealisms. This is a creation and a poem. The *Temeraire*,* though equally exquisite in its way, is only a natural incident poetically heightened it is truth and poetry. This is imagination and poetry. Yet, perhaps, Turner valued the *Temeraire* most, for he peculiarly reserved it in his will.

There can be, of course, no doubt that Turner selected this subject from the ninth book of the *Odyssey*. Yet, with his usual secretive sort of fun, he loved to mystify busybodies and dilettantes about it.

His friend, the Rev. Mr. Judkins, who is neither a busybody nor a dilettante, but a friend of Constable's, and a very clever landscape artist, was one day dining with Turner at a large party. A lady sitting next to the clerical artist, with the curiosity traditionally supposed to be peculiar to her sex, was full of the glories of the *Polyphemus*, the wonder of the last Exhibition. It was one perpetual whisper.

* National Gallery, London (see pp. 206–7)

'Wine? No, thank you; but oh, Mr. Judkins, do you— What do you think of Mr. Turner's great picture? And—a very little, if you please. Don't you now think it is a sweet picture?' &c, &c.

Turner, glum and shy, opposite, is watching all this. He sees where the lady's eyes fall after she addresses her whispers to Mr. Judkins. His little beads of eyes roll and twinkle with fun and slyness. Across the table he growls:—

'I know what you two are talking about, Judkins—about my picture.'

Mr. Judkins suavely waves his glass and acknowledges that it was. The lady smiled on the great man.

'And I bet you don't know where I took the subject from; come now—bet you don't.'

Judkins blandly replied,—

'Oh! from the old poet, of course, Turner; from the *Odyssey*, of course.'

'No,' grunted Turner, bursting into a chuckle; '*Odyssey!* not a bit of it. I took it from Tom Dibdin. Don't you know the lines:—

> "He ate his mutton, drank his wine,
> And then he poked his eye out."'

The lines may be in Dibdin—I never could find them; but such is the mystifying fun Turner was so fond of.(I, 316–17)

DEATH OF WILLIAM TURNER SENIOR

The old man latterly, (says Mr. Trimmer), was his son's willing slave, and had to strain [ie stretch] his pictures, and varnish them when finished, which made Turner say that his father began and finished his pictures for him. But I doubt if he varnished many pictures; few of them, I believe, were varnished at all; still, he was of great assistance to his son, and I think it was Mr. [Charles] Turner, the engraver, who told me that once making bold to enter Turner's studio, he found the old man on his knees colouring a canvas, when Turner made his appearance, and good-humouredly trundled out the visitor, telling him he was on forbidden ground. Turner was much attached to his father, and at his death stayed with us a few days at Heston for change of scene. He was fearfully out of spirits, and felt his loss, he said, like that of an only child. When at Sandycombe Lodge Turner senior was much respected, and I was told by the vicar that he was a regular attendant at the parish church. As he advanced in years, his son had him with him in London, and sold the place at Richmond, much to the old man's dislike. I have heard Turner censured for it; but he told my father that 'Dad' was always working in the garden and catching cold, and required looking after. Turner never appeared the same man after his father's death; his family was broken up. Phrenologically speaking, the father had the best skull of the two.[I, 163–4]

THE BENEVOLENT HOARDER [ROW OF 1829]

Mr. David Roberts, one of Turner's oldest friends, says:—

I think it must have been in the year 1823 or 1824 that being called on to attend a meeting of stewards of the Artists' General Benevolent Fund at the Crown and Anchor in the Strand, I first saw Turner; my impression at the time was anything but what I had in my imagination formed of this great painter. [...] Being seated round a table covered with green baize a little square-built man came in, to whom all paid respect; the business having begun, he joined in the conversation, and made some weak attempts at wit—at least I thought so, for no one seemed to laugh at his jokes but himself! So I asked who this very facetious little man was, and my astonishment on being told that it was 'The Great Turner' almost, without meaning a pun, turned my head.[II, 266]

It was in connexion with the Artists' General Benevolent Institution, that he himself had helped to found, that Turner's kind-heartedness shone out most conspicuously. But he was always for saving, for hoarding and scraping for future, perhaps distant, great emergencies. He was always for collecting and storing a treasure with which magnificent deeds of charity were to be done. He was a patient man, and looked forward to great benevolent schemes. 'But all this time,' said some, 'there are the widows and orphans of poor artists starving. We are planning a rich meal for our horses, but in the meantime the steed starves. This saving for future charity, and in the meantime being uncharitable, is too stoical for us; the groans of the poor reach our ears and wrack our hearts; let us open the granary of our benevolence, and not keep heaping up corn for famines that will never come.' But Turner would not change his plans; he was getting old and dogmatic; he was proud, and expected submission and respect to his views, especially as he was one of the founders. He could not help saving, it was in his blood; he had saved when it was necessary, he saved now because he did not know how to spend; he had saved for years for himself on principle, he saved now for others from habit.

The younger men were determined, with all respect to Turner, to overthrow this principle. They resolved to give their money nearly all away in contributions. Mr. Turner was treasurer, and kept his hand clenched beyond any one's strength to open; he lay at the door of the money room, whoever entered to take a handful must tread on Turner's body.

There was a growling conflict, but Turner could not be moved. His opponents were equally obstinate, for they felt they combated about a principle. Doggedly—for Turner was very obstinate—he abandoned the Society for ever. In vain Mr. Cockerell, one of the opposition, went to Queen Anne Street to discuss the matter with him. He would hardly see him; he growled; he would not even relent when Mr. Cockerell told him, 'that he would one day have to answer to the widows and orphans to whom he had refused bread.' As far as I can understand, Turner all but showed Mr. Cockerell the door, so hurt and indignant was he at what I dare say he called the ingratitude shown him by the Society. The Society then leaving the implacable Achilles, proceeded on their own way, and that way prospered. (II, 267–9)

ENGRAVING ON STEEL

Turner was at first a stern opponent to engraving on steel,* and had no notion of supplying plates for 'the million!' He called upon Sir Thomas Lawrence one day, at a

* Introduced by Thomas Lupton in the mid 1820s.

time when he had just received a proof, with which he was very much pleased. He showed it to Turner, and said, 'By the way. Turner, I wonder you don't have some of your drawings engraved on steel.' 'Humph! I hate steel.' 'But why?' 'I don't like it: besides, I don't choose to be a basket engraver!' 'A basket engraver! a basket engraver, Turner! what is that?' said the President. Turner looked at Lawrence, with that malicious leer which, in his little penetrating eyes, when he meant mischief conveyed more killing sarcasm than his words, and said, 'When I got off the coach t'other day at Hastings, a woman came up with a basketful of your *Mrs. Peel,** and wanted to sell me one for sixpence.' He disliked his works being sold cheap.(II, 147–8)

The illustrations to Rogers's *Italy* have never since been equalled.† Turner's best work is there engraved in the best manner and on the costliest paper. The figures and animals—such as the banditti, the dogs, and the monks, the boating party on Como, the goats on the Campagna, are among the best he ever drew. The *Alps* and *Lake of Geneva*, his *Moonlight*, and his *Rome*, are all quite gems. All that he liked to do best he seems to have done then. The

* Frick Collection, New York, NY † This illustrated edition of Samuel Rogers' long poem *Italy* was published in 1830 and included 25 vignettes by Turner. It was an immense success and went into six editions by 1859.

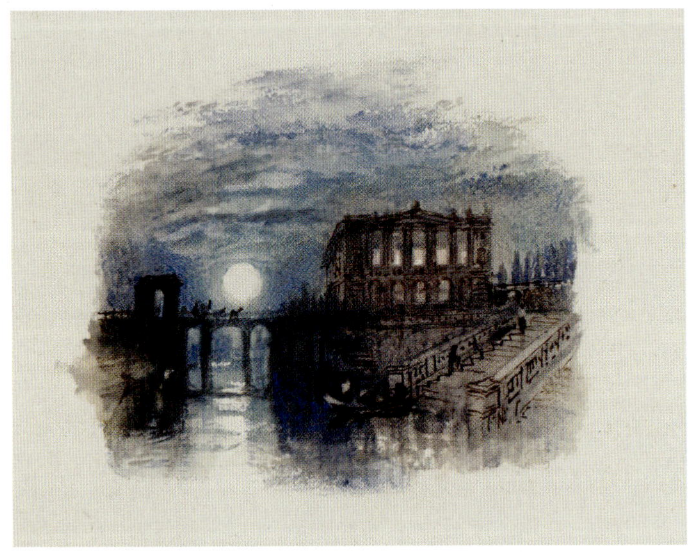

A Villa. Moon-Light (A Villa on the Night of a Festa di Ballo), vignette for Samuel Rogers' Italy, c. 1826–27

Moonlight is serener, the Rome more solid, the Venice more fairy-like than any one else's Rome, Venice, or Moonlight.[I, 242]

Turner did not care for the mere prosaic fact of any place; he was no local topographer; he did not draw for the townsmen or villagers. What he tried to do was to crowd into one drawing all the salient features of the whole neighbourhood. He knew how limited art was, and he thus sought to extend its frontier. If a steeple is a hundred feet high, it is sometimes necessary to draw it three hundred, to convey the effect of its being one hundred.(II, 235)

During some three years Turner was associated in the production of the *Rivers of France* with Mr. Leitch Ritchie. They travelled, however, very little in company; their tastes in everything but art being exceedingly dissimilar. 'I was curious,' says Mr. Ritchie,

> in observing what he made of the objects he selected for his sketches, and was frequently surprised to find what a forcible idea he conveyed of a place with scarcely a single correct detail. His exaggerations, when it suited his purpose to exaggerate, were wonderful; lifting up, for instance, by two or three stories, the steeple or rather stunted cone of a village-church; and when I returned to London, I never failed to roast him on this habit. He took my remarks in good part, sometimes indeed in great glee, never attempting to defend himself otherwise than by rolling back the war into the enemy's camp.(II, 236–7)

* *Overleaf: Saumur from the Île d'Offart, with the Pont Cessart and the Château in the Distance c. 1830. One of the watercolours made in preparation for Rivers of France*

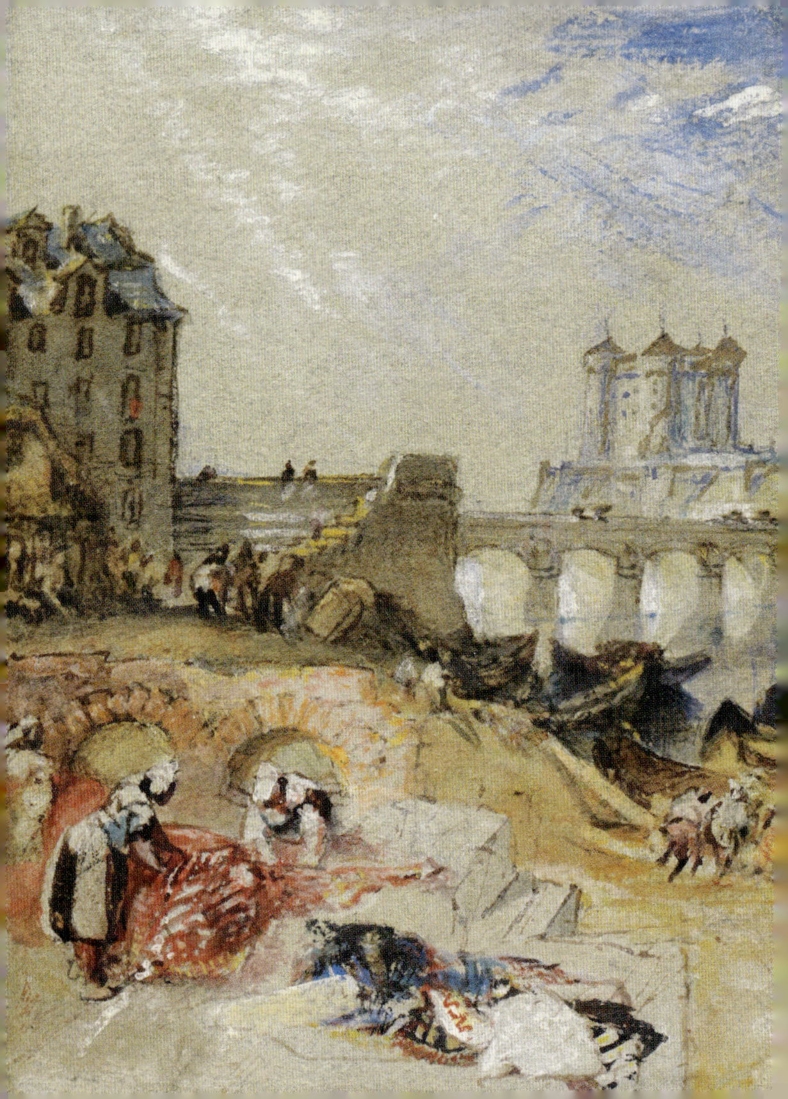

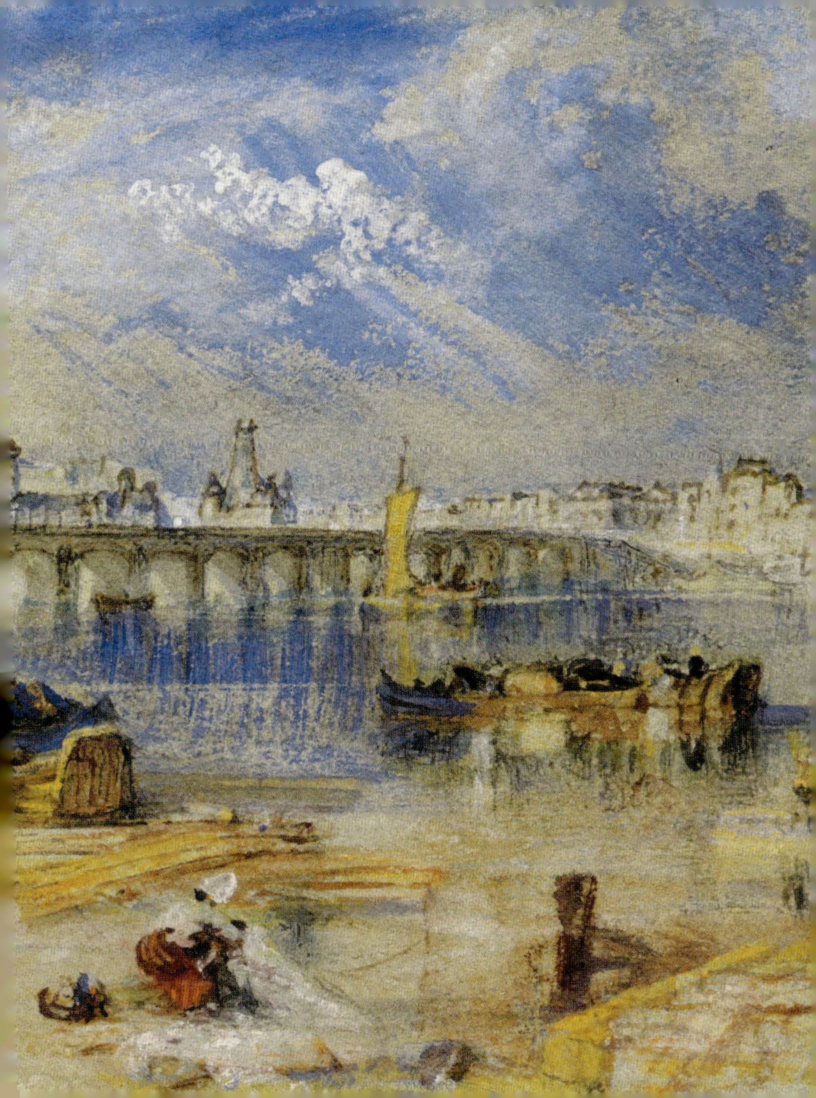

Mr. Lupton, the celebrated engraver, says:

> Turner was a man that not only considered that time was money, but he acted upon it, and worked from morning till night; indeed, it would be correct to say he laboured from sunrise to sunset. He would often ask his brother artists, sarcastically, if they ever saw the sun rise. These industrious habits, and his love of his profession, gave him a very long life, and accounts for the great number of his works left behind him, for it may be truly said he worked as many hours as would make the lives of two men of his own age.
>
> Turner was a great observer of all that occurred in his profession; of reserved manners generally, but never coarse (as has been said), though blunt and straightforward, he had a great respect for his profession, and always felt and expressed regret if any member of it appeared to waste or neglect his profession.[II, 36]

TURNER IN SCOTT-LAND

In the autumn of 1831 Turner was employed by Mr. Cadell to make a collection of twenty-four sketches for a new edition of Scott's poems, the publisher to retain the drawings. The painter had not seen the Trossachs or Loch Katrine till this year. Turner expressed his increased admiration of Scott after visiting the scenes Sir Walter had described, and personally testing their truth. He used to say Corriskin, in the Isle of Skye, was the grandest scene he had ever beheld.

It was at Corriskin that Turner all but perished while clambering about the crags. All I know of this escape is from the *Quarterly* reviewer of the time. In Vol. X. of Scott's *Poetical Works*, on the passage ending with the line 'the bleakest mountain side' in the 'Lord of the Isles,' I find the following note:—

> The *Quarterly* reviewer says, 'This picture of barren desolation is admirably touched, and if the opinion of Mr. Turner be worth anything, no words could have given a truer picture of this, one of the wildest of Nature's landscapes. Mr. Turner adds, however, that he dissents in one particular—but for one or two tufts of grass, he must have broken his neck, having slipped when trying to attain the best position for taking the view which embellishes this volume.'(I, 184–5)

Turner knew little of Scotch history, and cared, I should imagine, less. What he wanted was to paint

Overleaf: Corriskin (Loch Coruisk, Skye), 1831–34, reproduced about two thirds larger than life size. Turner can be seen sketching precariously.

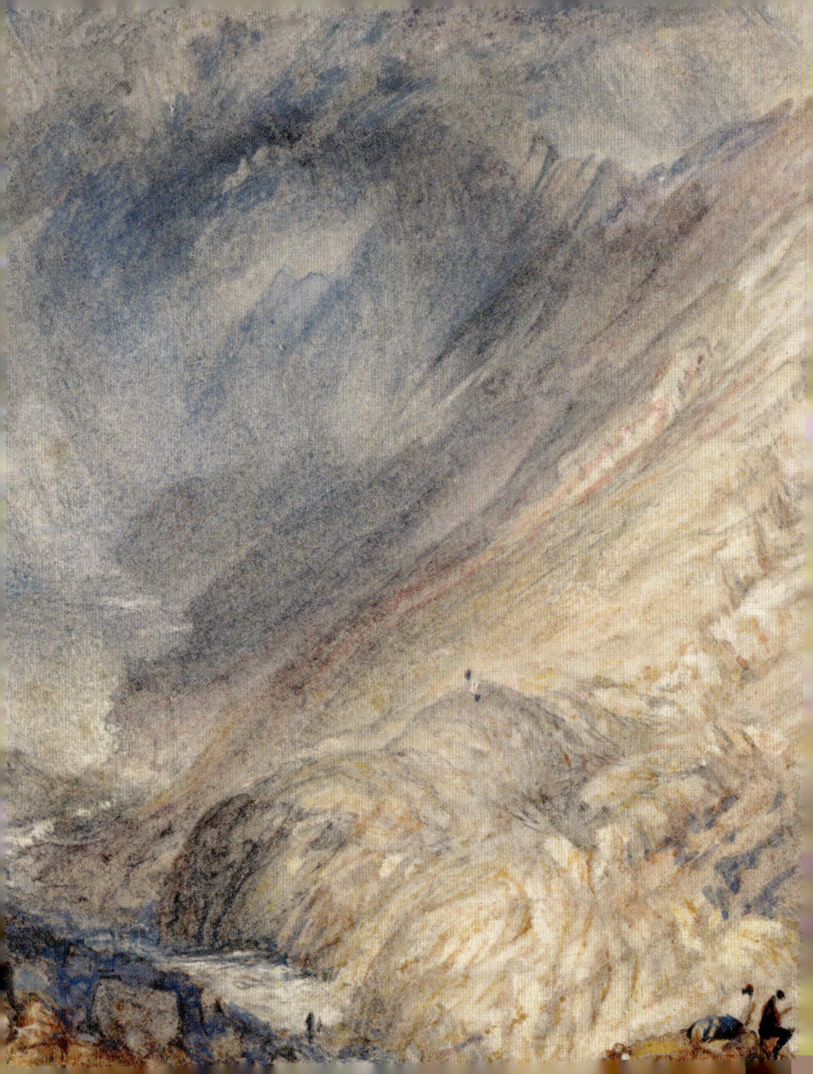

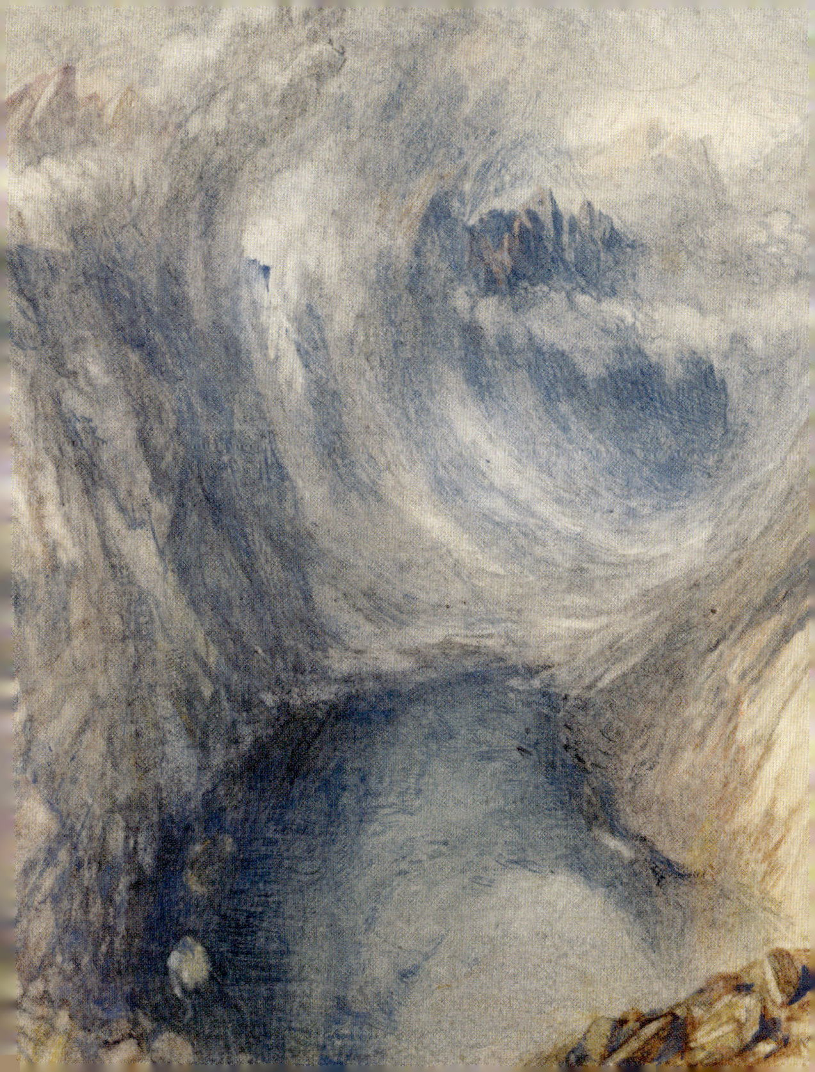

beautiful dreams of quiet lakes and of calm old castles, mouldering away majestically to the dust from which they sprang; and so he could do that, and carry off a good bagful of guineas to boot, he cared not for the Douglas of the Bleeding Heart, nay, nor for Bruce of Bannockburn himself. I do not say, far, far from it, that Turner had not read Scott's poems; no doubt he had, and enjoyed heartily the vigour and truth of their medievalism; but still his works show no especial appreciation of the poet, they are distinct creations, with a tender and exquisite beauty of their own; showing us the scenes, not as they were, but as they are—contrasting the feudal and the past as much as possible, and as sadly as possible, with the present.[(I. 188–9)]

Turner's *chef d'œuvre* is that tremendous scene, Loch Corriskin, in the Isle of Skye. In these upheaved waves and pinnacles of rock Turner revels, as he does in the mist that rolls up the receding glen, and darkens the small black grave of a lake. The danger of the scene is hinted by the precarious seat in which the painter sits, while his guide lies down and waits.[(I, 191–2)]

Many years ago (when Turner was making sketches for the *Provincial Antiquities*, Mr. Cadell, the Edinburgh bookseller, being with him), as they passed Norham, Turner took off his hat and made a low bow to the ruins,

* National Gallery of Scotland, Edinburgh (see preceding pages).

upon observing which, Cadell said, 'What the devil are you about now?' ' Oh!' replied Turner, 'I made a drawing or painting of Norham several years since [ie in 1797]; it took, and from that day to this, I have had as much to do as my hands could execute.'(I, 195)

Most probably this tour produced the *Norham Castle ('Summer's Morn')** exhibited at the Royal Academy, 1798, and used again in the *Liber* in 1816. It also served as an illustration to *Marmion*. I have seen several drawings of it by Turner; he generally brings the castle as a dark mass against the rising sun—cattle and boats in the foreground.(I, 196)

VARNISHING DAYS (2): CONSTABLE VS. TURNER

On these varnishing days Turner arrived very early, with his dirty chest of colours, his worn-out brushes, and an unclean palette, which would have shocked a Dutch painter. He sat on steps, or made a pile of boxes to stand on if his picture hung high.

Turner's fun was often professional.(II, 140)

My kind friend, Mr. Wilkie Collins, sends to me his boyish recollections of Turner. He (Mr. W. C.) used to go with his father to carry his paint-box, and make himself generally

* With Christie's, 5 July 2017, lot 105 (see pp. 60–1; and also pp. 264–5).

useful. On one of these occasions he remembers seeing Turner (not the more perfect in his balance for the brown sherry at the Academy lunch), seated on the top of a flight of steps, astride a box. There he sat a shabby Bacchus, nodding like a mandarin at his picture, which he, with a pendulum motion, now touched with his brush, and now receded from. Yet in spite of sherry, precarious seat, and old age. Turner went on shaping in some wonderful dream of colour, every touch meaning something, every pin's head of colour being a note in the chromatic scale.[II, 186]

That admirable, frank, and simple writer on art, the late Mr. [Charles Robert] Leslie, also sketches Turner on these pleasant days. He says:—

> Turner was very amusing on the varnishing, or rather the painting days, at the Academy. Singular as were his habits—for nobody knew where or how he lived—his nature was social, and at our lunch on those anniversaries he was the life of the table. The Academy has relinquished, very justly, a privilege for its own members which it could not extend to all exhibitors. But I believe, had the varnishing days been abolished while Turner lived, it would almost have broken his heart. When such a measure

* See p. 196.

was hinted to him, he said, 'Then you will do away with the only social meetings we have, the only occasion on which we all come together in an easy, unrestrained manner. When we have no varnishing days, we shall not know one another.'

In 1822 [actually 1832], when Constable exhibited his *Opening of Waterloo Bridge*,* it was placed in the School of Painting, one of the small rooms at Somerset House. A sea piece by Turner was next to it—a grey picture, beautiful and true, but with no positive colour in any part of it.† Constable's picture seemed as if painted with liquid gold and silver, and Turner came several times into the room while he was heightening with vermilion and lake the decorations and flags of the city barges. Turner stood behind him, looking from the *Waterloo* to his own picture; and putting a round daub of red lead, somewhat bigger than a shilling, on his grey sea, went away without a word. The intensity of the red lead, made more vivid by the coolness of his picture, caused even the vermilion and lake of Constable to look weak. I came into the room just as Turner left it. 'He has been here,' said Constable, 'and fired off a gun.' On the opposite wall was a picture, by Jones, of *Shadrach, Meshach and Abednego in the Furnace*.‡

* Tate, London † *Helvoetsluys; the City of Utrecht, 64, Going to Sea*, Tokyo Fuji Art Museum, Tokyo (see overleaf and also p. 36) ‡ Tate, London

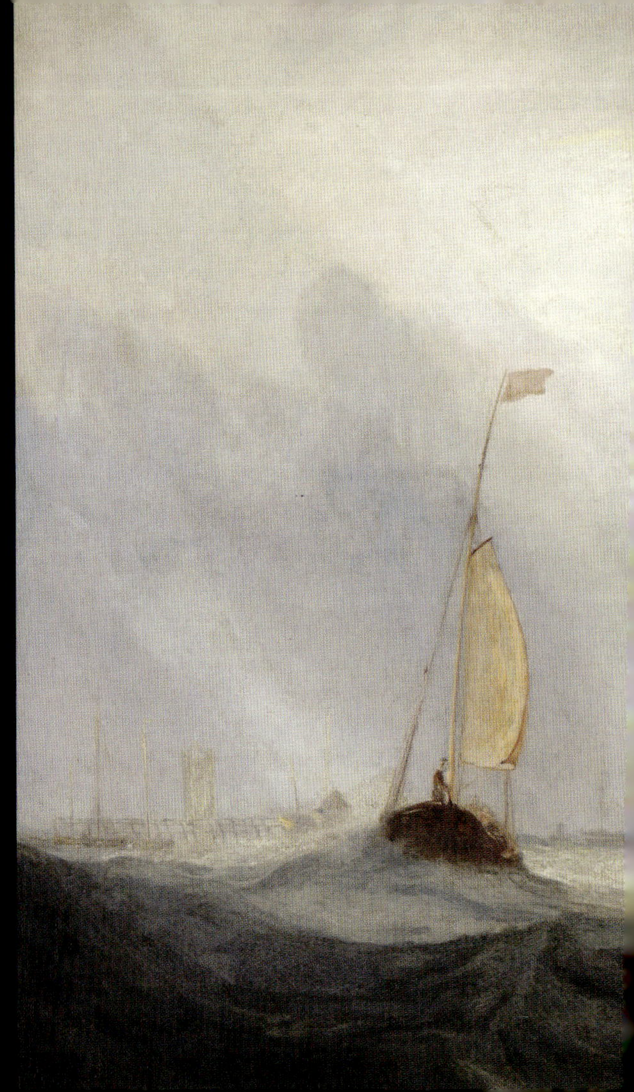

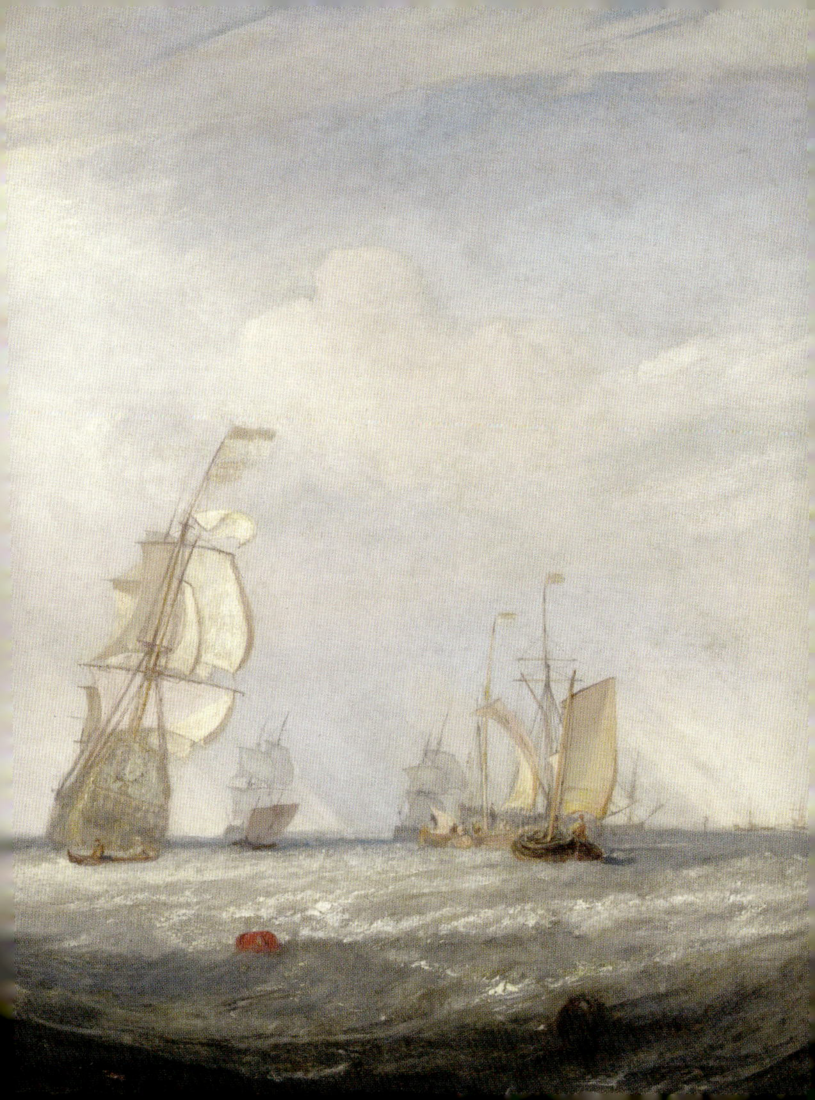

'A coal,' said Cooper, 'has bounced across the room from Jones's picture, and set fire to Turner's sea.' The great man did not come again into the room for a day and a half; and then, in the last moments that were allowed for painting, he glazed the scarlet seal he had put on his picture, and shaped it into a buoy.

In finishing the *Waterloo Bridge*, Constable used the palette knife more than the pencil. He found it the only instrument by which he could express, as he wished, the sparkle of the water.

This is a matchless story. The fact was, Turner did not much like Constable, and was not going to let himself be checkmated. What knowledge, too, it showed to suddenly alter the whole plan of his picture, and yet not to spoil it. Constable was secretly very severe on Turner's pictures, and in his violent sarcastic way would sometimes pretend to spit in disgust when they were mentioned. Leslie, his worshipper, acquired somewhat of the same prejudice; but his strong good sense soon mastered it. Once, Constable was pacing impatiently before a picture, the effect of which somehow or other did not please him. It was true to rules, but still there was something wanting (perhaps a mere red cap, a blue apron, or a tree stem); yet what it was he could not for the life of him tell. There was a line too

Previous pages: Helvoetsluys; the City of Utrecht, 64, Going to Sea, 1832

much or too little in the composition, that was certain. A speck of colour redundant or deficient, that was evident. At that moment Turner entered.

'I say, Turner,' cried Constable, 'there is something wrong in this picture, and I cannot for the life of me tell what it is. You give it a look.'

Turner looked at the picture steadily for a few moments, then seized a brush, and struck in a ripple of water in the foreground.

That was the secret—the picture was now perfect, the spell was completed. The fresh, untired eye of the great magician had seen the want at a glance.(II, 186–9)

CONSTABLE

Turner was too reserved to often praise, but he never uttered a word of critical disparagement or detraction. No restless poison of envy oozed perpetually from his tongue as it did from Constable's.

[Thomas] Stothard he would, however, openly praise; for he loved the gentle poetry which suffused all that good man did. ... Turner painted his *Boccaccio* picture* in distinct rivalry of Stothard, and he openly expressed his desire that Stothard, above all men, should like his pictures.

* *Boccaccio Relating the Tale of the Bird Cage*, 1832, Tate, London

[William] Etty, I believe, he did not like; Constable he personally had no relish for. I am afraid that Constable openly praised and secretly disliked Turner's works. (II, 35)

VARNISHING DAYS (3): GEORGE JONES

Two of the best stories extant about, the motives which led Turner to paint particular pictures are the following, which were kindly communicated to me by Mr. G. Jones, the painter's special crony and comrade. The first relates to Turner's picture of *The Burial of Wilkie*, that funeral picture in which every tone and tint is so attuned to the subject that the whole seems as if it were painted on crape.* The story dates the time back to when Wilkie, on his return to England, died near Gibraltar, and was buried in the sacred blue water close to Trafalgar. It strikingly shows Turner's depth of feeling, and his desire, without regard to buying or selling, to paint a monumental picture that might record his esteem for Wilkie's talent.

Shortly after Wilkie's death and burial at sea, the following conversation took place between Turner and his friend Jones.

T. I suppose nobody will do anything to commemorate Wilkie.

* *Peace – Burial at Sea*, Tate, London

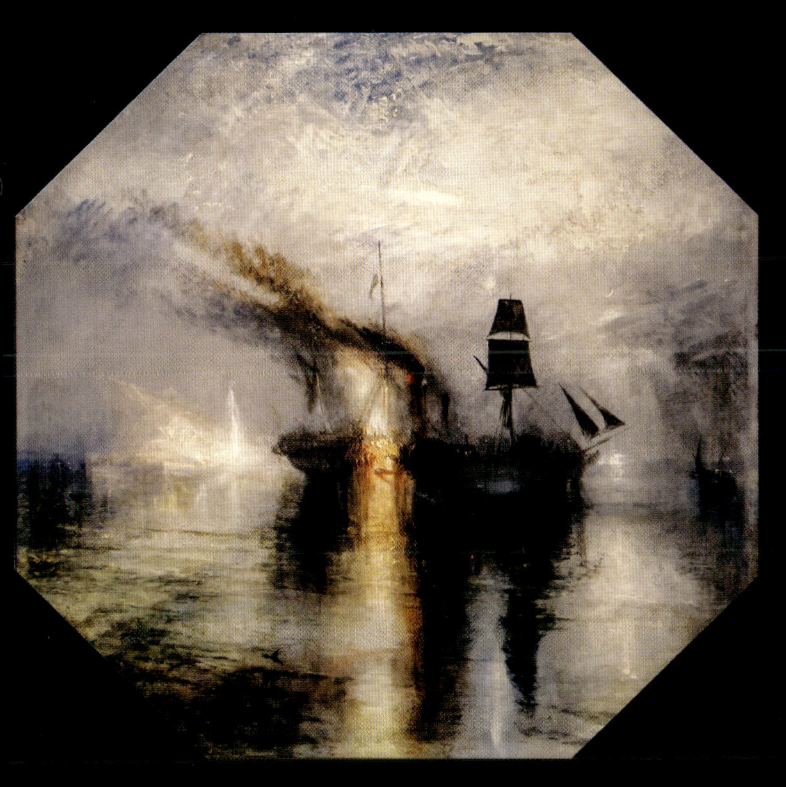

Peace – Burial at Sea, 1842

J. I shall pay a humble tribute by making a drawing representing his funeral.

T. How will you do it?

J. On the deck of the vessel, as it has been described to me by persons present, and at the time that Wilkie's body was lowered into the sea.

T. Well, I will do it as it must have appeared off the coast.

The picture by Turner and the drawing by Jones appeared in the ensuing Exhibition; the former under the title of *Peace—Burial at Sea*.

Turner painted the sails in the steamer as black as he could make them, which occasioned a remonstrance from [Clarkson] Stanfield, who justly thought the colour and effect untrue, upon which Turner said, 'I only wish I had any colour to make them blacker.' It is very like Turner, to have indicated mourning by this means, probably retaining some confused notions of the death of Ægeus and the black sails of the returning Theseus.

The second story relates to that swarthy crimson picture *The Fiery Furnace*.

The dialogue between the same persons is worthy of notice, as proving Turner's willingness to be on the most social terms with his brethren.

Turner asked his friend what he intended to paint for the ensuing Exhibition of 1832.

J. The fiery furnace, with Shadrach, Meshach, and Abednego.

T. A good subject; I'll do it also; what size will you do it?

J. Kit-cat.*

T. I'll paint it Kit-cat size too. Will you have an upright or a long picture?

J. Upright.

T. I'll paint it upright. What will you paint it on?

J. On panel.

T. I'll paint it on panel. Have you ordered a panel?

J. No.

T. Then order two, and tell the maker to send one of them to me, but remember that if I come into your room while you are painting that subject, you hide it instantly.

The pictures were painted and exhibited in 1832. The members of the Academy were surprised to find that they had been executed with the most perfect sympathy.† [II, 183–184]

* 36 x 28 inches (91 x 71 cm) † *Shadrach, Meshach and Abednego in the Burning Fiery Furnace*, 1832, Tate, London, and George Jones, *The Burning Fiery Furnace*, 1832, Tate, London (see following pages)

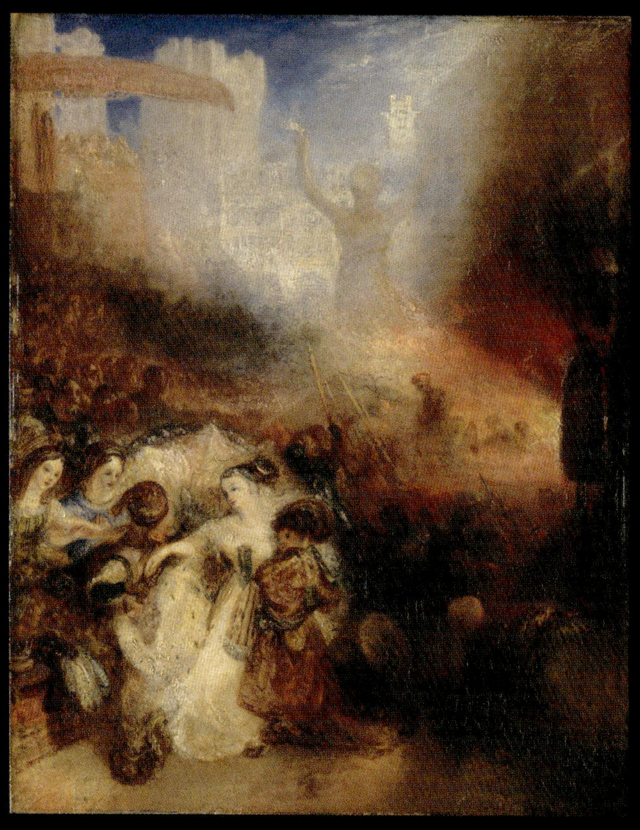

Shadrach, Meschach and Abednego in the Burning Fiery Furnace, 1832.

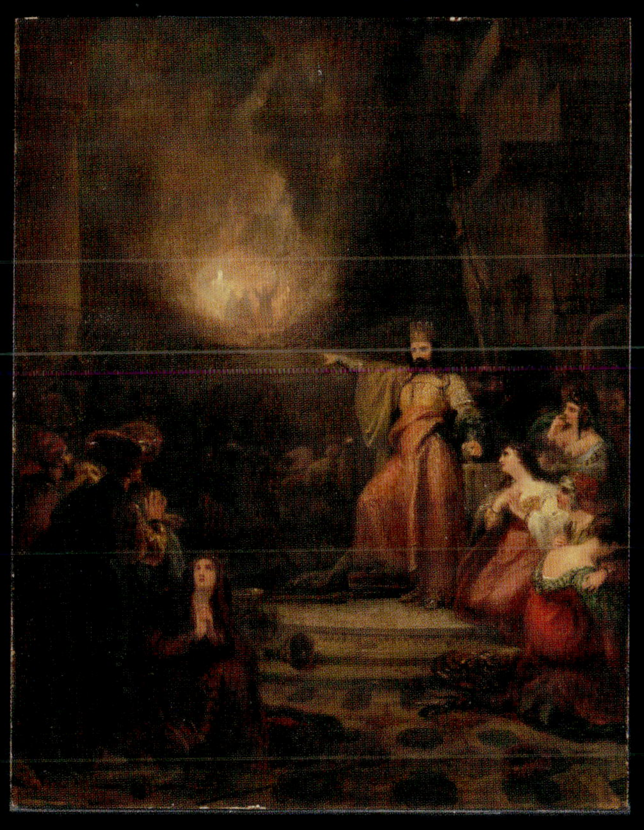

George Jones, The Burning Fiery Furnace, 1832

CHANTREY AND THE FIRE OFFICE

On one of those pleasant varnishing days of old the weather was very raw and cold; Chantrey, brimming over with fun as usual, went up with his beaming red face to a picture of Turner's which was specially luminous with orange chrome. Pretending to warm his hands at it, as at a fire, the sculptor said:—

'Why, Turner, this is the only comfortable place in the room. By-the-bye, is it true, as I have heard, that you've got a commission at last to paint a picture for the Sun Fire Office?'

Turner would have chewed the cud of this joke for days in his old-fashioned chuckling way.[II, 256–7]

NEW PATRONS

In reviewing Turner's career, it should be carefully observed that the nobility of England were not sufficiently advanced in a knowledge of art to be able to understand Turner's genius, only two or three—Lord de Tabley, Lord Egremont, Lord Yarborough, Lord Harewood, and a few others—ever patronized him, and they only stintingly. It was the great public he had to appeal to with his engravings. He earned his fortune by engraving, and not by his pictures. From exhibition to exhibition his great pictures returned unsold. It was the Manchester merchants who first began to buy his Venetian pictures; and at the very time tenth-rate Caraccis and disgusting Dutch pictures were being bought by hundreds to fill our noblemen's galleries.

Never let us forget that it was the Reform Bill that gave birth to modern art—that threw open our exhibitions, and that originated our galleries of modern pictures. Before that, ancient dead art was dominant, except in portrait-painting. Wilson and Barry all but starved; Gainsborough's landscapes would not sell; and Hilton was neglected.[(I, 353–4)]

It is to the middle class of England, from whom Shakespeare and our greatest men have sprung, that English art owes its present flourishing condition. From them Turner obtained his most generous commissions, for taste that had grown paralysed in drowsy country seats began now to bloom again amid factory smoke and the roar and buzz of wheels, amid cotton fluff, and in the vaporous Manchester engine rooms.[(II, 238)]

THE MONEY SPIDER

He would sell nothing but at his own rate; he would save up his money for royal deeds of posthumous charity. As to his ceaseless thoughts on charitable objects, his own friend, Mr. Jones, testifies. He says:—

> During twenty-five years, he indulged the pleasing hope that he should leave a testimony of his good will and compassion for unfortunate artists. To his intimate friends he constantly talked of the best mode of leaving property for the use of the unsuccessful; he wished his survivors to employ his property in building houses for the above-named purpose; he did not like to call them almshouses, but had selected the denomination of 'Turner's Gift.' His benevolence was conspicuous whenever he was tried, though he often used terms of harshness in which his feelings had no part; but he hated idleness, extravagance, and presumption. He thought that artists had not time for the duties and pleasures of domestic festivity, yet believed that they should often meet to strengthen fraternal feeling without much expense; therefore was zealous in support of the Academy Club, tried to establish an artists' dinner at the Athenæum, and left £50 in his will to be expended annually on a dinner for the members on the anniversary of his birthday.'(II, 157–8)

VARNISHING DAYS (4): A VENETIAN PAINTING

Of one of his small pictures of Venice now in the Vernon Gallery, a pleasant story is told, which shows his good-nature and his love of practical joking.

The picture in question, one of those so full of vivid reflections (not always quite true to fact), was hung next a view of Ghent, by his old friend, George Jones, R.A. On the varnishing day at the Academy, Turner, who delighted in these social moments of working and chatting amongst comrades, said to his friend:

'Why, Joney, how blue your sky is! but I'll out-blue you.'

And immediately scrambling upon a box, joking and chuckling, he deepened the sky of his Venice with a scumble of ultramarine.

'I've done you now, Georgey,' he said, as he passed on to another picture.

In his absence, as a joke, Jones determined to baffle the great man, and instantly set to work and painted the sky of Ghent a blank white, which, acting as a foil, made Turner's Venetian sky look preposterously blue.

* *Bridge of Sighs, Ducal Palace and Custom-House, Venice: Canaletti Painting*, 1833, Tate, London † George Jones, *Ghent*, 1833, current location unknown

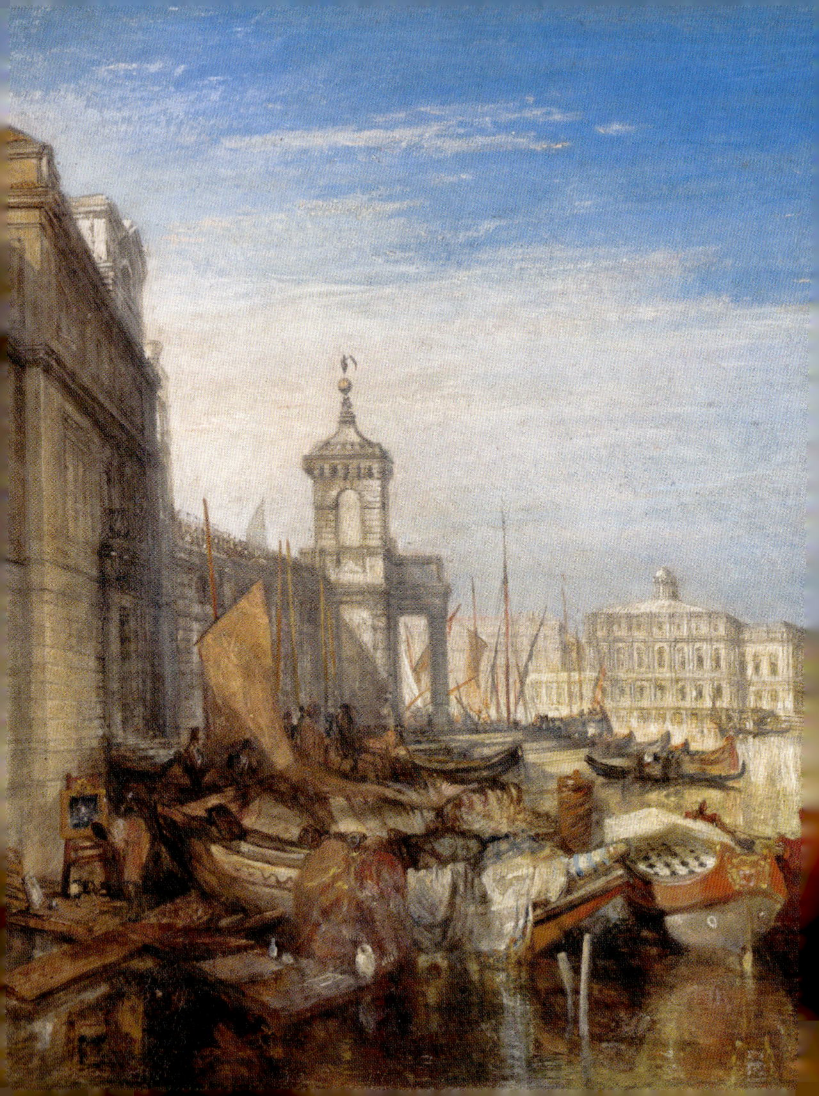

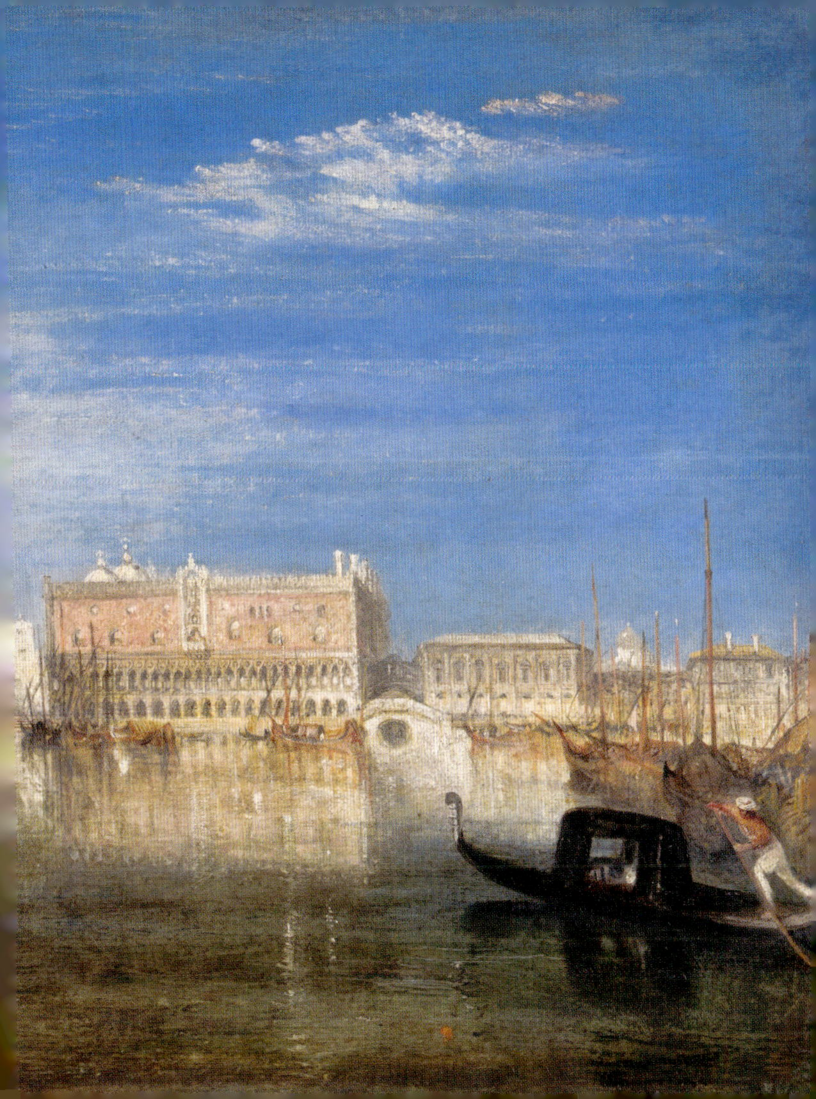

The next day, Turner laughed heartily when he returned to his picture to find himself again checkmated.

'Well, Joney,' he said, 'you have done me now. But it must go,' and went to work briskly and merrily at the water, ships, and fairy-like buildings, never altering the sky any more.

For this dream of Venice Mr. Vernon gave Turner two hundred guineas; and this price the painter evidently thought extravagant, for he was heard to say—

'If they will have scraps, they must pay for them.'

By which oracle, I suppose, Turner meant that the picture was only a fragment of an harmonious whole—a merry, fanciful sketch; and it is certain that he despised such studies in comparison with his earlier and more solid, though less poetical works.(II, 241–2)

VARNISHING DAYS (5): THE BURNING OF THE HOUSES OF PARLIAMENT

In 1835, [John] Scarlett Davis, a well-known artist of that day, wrote to his friend [Joseph Murray] Ince, a favourite pupil of David Cox, and now a comparatively forgotten man, who realized a considerable fortune by his profession. He says:—

Previous pages: Bridge of Sighs, Ducal Palace, and Custom-House, Venice: Canaletti Painting, 1833

I have no artistical chat for you, further than that Turner has painted a large picture of the *Burning of the Two Houses of Parliament*;* but I have heard it spoken of as a failure—a devil of a lot of chrome [yellow]. He finished it on the walls the last two days before the Gallery opened to the public, and I am told it was good fun to see the great man whacking away with about fifty stupid apes standing round him, and I understand he was cursedly annoyed—the fools kept peeping into his colour-box and examining all his brushes and colours.(I, 327)

[Ruskin expands on this incident, relating that]

The Burning of the Houses of Lords and Commons was almost entirely painted on the walls of the Exhibition. His facility at this period of his life was astounding. He would frequently send his canvas to the British Institution with nothing upon it but a grey groundwork of vague, indistinguishable forms, and finish it upon the varnishing day into a work of great splendour. Likewise at the Academy he frequently sent his canvas imperfect and sketchy, trusting entirely to varnishing days for the completion of his picture. It was astonishing what he

* Cleveland Museum of Art, Cleveland, OH

Overleaf: The Burning of the Houses of Lords and Commons, 16 October 1834, 1835

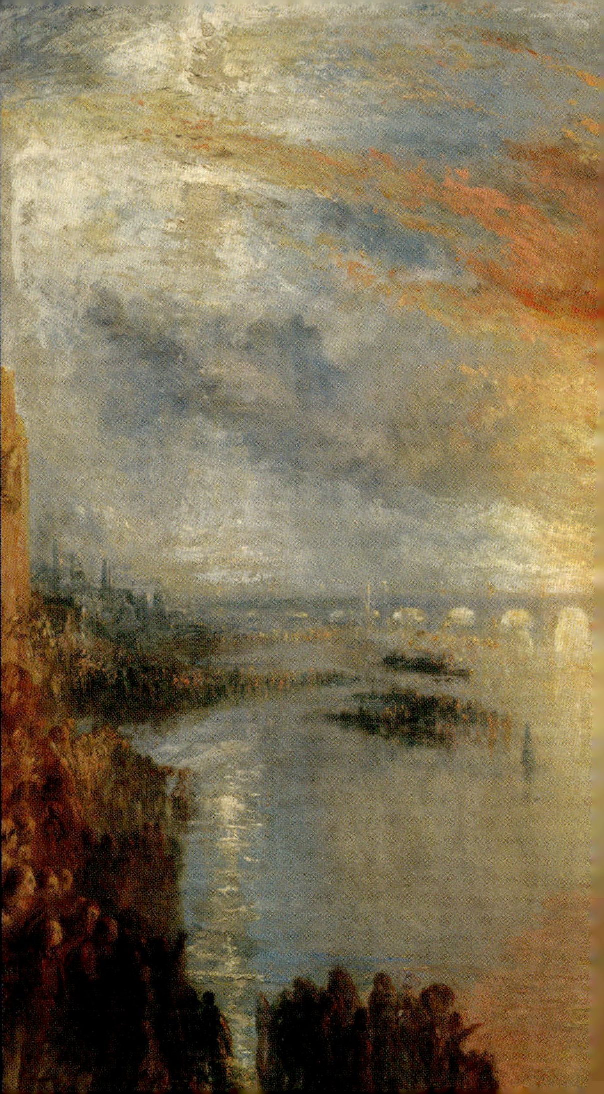

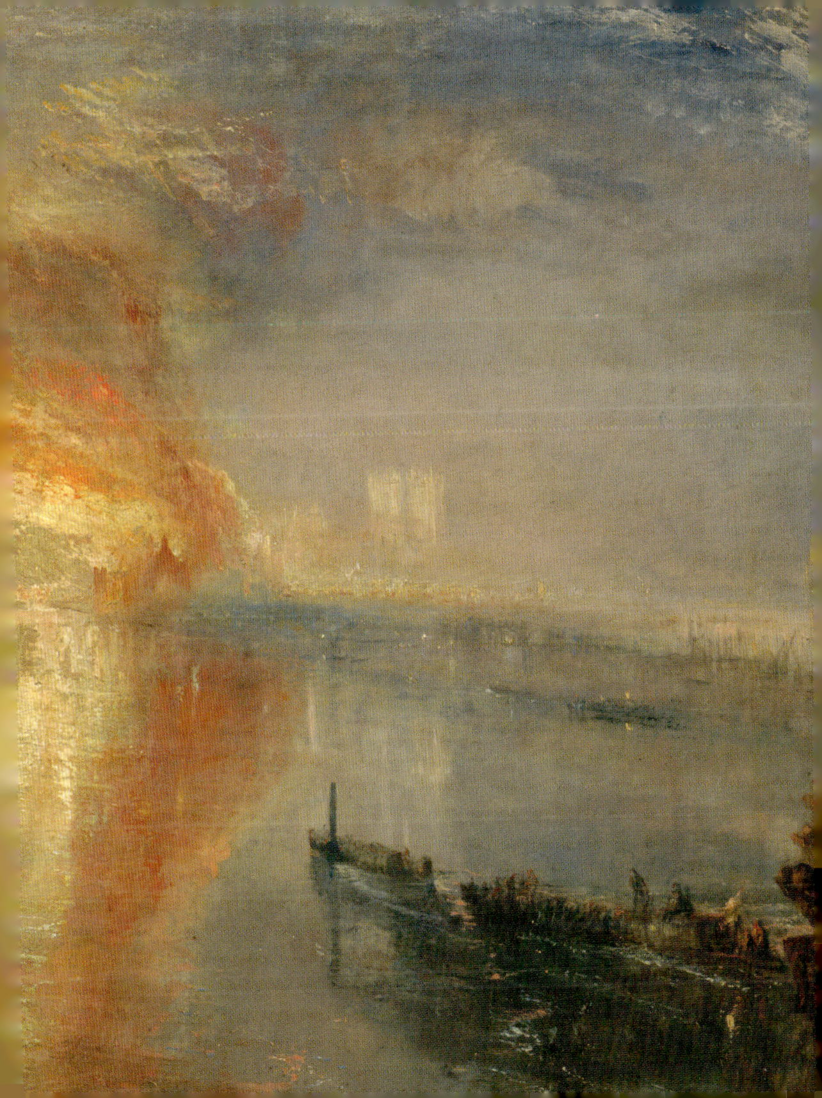

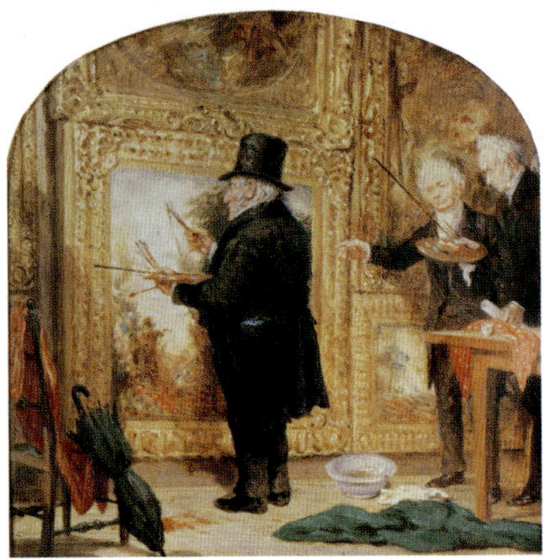

William Parrott, Turner on Varnishing Day, 1840

accomplished on those days … Turner was always the first at the Academy on those occasions, arriving there frequently as early as four o'clock, and never later than six; and he was invariably the last to quit in the evening. He might be seen standing all day before his pictures; and, though he worked so long, he appeared to be doing little or nothing. His touches were almost imperceptible; yet his pictures were seen, in the end, to have advanced wonderfully. He acquired such a mastery in early life, that he painted with a certainty that was almost

> miraculous. Although his effects were imperceptible on a near inspection of the picture, he knew unhesitatingly how to produce them without retiring from his work to test the result. He was never seen, like Sir Thomas Lawrence and others, to be perpetually walking about, but kept hard at work, nose to the canvas, sure of his effects.(II, 166–7)

INDIFFERENT

One element in Turner's success was his indifference to praise. Though proud of his works, he was not a vain man. He never suffered from the disappointments arising out of a premature desire for fame. He did not appear to be pleased with Mr. Ruskin's superlative eulogies, says Mr. P. Cunningham. 'He knows a great deal more about my pictures than I do,' said Turner; 'he puts things into my head, and points out meanings in them that I never intended.' It was not easy to draw his attention to the admiration of his own pictures. A well-known collector [Benjamin Windus] with whom the artist had long been intimate, once invited him to be present at the opening of a new gallery which was hung round with his most beautiful drawings. To the disappointment of the connoisseur, Turner scarcely noticed them, but kept his eye fixed upon the ceiling. It was panelled, and neatly grained in oak. 'What are you

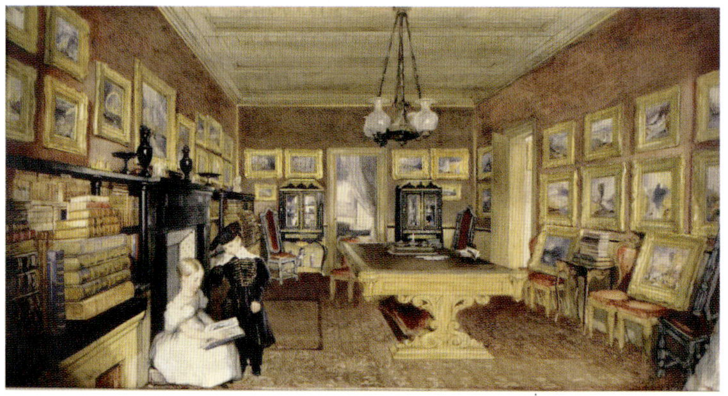

John Scarlett Davis, Interior of 'The Library at Tottenham', the seat of Benjamin Godfrey Windus, 1835

looking at so intently?' said the host. 'At those boards,' was the reply; 'the fellow that did that must have known how to paint.' And nothing would induce him to turn to the magnificent pictures that sparkled on the walls. He never talked about his own pictures, but would occasionally give hints to other artists; and when these were adopted, they were always certain improvements. We never heard of his saying anything, however, that would give pain, though he felt keenly the ignorant criticisms and ridicule with which his own pictures were sometimes treated.

Turner's was a good and kind nature; he was not the

sordid hunks and miser the scandal of the time made him. He used to say to an intimate friend:

'Don't wish for money; you will not be the happier, and you know you can have any money of me you want.'(II, 130–1)

TRAVELLING WITH H. A. J. MUNRO, 1836

Of all Turner's tours, we have most records of that which he took with [the wealthy Scottish collector] Mr. Munro in 1836. The very circumstance that gave rise to the tour is a proof of the painter's almost womanly tenderness for those he really received into friendship. A great and serious depression of spirits had fallen on Mr. Munro, and it became gradually a burden he could not shake off. Turner proposed a sketching tour to divert his friend's mind into fresh channels. They started through a part of France which Turner wanted to visit, and after visiting Chamonix and Mont Blanc, which Turner had a great desire to see, they went by the Valley of Aosta into Italy, returning home afterwards by Turin.

Mr. Munro found that Turner enjoyed himself in his way—a sort of honest Diogenes way. He disliked teasing questions as to how he got this or that colour. On one occasion, in the Aosta Valley, Turner was dissatisfied with a sketch. He altered and sponged till the drawing got a sort of white greenness about it which was not pleasant. He

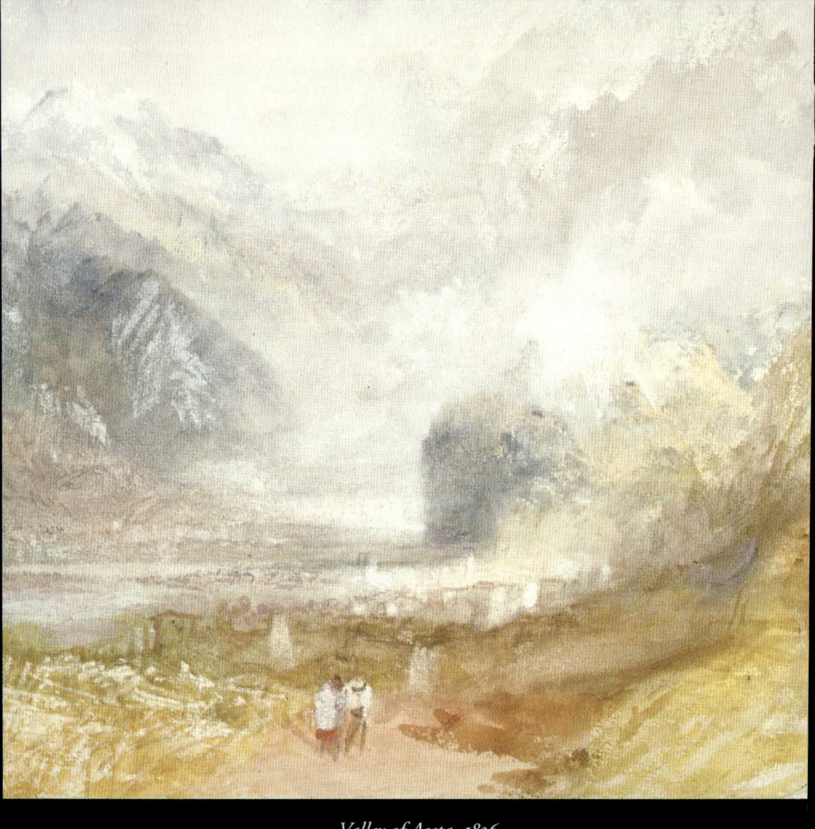

Valley of Aosta, 1836

got quite fretful about this, and began to abuse colour-sketching, saying, 'I could have done twice as much with the pencil.'

His first inquiry in the morning, when they started to sketch, was always, 'Have you got the sponge?' because it was with the sponge he obtained many of his misty and ærial effects.

He never rhapsodized about scenery, but set hard at work at some distance from Mr. Munro, silent, concentrated (and generally a good deal higher), so as to obtain more distance and more of a bird's-eye view. He took quick sketches, and then finished them afterwards quietly (by help of his tremendous memory) at the inn. He had a horror of what he said Wilson called 'being too mappy.' If you bore with his way, it was easy to get on very pleasantly with him; indeed, there was a sort of half resolution come to that Turner and Mr. Munro should visit the East together.[(I, 229–30)]

It was in this tour Turner made a sketch* which he afterwards turned into his picture (now in Mr. Munro's gallery) of the *Avalanche*, one of his grandest and wildest flights of imagination.†[(I, 231)]

* Museum of Fine Arts, Boston, MA † Art Institute of Chicago, Chicago, IL

Overleaf: Valley of Aosta: Snowstorm, Avalanche, and Thunderstorm, 1836

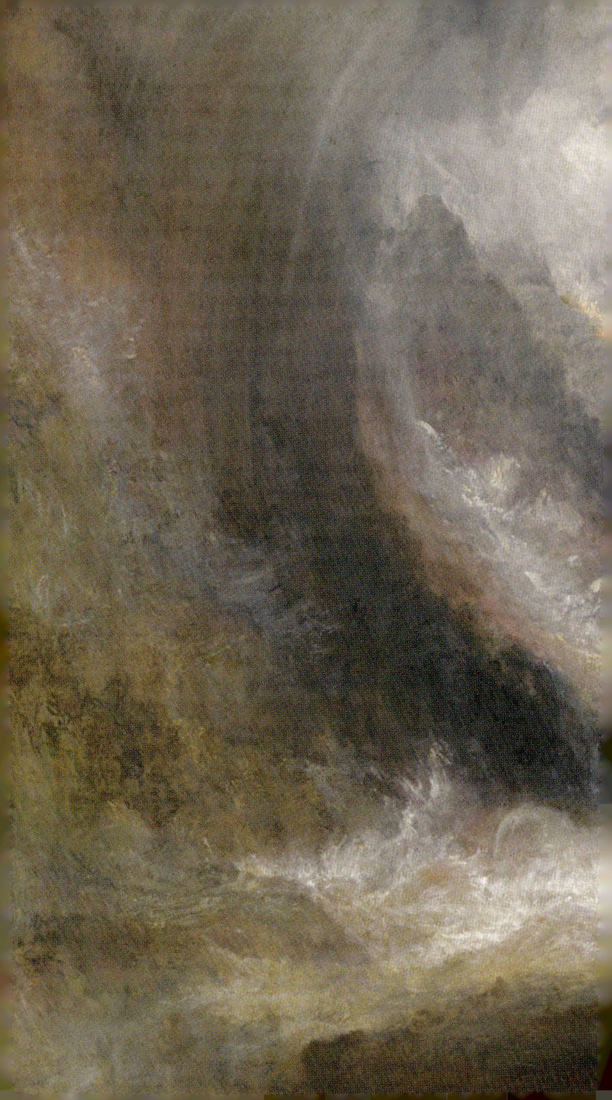

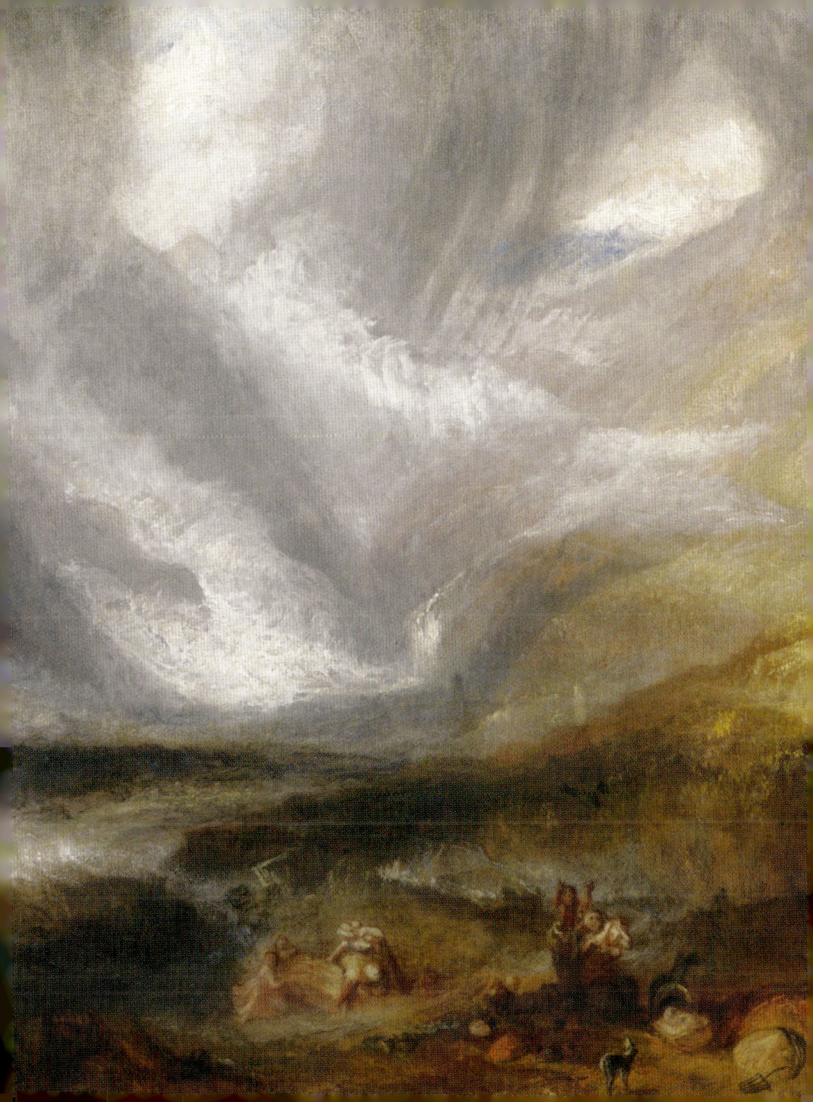

THE *OLD TEMERAIRE*

From the day that, as a boy, he first boated up and down the Thames, to the day that, at Chelsea, he turned his dying eyes on the river that he loved, Turner had all an Englishman's love for the water.

He loved the Thames and its 'black barges, patched red sails, and every possible condition of blue and white fog'; he loved them, because he had a tenacious love all his life through for what had been known to him in childhood.[I, 333]

The *Temeraire* picture* was exhibited by Turner at the Royal Academy in 1839. The subject was suggested to the painter by [Clarkson] Stanfield.† In 1838 Turner was with Stanfield and a party of brother artists on one of those holiday excursions in which he so delighted, probably to end with whitebait and champagne at Greenwich. It was at these times that Turner talked and joked his best, snatching now and then a moment to print on his quick brain some tone of sky, some gleam of water, some sprinkling light of oar, some glancing sunshine cross-barring a sail. Suddenly there moved down upon the artists' boat the grand old vessel that had been taken prisoner at the Nile, and that led the van at Trafalgar. She loomed pale

* National Gallery, London † Turner is now thought to have been travelling abroad when this event took place.

and ghostly, and was being towed to her last moorings at Deptford by a little fiery, puny steam-tug.

'There's a fine subject, Turner,' said Stanfield.

So Turner painted it, and it proved one of his most poetical pictures.(I, 335–6)

Mr. Ruskin considers this picture of 1839 the last picture Turner executed with his entire and perfect power. The *Polyphemus*, painted in 1829, he claims as marking the beginning of Turner's central and best period of ten years. Singularly enough, the picture of 1829 is a sunrise; the picture of 1839 a sunset.

I extract from the *Athenæum* of three years ago a criticism of mine on this picture, chiefly considered as a matchless tableau of colour:

> The crown and paragon of the collection is the *Fighting Temeraire tugged to her last Berth*, which stands out from amongst them as a great flame-coloured Mexican cactus, the very emperor of flowers, would do in a nosegay of simple primroses. We place it first of all his works, because it excels in colour all landscapes, we might almost say, in the world;—we place it first, because it excels in colour, and it was as a colourist that Turner excelled almost all painters. It is wonderful for all the qualities of colour, for brilliancy, contrast, breadth, tone, transparency,

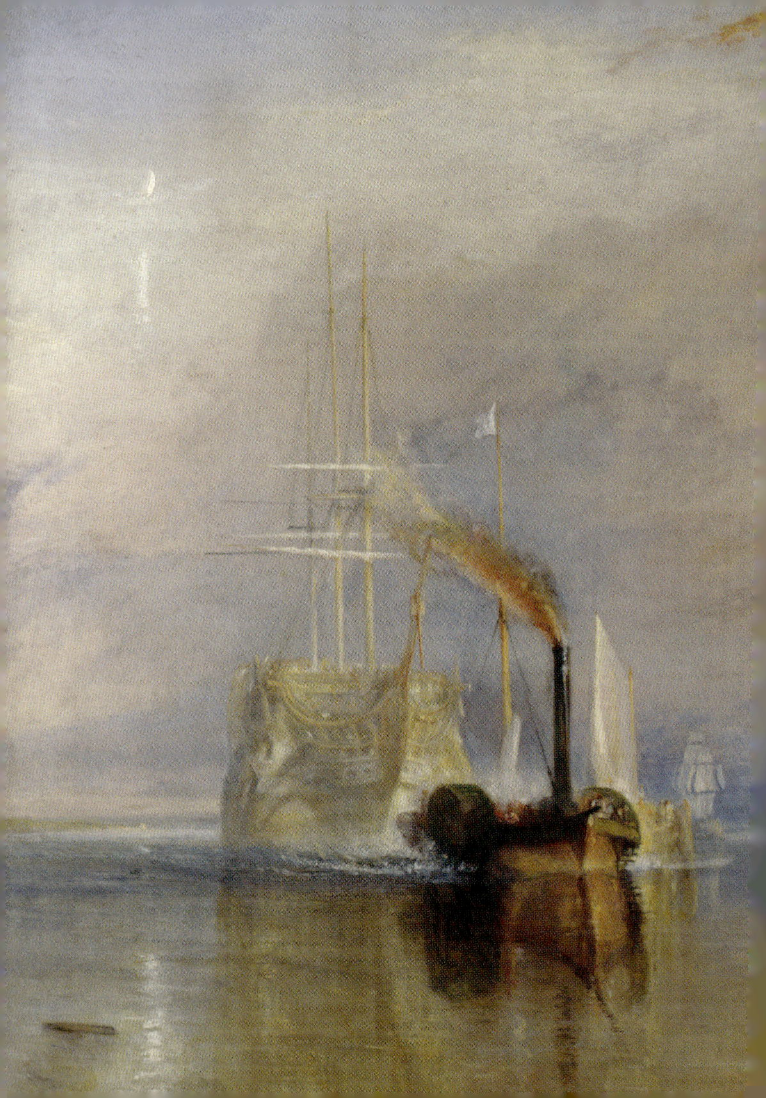

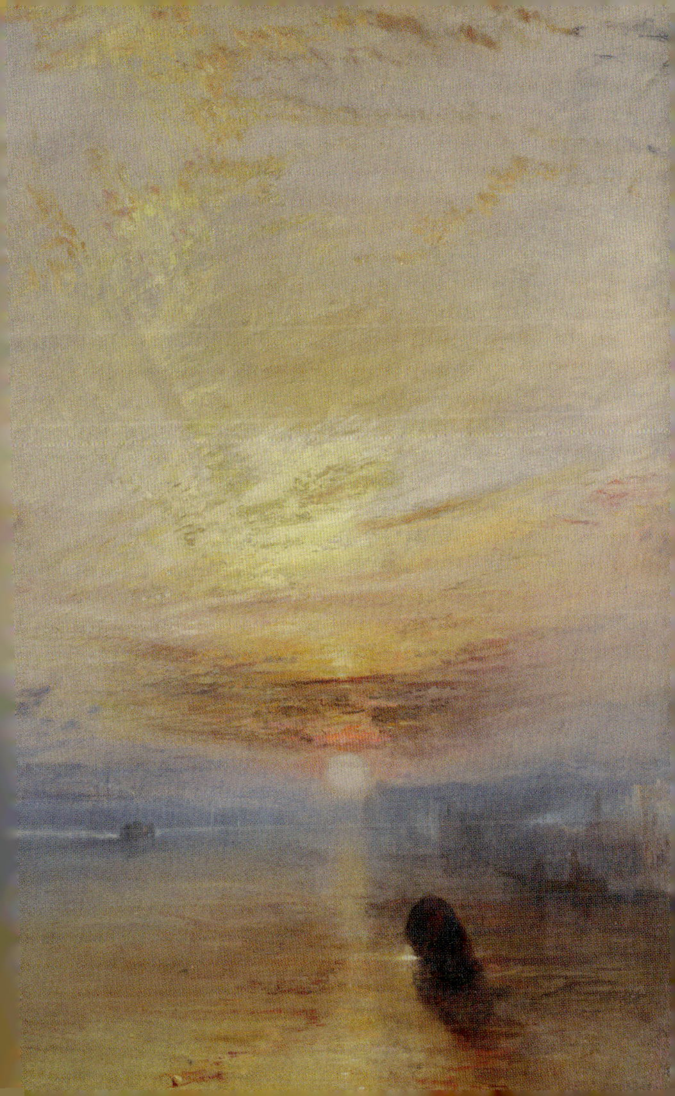

and light. And these fantasies are lavished on one of the simplest of heroic themes:—an old man-of-war being towed to her last moorings,—her grave,—where, her life well spent, she will return to those primitive elements from whence her oaks first sprang. She is towed by a steamer, late in the sunset, which is smouldering fiercely out of the sky; beyond the whirlpool of crimson and yellow, and flame-streaks of vermilion, a blue haze is creeping up the river to meet the night. Grand and warrior-like, stern, like an unconquered veteran, proud of trophy and scar, the *Temeraire* moves on, with its lance-like masts erect, its broad, pale, spectral hull looming stupendous and threatening over a water red as with the blood of past battles. A grand and touching sight is the old ship, so vast and thunderous in its sleeping and now well-nigh exhausted might,—so staunch, so true, and indomitable it is. The tug seems to convoy it gently and lovingly, as the enormous bulk whitens and troubles the water.[II, 337–8]

In no picture we have ever seen can you pass through so far, and yet come to no wall that orders back the impatient and forth-flying imagination. Through a thousand semitones and half-notes of

Previous pages: The Fighting Temeraire tugged to her last berth to be broken up, 1838

> grey and neutral tint we reach the sovereign colours that rule the picture. The very relaxations and freedoms of the drawing seem true to the aerial witchery and beguilement of such an hour and such an evening.[(I, 339)]
>
> As a picture it is the most glorious consummation of colouring ever painted by English fingers, or seen by English eyes. In exquisite transparency it surpasses water-colours; in strength and purity it transcends oil. It is the noblest English poem, founded on English scenery and English events, ever thrown on canvas. He who painted this deserves indeed a central seat in our wide Pantheon.[(I, 339–40)]

At Deptford she was to cease to be a ship, and to become a hospital hulk for the sailors of all nations. But Turner looked at her not as an old friend going to the grave, but as an old warrior going to his rest; he did, to celebrate its grand apotheosis, turn the sky and earth into a gory battle-field, and in gorgeous sunset she moves in pomp to her burial. In Turner's eyes she was then no longer the pale ghost of her former self, but a warship moving through the sulphurous flame at Trafalgar, with the blood oozing through her planks as the wine pours from the wine-press at vintage-time. He knew, when he painted this picture, that he should touch the heart of England, because his own heart was touched as he painted.[(I, 340)]

[Thornbury relates attempts to buy the *Temeraire*, describing it as 'this Koh-i-noor of a picture':]—

Some years after the Exhibition, Mr. Leslie tried to buy it for Mr. James Lenox, of New York; but Turner would not part with it. In 1831 [sic] it had already been mentally placed by him among the pictures he would leave to the nation. Sacks of gold would not have shaken him on this point.(I, 342)

LATER TRAVELS

The Swiss and Venetian sketches are very numerous. Turner drew Lausanne, bathed in a rosy sunset; a morning view, looking from Brennen [Brunnen]; Fluelen on the Lake of Lucerne, looking from Kussnach towards the Bernese Alps; and Mons Pilatus, dark against the sunset. Then comes his last visit to Venice; and for the hundredth time he sits down to make notes of San Giorgio, Santa Maria del Salute, the Bridge of the Riva del Schiavoni, and the lagoon between San Giorgio and the Cantieri.(I, 323)

Mr. Ruskin had given Turner, on one of his late tours, a commission for a drawing of Venice, but it was so unfinished that it did not please him.(II, 284–5)

Opposite: The Church of Santo Stefano, Venice, from the Rio del Santissimo, 1840

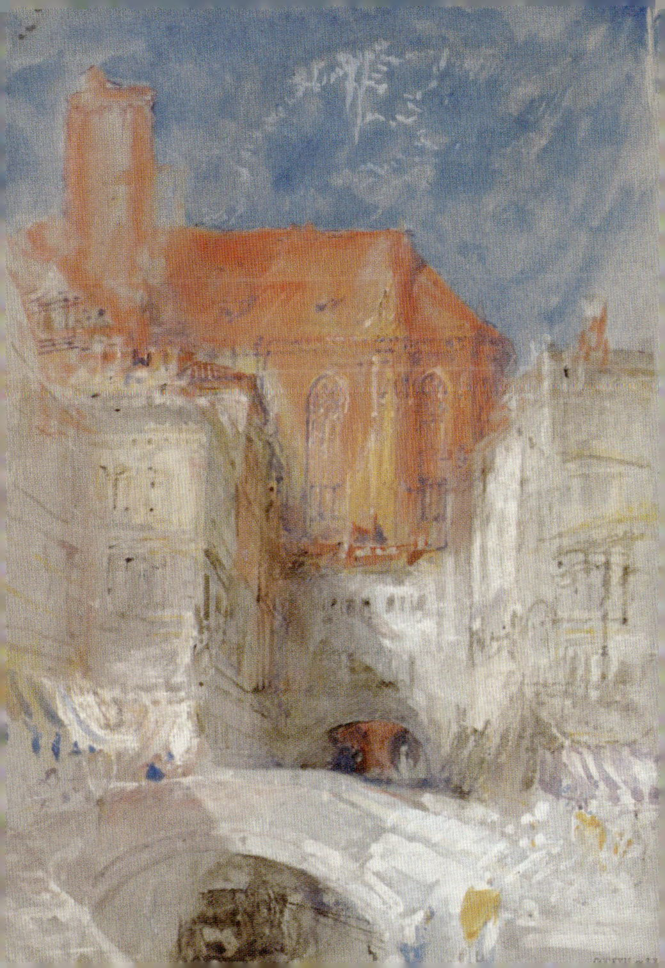

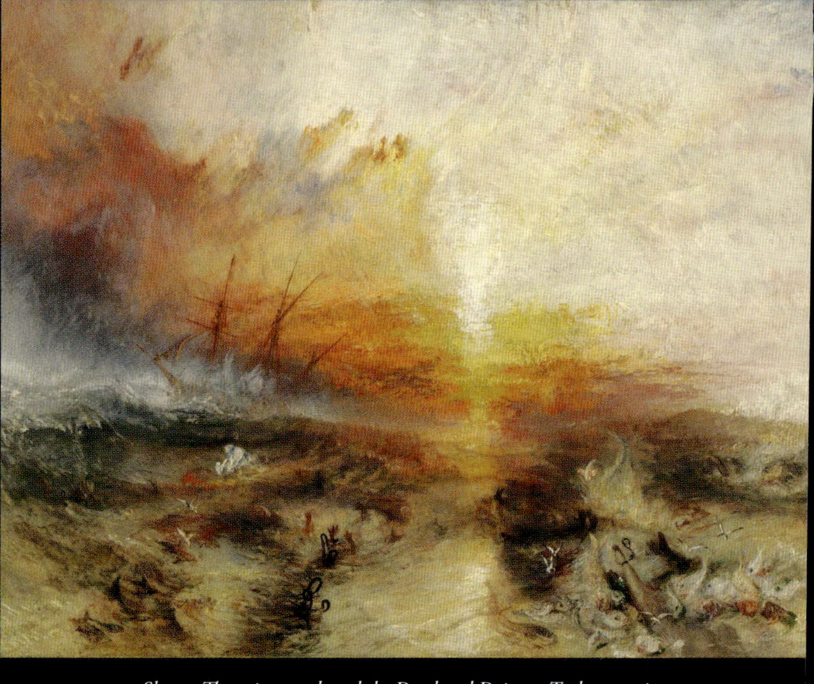

Slavers Throwing overboard the Dead and Dying—Typhon coming on
('The Slave Ship'), 1840

THE *SLAVE SHIP*

Generally speaking, I have abstained from quoting any passages of Mr. Ruskin's for their mere poetry, unless they really contained some exposition of Turner's style and mind; but the following I cannot pass by, especially as I have not myself seen the picture alluded to.

> But I think the noblest sea that Turner has ever painted, and if so, the noblest certainly ever painted by man, is that of the *Slave Ship*, the chief Academy picture of the Exhibition of 1840. It is a sunset on the Atlantic, after prolonged storm; but the storm is partially lulled, and the torn and streaming rain clouds are moving in scarlet lines to lose themselves in the hollow of the night. The whole surface of sea included in the picture is divided into two ridges of enormous swell, not high nor local, but a low, broad heaving of the whole ocean, like the lifting of its bosom by deep-drawn breath after the torture of the storm. Between these two ridges the fire of the sunset falls along the trough of the sea, dyeing it with an awful but glorious light, the intense and lurid splendour which burns like gold, and bathes like blood.'(II, 335)

MR RUSKIN AND *MODERN PAINTERS*

Latterly, there have been gainsayers, with whom I have no sympathy, treasonable enough to think that though equally eloquent, industrious, acute, and original, Mr. Ruskin has become almost too voluminous and episodical, interlarding his commentaries on Turner with too much of Scriptural quotation, and growing almost too subtle in reasoning, and too technically and laboriously scientific. There are even heretics daring enough to doubt whether Turner ever plunged so deeply into geological theories, mythological mysteries, abstruse spiritualisms, and Biblical allegories as is made out. For myself, I do not think he went much further than Lemprière for his *Polyphemus*, and some poor translation of Ovid for his *Liber* subjects. He had meaning in all he did, but it needed no Swedenborg interpretation to discover such meaning.(II, 210)

[C. R. Leslie is quoted as follows:]

> I was equally delighted and surprised when I heard that a very young man had come forward, with extraordinary ability, knowledge and love of Nature, as the champion of Turner, at a time when (excepting by painters) his transcendent powers were little felt or understood. But I own I was disappointed,

> when I read Mr. Ruskin's *Modern Painters*, at one of the modes he adopted in the vindication of the great artist's just claim to admiration.
>
> It was unnecessary and unsafe to the reputation of Turner to assume that he had fewer faults than other great painters, and to contrast his beauties with the faults, often indeed imaginary of Claude, the Poussins, Cuyp, or Canaletti; unnecessary, because his excellences are of so high an order that his greatest admirers may fearlessely acknowledge all the defects with which he may be charged… (II, 201–2)

SOAPSUDS AND WHITE-WASH

We have no recollection of any other picture than one of Turner's by an artist of reputation, in which snow is represented 'in action.'*

The critics of all kinds, learned and unlearned, were furious when it was exhibited; some of them described it as a mass of 'soapsuds and white-wash.' 'Turner,' says Mr. Ruskin,

> was passing the evening at my father's house, on the day this criticism came out; and after dinner, sitting in his arm-chair by the fire, I heard him muttering

* *Snow Storm: Steam-Boat off a Harbour's Mouth,* 1842, Tate, London

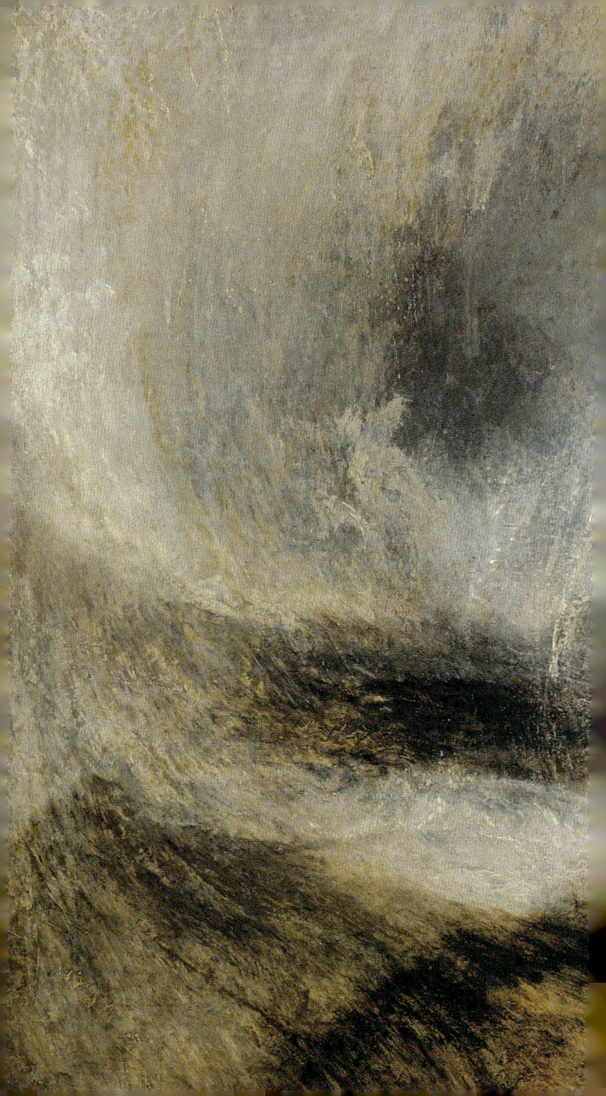

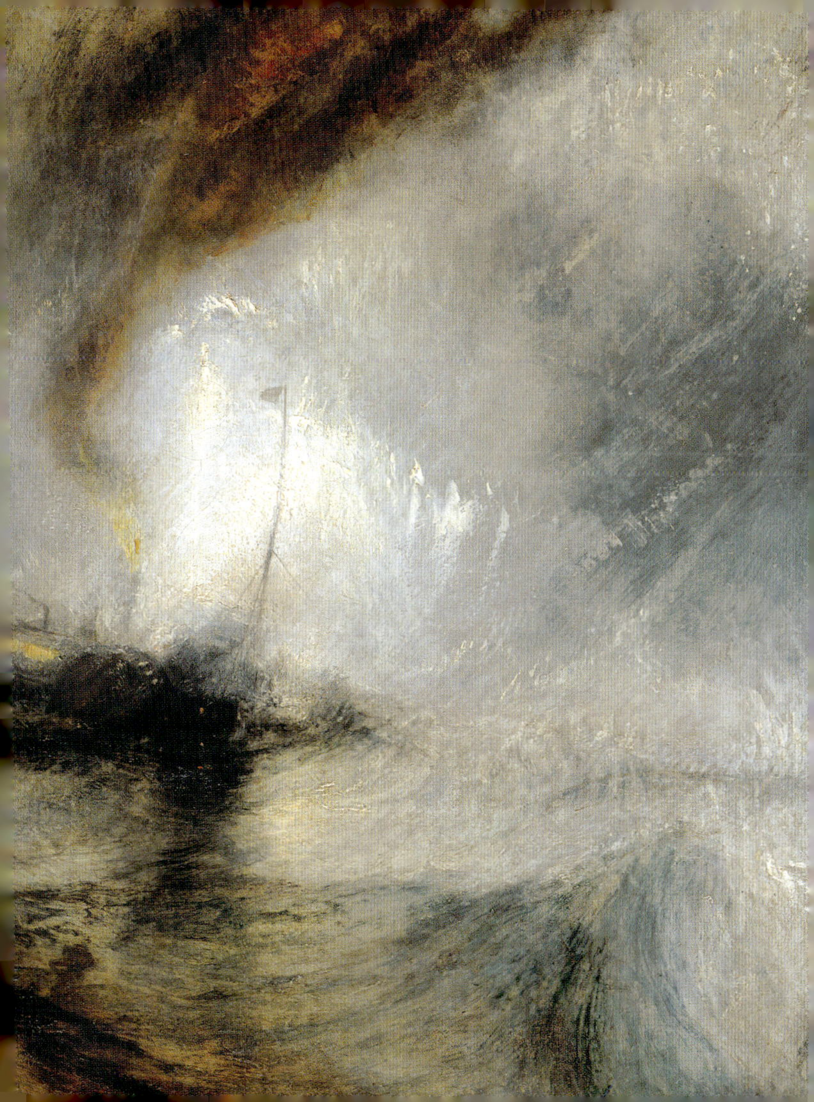

> low to himself, at intervals, 'Soapsuds and whitewash,' again, and again, and again. At last I went to him, asking why he minded what they said. Then he burst out, 'Soapsuds and whitewash! What would they have? I wonder what they think the sea's like? I wish they'd been in it.'
>
> It is thus, too often, that ignorance sits in judgment on the works of genius.(II, 206–7)

I cannot find a better place than here to insert an admirable anecdote furnished to Mr. Ruskin, by the Rev. Mr. [Charles] Kingsley. He says:

> I had taken my mother and a cousin to see Turner's pictures, and as my mother knows nothing about art, I was taking her down the gallery to look at the large *Richmond Park*;* but as we were passing the *Snow Storm*, she stopped before it, and I could hardly get her to look at any other picture; and she told me a great deal more about it than I had any notion of, though I have seen many snow-storms. She had been in such a scene on the coast of Holland during

* Probably *Richmond Hill, on the Prince Regent's Birthday*, 1819, Tate, London

Previous pages: Snow Storm: Steam-Boat off a Harbour's Mouth Making Signals in Shallow Water, and going by the Lead. The Author was in this Storm on the Night the 'Ariel' left Harwich, 1842

the war. When, some time afterwards, I thanked Turner for his permission for her to see the pictures, I told him that he would not guess what had [most] caught my mother's fancy, and then named the picture; but he said,

'I did not paint it to be understood, but I wished to show what such a scene was like. I got the sailors to lash me to the mast to observe it. I was lashed for four hours, and I did not expect to escape; but I felt bound to record it if I did. But no one had any business to like the picture.'

'But,' said I, 'my mother once went through just such a scene, and it brought it all back to her.'

'Is your mother a painter?'

'No.'

'Then she ought to have been thinking of something else.'[(I.334–5)]

A CRITIC CHASTENED

I am afraid the tradition is too true, that that great and bitter satirist of poor humanity's weaknesses, Mr. Thackeray, had more than a finger in thus lashing the dotage of a great man's genius. Long after, I have heard that Mr. Thackeray was shown some of Turner's finest water-colour drawings, upon which he exclaimed: 'I will never run down Turner again.' But the blows had already gone to the old man's heart, and it did no good to lament them then.

Of Turner's sensitiveness to criticism, Mr. Ruskin says, with deep feeling,

> To censure, Turner was acutely sensitive; owing to his own natural kindness, he felt it for himself or for others, not as criticism, but as cruelty. He knew that however little his higher power could be seen, he had at least done as much as ought to have saved him from wanton insult, and the attacks upon him in his later years were to him not merely contemptible in their ignorance, but amazing in their ingratitude—'A man may be weak in his age,' he said to me once, at the time when he felt he was dying, 'but you should not tell him so.' What Turner might have done for us, had he received help and love instead of disdain, I can hardly trust myself to imagine.[II, 196–7]

WIDER CRITICISMS

Among the German critics, Dr. Waagen stands pre-eminent for pompous blundering. He has one of those routine minds, unoriginal, bound by precedent and convention, and holding to the old and safe. Here is his dictum, which is evidently founded on a very scanty knowledge of Turner's works, especially of his divine water-colour drawings, without which no one can judge of his greatness. Dr. Waagen is no Solomon in his utterances, as the following will show:—

> It appears to me that Turner was a man of marvellous genius, occupying some such place among the English landscape painters of our day as Lord Byron among the modern English poets. In point of fact, no landscape-painter has yet appeared with such versatility of talent. His historical landscapes exhibit the most exquisite feeling for beauty of lines and effect of lighting; at the same time he has the power of making them express the most varied moods of nature—a lofty grandeur, a deep and gloomy melancholy, a sunny cheerfulness and peace, or an uproar of all the elements. Buildings he also treats with peculiar felicity; while the sea, in its most varied aspect, is equally subservient to his magic brush. His views of certain cities and localities inspire the spectator with poetic feelings such as no other painter ever excited in the same degree, and which is chiefly attributable to the exceeding picturesqueness of the point of view chosen, and to the beauty of the lighting. Finally, he treats the most common

little subjects, such as a group of trees, a meadow, a shaded stream, with such art as to impart to them the most picturesque charm. I should therefore not hesitate to recognise Turner as the greatest landscape painter of all times; but for his deficiency in one indispensable element in every perfect work of art—namely, a sound technical basis. It is true that the pictures and drawings of his earlier and middle period overflow with an abundance of versatile and beautiful thoughts, rendered with great truth of nature; but at the same time his historical landscapes never possess the delicacy of gradation and the magical atmosphere of Claude, nor his realistic works the juicy transparency and freshness of a Ruisdael; while many of his best pictures have lost their keeping by subsequent darkening, and with it a great portion of their value. In his later time, however, he may be said to have aimed gradually rather at a mere indication than a representation of his thoughts, which in the last twenty years of his life became so superficial and arbitrary, that it is sometimes difficult to say what he really did intend. Not that I overlook even in these pictures the frequent extraordinary beauty of composition and lighting, which render them what I should rather call the beautiful souls of pictures. The raptures, therefore,

> of many of Turner's countrymen, who prefer these pictures to those of his early period, I am not able to share, but must adhere to the sober conviction that a work of art executed in this material world of ours must, in order to be quite satisfactory, have a complete and natural body, as well as a beautiful soul.(II, 191–3)

THE GALLERY ON QUEEN ANNE STREET IN THE 1840S

Everything about the Gallery in Queen Anne Street seemed of a piece to those who went with a scornful and Pharisaical determination to find there the miser and the misanthropist.(II, 177) 'Nobody ever seemed to enter the house', says Mr. Rippingille, 'and while all the houses round it from time to time smartened themselves up, this alone remained unchanged.' It looked cold, dirty, and forsaken, like a bankrupt's warehouse; 'nor was anything alive,' says the bitter writer,

> ever seen in it, pass when and as often as you would, but an old tabby cat, lying upon a bit of ragged green baize on a table at the area window, and sometimes an old woman in a mobcap, who looked like a being of the last century, or the other world.(II, 173)

JAMES ASTBURY HAMMERSLEY'S VISIT TO THE GALLERY IN 1844

I rang, and tardily enough the well-known old housekeeper opened the door to me, and I was placed in what I suppose was Turner's dining-room. I waited there for a short time, all eyes, all ears, when I heard a shambling, slippered footstep down a flight of stairs—slow, measured, yet as of one who was regardless of style or promptitude—what the world calls shambling, in fact. When the door opened, I, nobody, stood face to face with, to my thinking, the greatest man living. I shall attempt no description; you know how he looked. I saw at once his height, his breadth, his loose dress, his ragged hair, his indifferent quiet—all, indeed, that went to make his physique and some of his mind; but, above all, I saw, felt (and still feel) his penetrating grey eye!

Remaining only a moment longer in the cold and cheerless room, at his request I followed him into his gallery, which you, doubtless, remember well. The room was even less tidy than the one we had left—indeed, was an art chaos, all confusion, mouldiness, and wretched litter—most of the pictures, indeed

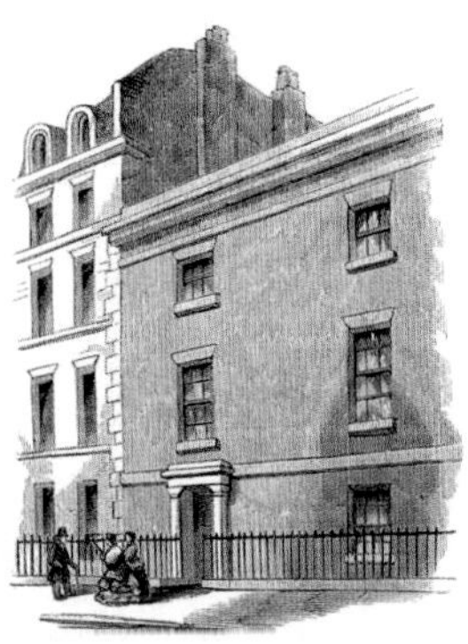

Turner's house in Queen Anne Street, c. 1859

all those resting against the wall, being covered with uncleanly sheets or cloths of a like size and character. Turner removed these protections to his pictures, and disclosed to my wondering and reverent observation many of those works which are now known so generally; among them, and the most prominent, being the *Opening of the Walhalla*.[II, 119]

On the 26th of November, 1844, I paid my second visit to the Turner Gallery. I shall not readily forget this visit, though it began and ended in something less than ten minutes. I entered the dingy dining-room as before, and was immediately joined by Turner, who, as before, led me up to his gallery.

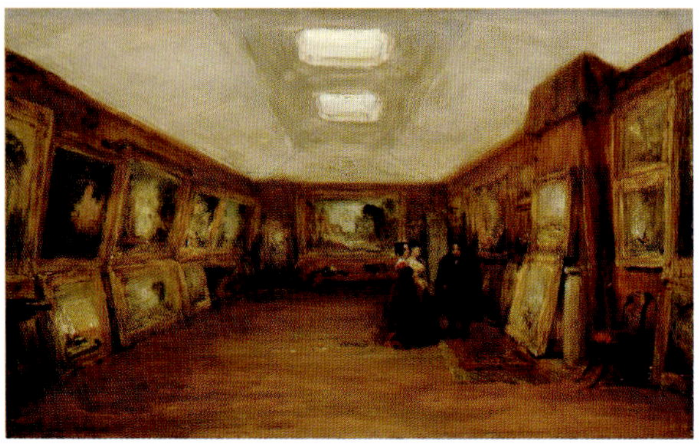

George Jones, Interior of Turner's Gallery: The Artist showing his Works (including Dido Building Carthage and possibly Dido and Æneas), c. 1852

Our proceedings then resembled our proceedings on the former visit, distinguished from it, however, by the exceeding taciturnity, yet restlessness of my great companion, who waved about and occasionally clutched a letter which he held in his hand. I feared to break the dead silence, varied only by the slippered scrape of Turner's feet as we paced from end to end the dim and dusty apartment. At last he stood abruptly, and turning to me, said, 'Mr. Hammersley, you must excuse me; I cannot stay another moment; the letter I hold in my hand has

> just been given to me, and it announces the death of my friend [the landscape painter Augustus Wall] Calcott.' He said no more; I saw his fine grey eyes fill as he vanished. I left at once.(II, 119–121)

FRUSTRATED HOPES

'Many stories,' says Mr. Jones, 'are told of Turner's parsimony and covetousness,'

> but they are generally untrue; he was careful, and desired to accumulate; he acknowledged it, often added to the jokes against himself, and would say, with an arch expression of countenance, when congratulated on the successful sale of a picture, 'Yes, but there is the frame, or the carriage, or the time spent in alteration or varnishing'; but these were indulgences in the ridiculous, which always excited mirth and gave him pleasure; cruelty and unkindness he never felt, a proof of which was discovered after his death.(II, 132)

Turner's main undeviating thought was to benefit art, and to found almshouses near where he had once lived for the poor foot-sore common soldiers in the great army of Art. No paltry vanity hung round the neck of this great-hearted, yet I fear unhappy man. For this he had lived like the half-starved steward of a miser's property. For this he had let his house grow into a den, and had worked like a miner amid a sordid gloom. For poor broken old men of no talents, the world's failures, he had ground down insolent publishers. For weeping widows and orphans he had wrangled about additional shillings for picture-frames and cab-hire; to pay for poor artists' funerals, he had toiled and travelled; to chase the wolf from other men's doors, he had consented to men calling him 'miser, Jew, and dog'.(II, 127)

TURNER'S PRICES

Apropos of prices, we are told that one day Mr. [Joseph] Gillott, the well-known manufacturer [of steel pen nibs] of Birmingham, sallied forth from his hotel, determined at any price to obtain admission to the enchanted house in Queen Anne Street. He was rich, he was enthusiastic—he believed strongly in the power of the golden key to open any door. He arrived at the blistered dirty door of the house with the black-crusted windows. He pulled at the bell; the bell answered with a querulous, melancholy tinkle. There was a long inhospitable pause; then an old woman with a diseased face looked up from the area, and presently ascended and tardily opened the door, keeping the filthy chain up, however, as a precaution. She snappishly asked Mr. Gillott's business. He told her in his blandest voice. 'Can't let 'ee in,' was the answer, and she tried to slam the door. But during the parley the crafty and determined Dives had put his foot in, and now, refusing to any longer parley, he pushed past the feeble enraged old she-Cerberus, and hurried upstairs to the gallery. In a moment Turner was out upon him like a spider on another spider who has invaded his web. Mr. Gillott bowed, introduced himself, and stated that he had come to buy. 'Don't want to sell,' or some such rebuff, was the answer; but Gillott shut his ears to all Turner's angry vituperations.

'Have you ever seen our Birmingham pictures, Mr. Turner?' was his only remark.

'Never 'eard of 'em,' said Turner.

Gillott pulled from his pocket a silvery fragile bundle of Birmingham bank-notes (about £5000 worth).

'Mere paper,' said Turner, with grim humour, a little softened, and enjoying the joke.

'To be bartered for mere canvas,' said Gillott, waving his hand at the *Building of Carthage* and its companions.

'You're a rum fellow!' said Turner, slowly entering into negotiations, which ended in Gillott eventually carrying off in his cab some £5000 worth of Turner's pictures.*(I, 388–9)

* See p. 37

Overleaf: Approach to Venice, 1844, once owned by Joseph Gillott

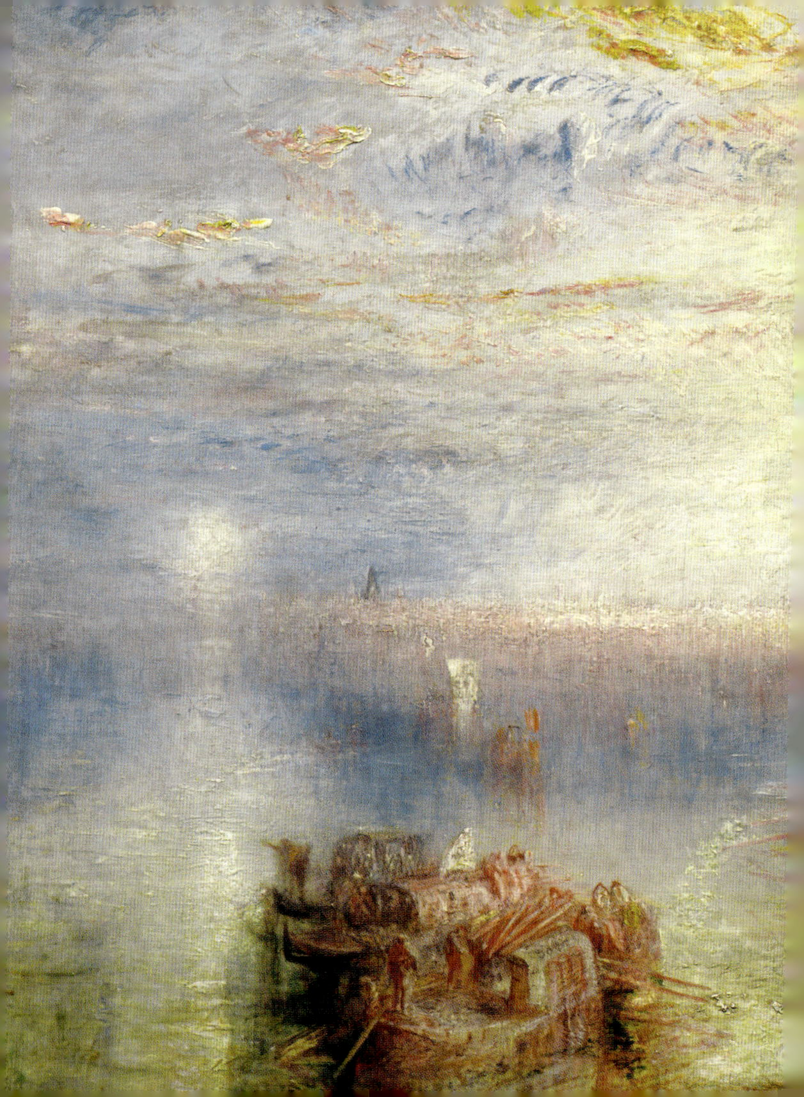

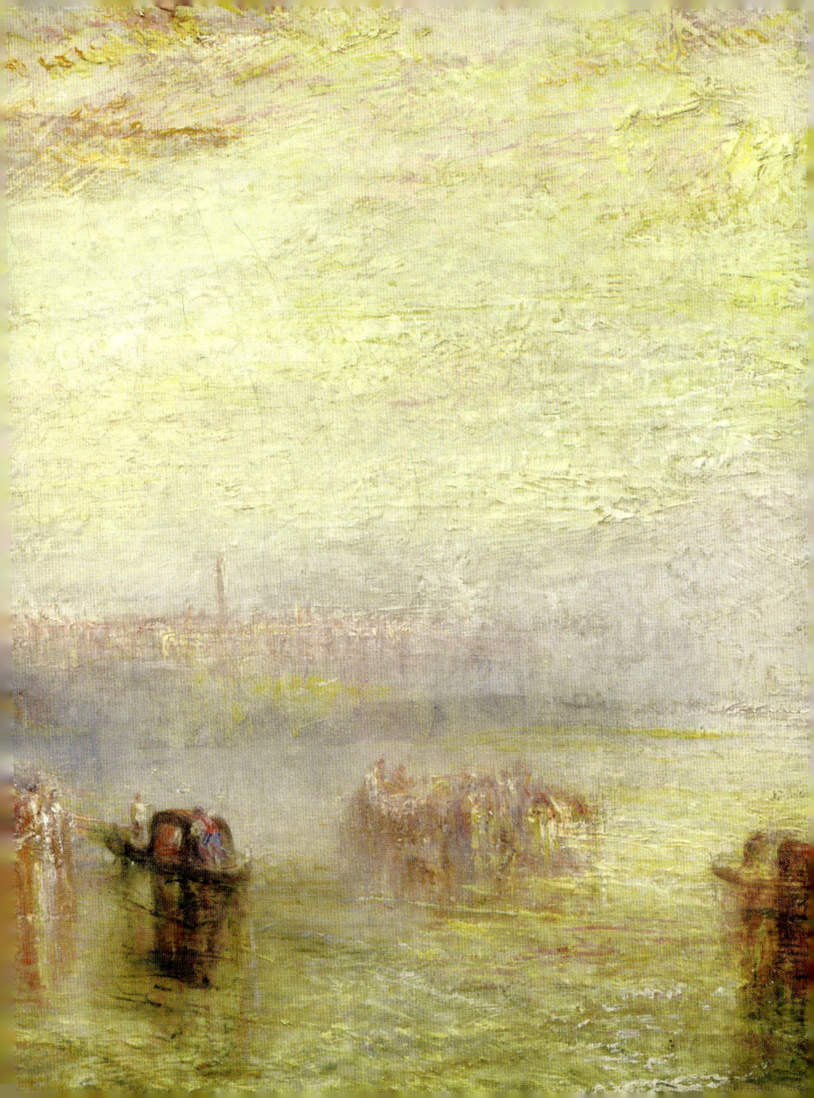

We have already seen him refuse £2000 for the *Rise of Carthage* from a private purchaser; we shall now see him refuse £2500 from a body of eminent public men, who wish to present the picture to the nation. He has but to keep silent, to forget his generous intention, and pocket the money. His change of purpose will never be known; he has other pictures to leave.

At a great meeting at Somerset House, where Sir Robert Peel, Lord Hardinge, &c, were present, it was unanimously agreed to buy two pictures of Turner, and to present them to the National Gallery, as monuments of art for eternal incitement and instruction to artists and all art-lovers.* A memorial was drawn up and presented to Turner by his sincere old friend, Mr. Griffiths, who exulted in the pleasant task. The offer was £5000 for the two pictures, the *Rise* and *Fall of Carthage*.

Turner read the memorial, and his eyes brightened. He was deeply moved: he shed tears; for he was capable, as all who knew him well know, of intense feeling. He expressed the pride and delight he felt at such a noble offer from such men; but he added, sternly, directly he read the word 'Carthage'—

'No, no; they shall not have it.'

* Judy Egerton has proposed this account unreliable: *National Gallery Catalogues: The British Paintings*, 1998, pp. 279–80 n. 48.

On Mr. Griffiths turning to leave, he called after him and said:—

'Oh! Griffiths, make my compliments to the memorialists, and tell them *Carthage* may some day become the property of the nation.'

One of his oldest friends tells me that the week Turner sold a picture he used to always appear dejected and oppressed; and if he was pressed to say why he appeared so low, he would say, sorrowfully:—

'I've lost one of my children this week.'[(I, 394–5)]

LAST WORKS

Some of Turner's enemies accuse him (I think very unjustly) of latterly taking advantage of his name, and selling at large prices experiments that had cost him neither labour nor thought.

I see no fraud or injustice in Turner selling his later pictures. They were bought voluntarily by men with their eyes open. If they were slight, they were wonderful; they were what no one else could do; they were gorgeous ideals of colour and effect; they were efforts to carry art beyond its hitherto known limits. Turner did not know that they were unworthy of him; his sight and brain were failing, but there was still the lifetime of a great man in each of them; they were what only a man at the end of life could

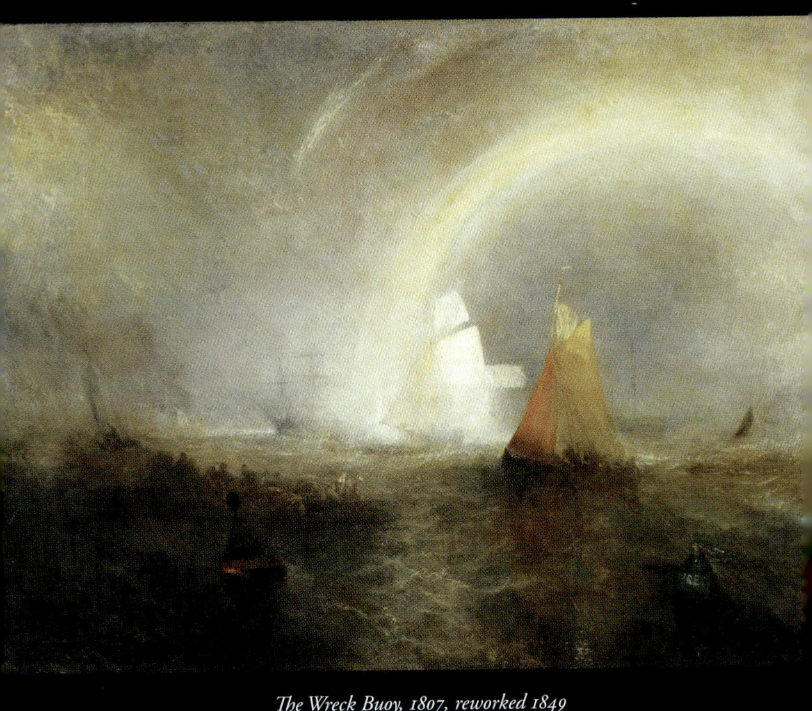

The Wreck Buoy, 1807, reworked 1849
'The last oil he painted before his noble hand forgot its cunning'
(John Ruskin)

do; and after all, as even his enemies avow, the worst of them were of great interest, wonderful proofs of power, failing only because trying for impossibilities. They had a value as riddles, experiments, and prophecies.(II, 244–5)

DRAWN INTO SOCIETY

I have heard people, friends of Turner, assert that Mr. Ruskin's book killed him, by increasing his fame, leading him more into society, and so altering his food, his hours, and his habits.

Latterly, Turner was always to be seen between ten and eleven at the Athenæum, discussing his half-pint of sherry. As his health failed, he became very talkative after his wine, and rather dogmatic.

In earlier days he was always shy, especially before ladies; but if thoroughly at his ease and once roused, or got in a vein of joking, he became very social and amusing. He was rather desirous to obtain a repute for general knowledge, and was a reader of all the best books and reviews of the day. The *Edinburgh Review*, in its best days, was one of his special favourites.(II, 264–5)

I am sorry to own that I cannot say very much for Turner's moral character. A selfish and brooding solitary life and naturally strong passions could not be expected to lead to anything but a selfish and vicious old age. Latterly,

Turner resorted to wine while he painted, to rouse his imagination; and at Chelsea I fear he gave way to even more fatal drinking.

Nor were these his only excesses. He would often, latterly, I am assured on only too good authority, paint hard all the week till Saturday night; he would then put by his work, slip a five-pound note in his pocket, button it securely up there, and set off to some low sailors' house in Wapping or Rotherhithe,* to wallow till the Monday morning left him free again to drudge through another week. A blinded Samson, indeed—a fallen angel, forgetful of his lost Paradise.

Turner left four illegitimate children, and bequeathed money to the mistress with whom he had spent the later years of his life.

'I once,' says a friend, 'heard Mr. Crabb Robinson (the friend of Wordsworth) casually mention a remark dropped by the late Miss Maria Denman, when the two were out for an excursion with Rogers (I think), and had put up at an inn in a village near London. "That," said the lady, pointing to a youth who happened to pass, "is Turner's natural son."'"† (II, 167–8)

* Turner inherited The Ship and Bladebone pub on New Gravel Lane, and was most likely visiting the area to collect his income. † Nothing further has substantiated this claim.

JOHN JABEZ EDWIN MAYALL AND PHOTOGRAPHY

One of the most interesting proofs of the perpetual growth of Turner's mind is the following account of the interest he took in the science of optics and in the science of photography. It is kindly furnished to me by that eminent professor of the progressing and wonderful art, Mr. Mayall, of Regent Street:—*

> Turner's visits to my atelier were in 1847, '48, and '49. I took several admirable daguerreotype portraits of him, one of which was reading, a position rather favourable for him on account of his weak eyes and their being rather bloodshot. I recollect one of these portraits was presented to a lady who accompanied him. My first interviews with him were rather mysterious; he either did state, or at least led me to believe, that he was a Master in Chancery, and his subsequent visits and conversation rather confirmed this idea. At first he was very desirous of trying curious effects of light let in on the figure from a high position, and he himself sat for the studies. He was very much pleased with a figure-study I had

* Mayall only opened his studio at 224 Regent Street around 1852; the incidents described here must have taken place at his premises at 433 West Strand.

just completed of *This Mortal must put on Immortality*; he wished to bring a lady to try something of the kind himself. This was in 1847; and I believe he did fix a day for that purpose. However, it happened to be a November fog, and I could not work. He stayed with me some three hours, talking about light and its curious effects on films of prepared silver. He expressed a wish to see the spectral image copied, and asked me if I had ever repeated Mrs. Somerville's experiment of magnetizing a needle in the rays of the spectrum. I told him I had.

I was not then aware that the inquisitive old man was Turner, the painter. At the same time, I was much impressed with his inquisitive disposition, and I carefully explained to him all I then knew of the operation of light on iodized silver plates. He came again and again, always with some new notion about light. He wished me to copy my views of Niagara—then a novelty in London—and inquired of me about the effect of the rainbow spanning the great falls. I was fortunate in having seized one of these fleeting shadows when I was there, and I showed it to him. He wished to buy the plate. At that time I was not very anxious to sell them. I told him I had made a copy for Sir John Herschel, and with that exception did not intend to part with a copy. He told me he should like to see Niagara, as it was the greatest wonder in nature; he was never tired of my descriptions of it. In short, he had come so often, and in such an unobtrusive manner, that he had come to be regarded by all my people as 'our Mr. Turner'.(II, 259–61)

I recollected putting aside a rather curious head of him in profile, and, you may be sure, on the following morning after this interview I lost no time in looking up the portrait, which, I regret to say, one of my assistants had without my orders effaced. I am almost certain you will be able to trace some of the daguerreotypes of him, for I made at least four, for which he paid me;* and some I rubbed out where we had tried the effect of a sharp, narrow cross light, in which some parts of the face were left in strong shadow.(II, 261–2)

He sent me many patrons. I used to hear about him almost daily. When somewhat desponding of my success one day, I told him London was too large for a man with slender means to get along. He sharply turned round and said, 'No, no; you are sure to succeed; only wait. You are a young man

* A daguerreotype purporting to be by Mayall, and to depict Turner, was exhibited in 2017, but has not yet been definitely documented. See *The Times*, 20 May 2017.

yet. I began life with little, and you see I am now very comfortable.' 'Yes,' I replied; 'and if I were on the same side of Chancery you are, perhaps I might be comfortable also.' I was at that time fighting the battle of the patent rights of the daguerreotype. He smiled and said, 'You'll come out all right, never fear.' My recollection now is, that he was very kind and affable to me, rather taciturn, but very observant and curious; he would never allow me to stop working when he came, but would loiter and watch me polish the plates and prepare them, and take much interest in the result of my labours.

I recollect Mr. [William] Spence, the naturalist [F.R.S.], sitting to me [*c.* 1847], and was much struck at the time with the resemblance of the two heads. I mentioned this to Turner, and I showed him the portrait of Mr. Spence. Mr. Spence was stouter. Turner stooped very much, and always looked down; he had a trick of putting his hand into his coat-pocket, and of muttering to himself.

Whatever others may have said of his parsimonious habits, I cannot recollect one act of his that would lead me to infer he was other than a liberal, kindhearted old gentleman.(II, 262–3)

TWILIGHT AT CHELSEA

Many of the Academicians knew that Turner had latterly another home besides the murky house in Queen Anne Street; but they did not dare to express openly their curiosity. He was evidently taken more care of; he was better dressed; he was more cleanly and tidy than in former years; he even ventured on a red velvet waistcoat, and his linen had more daylight whiteness about it than it had had for years.

Turner was not an exhibitor at the Royal Academy Exhibition of 1851. This was a sign of declining health that his friends did not fail to notice with alarm. He came, however, to the private view: those who saw him thought him breaking up fast. It was evident that he could not live the year out. He was shaky; he was feeble; he was no longer the sturdy, dogged, strange being; he was the broken, decrepit old man.

Not appearing for a long time at the Academy meetings, at which he had hitherto been so constant, some of his friends became alarmed, and one of them (Mr. David Roberts) wrote to Queen Anne Street, stating how all his brethren regretted his absence from their meetings, and to beg him, if he was ill and could not attend, to let him know, that he might come and see him, reposing the most perfect confidence in him, should it be his wish that the place of his residence should remain private.

Turner did not reply; but some two weeks after he appeared at Mr. Roberts' studio in Fitzroy Square, sadly broken and ailing. He was evidently deeply moved by the letter his friend had written, for he said—

'You must not ask me; but whenever I come to town I will always come to see you.'

> I tried to cheer him up, but he laid his hand upon his heart and replied, 'No, no; there is something here which is all wrong.' As he stood by the table in my painting-room, I could not but help looking attentively at him, peering in his face, for the small eye was as brilliant as that of a child, and unlike the glazed and 'lack-lustre eye' of age. This was my last look. The rest is soon told. None of his friends had seen him for months; indeed, I believe I was the last, together with his friend George Jones, who I afterwards learnt had that day also called on him.
>
> He only called once after this, which was some two months before his death. He died in December of that year.

But there was one who mourned and wondered at Turner's absence more than any of his other friends could, and that was his old housekeeper in Queen Anne Street,

Mrs. Ellen Danby*—the guardian of his murky house—his faithful old servant for so many long years of rain and sunshine. She was deeply troubled at Turner's mysterious disappearance; she knew he must be ill, but yet knew not how to find him amid the labyrinths of London. At last, one day, as she was brushing an old coat of Turner's, in turning out a pocket she found and pounced on a letter directed to him, and written by a friend who lived at Chelsea. There, then, she felt sure he must be; it was for her to sally forth and discover him.

This poor old lady, with another as infirm and old as herself, resolved at last to set out on a voyage of discovery, How they reached there 'deponent knoweth not,' but they did reach the cottage by the river-side, and finding that the adjoining cottage sold ginger beer, the two old dames craftily treated themselves to a bottle of the same, got into a diplomatic gossip with the seller of ginger beer, and by dint of the outlay of twopence and a little pumping, were quite satisfied that the lady and the old gentleman who

* This may be a further example of Thornbury's sloppiness, and the correct identity is presumably Hannah Danby, Turner's cancer-stricken housekeeper. However, the identity of the second elderly woman subsequently mentioned has not been resolved. Two potential candidates are Maria Tanner and Eleanor Harpur (who, with her husband Henry, had travelled with Turner up the Rhine in 1840); see Franny Moyle, *Turner*, p. 435.

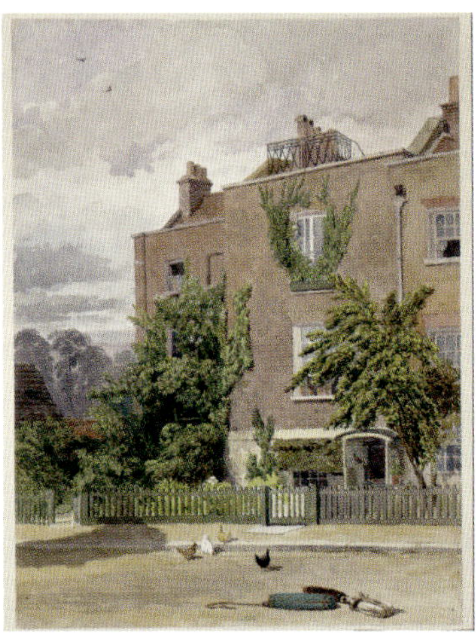

John Wykeham Archer, House of J. M. W. Turner at 6 Davis Place, Chelsea, 1852. Turner had the roof flattened to make a balcony from which he could enjoy the views of the river.

lived next door must be the great painter and his landlady; but what must have grieved them much was that the gentleman had been very unwell, and little out for the last two months. Having ascertained this, the two got home as they best could, and Mrs Danby contrived to apprise a relative and one of the executors, Mr Harpur, of her discovery. Mr Harpur lost no time in finding out the Chelsea cottage—only in time to find Turner fast sinking. On the following day he breathed his last.(II, 272–4)

Turner, some time before this, feeling dangerously ill, had sent for a well-known doctor from Margate, whom he had before employed, and in whom he had confidence. The sick man, who had once said that he would give all his money if he could but be twenty once again, watched the doctor's face with eager anxiety. He was told that death was near. 'Go downstairs,' he said to the doctor; 'take a glass of sherry, and then look at me again.' The doctor did so, but the reply was the same. Turner would not believe that the awful change was so near. I fear he had no religious hope to cheer him at that hour. The dreadful despairing fear of annihilation pressed upon the heart of this great man, who had done so much to make men love God's beautiful world. His fame and his wealth seemed to him then but poor worthless things.

The day he died—nay, I believe the very hour almost that he died—his landlady [Mrs Sophia Booth] wheeled Turner's chair to the window, that he might see the sunshine he had loved so much, mantling the river and glowing on the sails of the passing boats.(II, 274–5)

Overleaf: Sunrise over the Sea, perhaps at Margate, c. 1845. Sheet from one of the sketchbooks left by Turner in Sophia Booth's lodgings

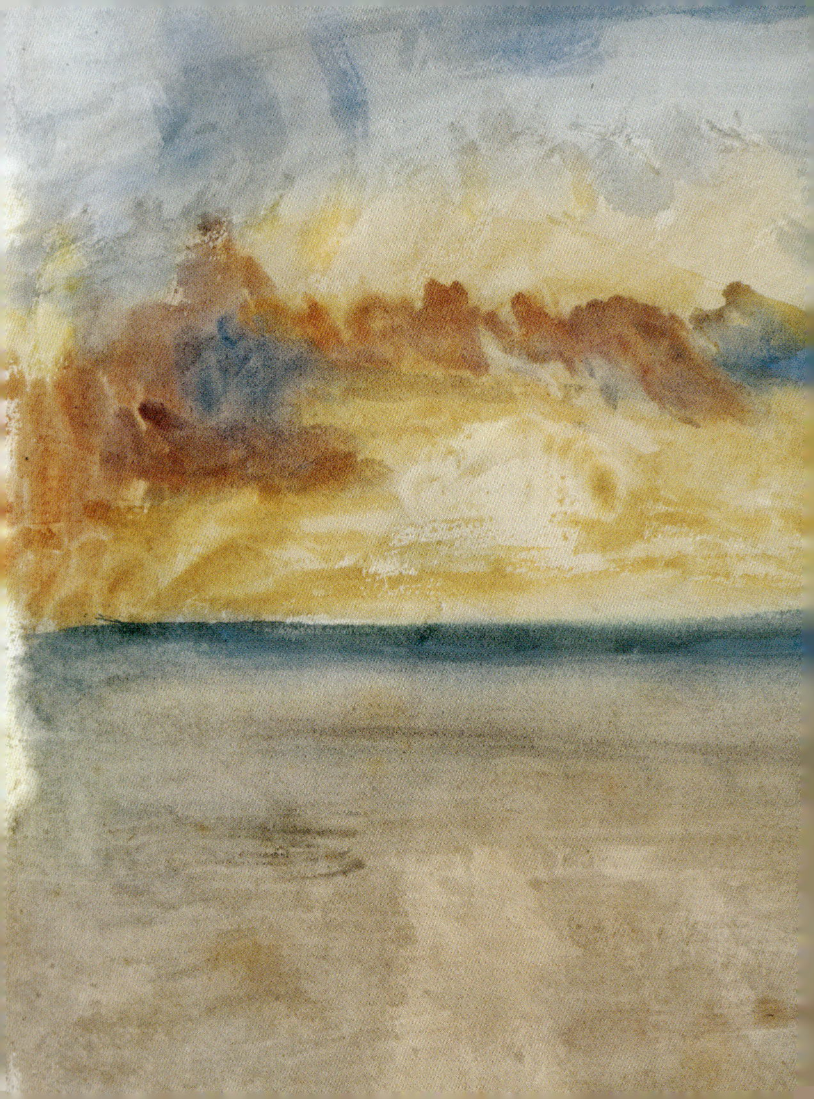

THE LAST SUNSHINE

In the streets of Chelsea, and all along the shore of the Thames, Turner was known to the street-boys as 'Puggy Booth', and by the small tradesmen he was designated 'Admiral Booth'; for the story ran that he was an old admiral in reduced circumstances. I am told that up to the period of his very last illness Turner would often rise at daybreak, leave his bed, with some blanket or dressing-gown carelessly thrown over him, and go up on the railed-in roof to see the sun rise and to observe the colour flow, flushing back into the pale morning sky. To me, there is in this tenacity of the dying man to his old love something very touching, something very sublime. To him nature could never cloy; he still, with the true humility of genius, felt how much he had to learn, and how inimitable was the beauty of the world he had tried to depict.

The old painter died with the winter-morning sun shining upon his face as he was lying in his bed. The attendant drew up the window-blind, and the morning sun shone on the dying artist—the sun he had so often beheld with such love and such veneration. The sun of the *Building of Carthage* and of the *Frosty Morning* shone still with unfading brightness, and the painter who had so often tried to picture its globe of living flame lay lifeless in an upper room of the river-side cottage—not far from the spot where he had first floated out in a boat to study nature—not far from that Lambeth Palace which was the subject of his first water-colour drawing—not a great way from that Battersea which had been the subject of his first effort in oil—no longer the bright-eyed, ambitious boy, full of living genius and young hope, but the wrinkled, faded, worn-out old man, rich, famous, now only cumbering the earth till the vault can be opened for him to be at rest, in his regal mausoleum, between Reynolds and Barry.(II, 276–7)

THE EMPTY GALLERY

From my kind friend, Mr. Trimmer, I am indebted for the following interesting account of the appearance of Turner's house after his death:—

> I had often visited Turner, partaken with my father a déjeûner *à la fourchette*, and had had my pockets crammed with biscuits, after the olden fashion. Now, when I entered, all was altered, the master-mind was gone, the mainspring had snapped. The same aged attendant let us in, but all was the silence of death. I will describe the interior. First, the entrance hall. Here were several casts, from the antique, of Centaurs in conflict with the Lapithæ, and a picture of Sir Joshua, all very trite and depressing.

Turning to the right was the dining-room, over the fire-place a small model of a female figure, and a small Wilson obscured by smoke, quite in keeping with the sombre walls. In Turner's time there was also a picture of Tassi, Claude's master. Backwards stretched a large unfurnished room filled with unfinished pictures; then a larger and drearier room yet; lastly, a back room, against the walls of which stood his unfinished productions, large full-length canvasses placed carelessly against the wall, the damp of which had taken off the colours altogether, or had damaged them. Some canvasses had a coat of white run over the ground, doubtless the work of Turner senior; the next stage was patting in large masses of black and white, apparently with the spatula; at least, the brush seemed used but sparingly. Turner is said to have laid in his dead-colouring with body colour, but so far as my inspection extended, I saw no traces of it; it rather seemed fat oil. In common with the great masters, the colours were well loaded, both lights and darks, but of a darker tint than when finished. Among them was an extraordinary picture of the *Carnival*,* red and

* Possibly *Shadrach, Meschach and Abednego in the Burning Fiery Furnace* (see p. 184) or the unfinished *Dinner in a Great Room* (Tate, London)

black predominating. Here Turner revelled in all his luxury. A little before his death (I think Mr. Griffiths is my authority, and he was one of Turner's oldest friends and associates), Turner used to go to the top of the house he lodged in to see the fireworks at Vauxhall.

There were there many pictures condemned by a discerning public. Many of Turner's admirers say that there are parts of these no one could do but Turner. I must confess that I can see no merit in them. Some of the figures, with all the defects of Rembrandt immensely exaggerated, showed an absence of all drawing, and effects of light and shade unrealized by Nature and outraging all analogies.

Then we went into Turner's sleeping apartment; it is surprising how a person of his means could have lived in such a room; certainly he prized modern luxuries at a very modest rate.

TURNER'S PAINTING ROOM

When making an inspection of Turner's residence, I reserved his studio as the finale. This, during his lifetime, was enshrined in mystery, and the object of profound speculation. What would his brother brush-drivers have given some thirty years before, to have forced an entrance when Turner was at the height of his fame! Often had I seen him emerge from that hidden recess when shown into his gallery. That august retreat was now thrown open; I entered. On a circular table lay his gloves and neck-handkerchief. In the centre of the table was a raised box with a circle in the centre with side compartments; a good contrivance for an artist, though I had never seen one of the kind before. In the centre were his colours, the great object of my attraction. I remember, on my father's once observing to Turner that nothing was to be done without ultramarine, his saying that cobalt was good enough for him; and cobalt to be sure there was, but also several bottles of ultramarine of various depths; and smalts of various intensities, of which I think he made great use. There was also some verditer. The next object of interest was the white; there was a large bottle of *blanc d'argent*, and another of flake white. I had observed that Turner used silver white before making this inspection. His yellow pigments consisted of a large bottle of chrome. There were also a bottle of tincture of rhubarb and some iodine, but whether for artistical or medicinal use I cannot say. Since writing the above, I was told by his housekeeper that ultramarine was employed by him very sparingly, and that smalt and cobalt were his usual blues. She was in the habit of setting Turner's palette. The palette—at least that in use, for he possessed two large splendid ones—was a homely piece of square wood, with a hole for the thumb. Grinding colours on a slab was not his practice, and his dry colours were rubbed on the palette with cold-drawn oil. His colours were mixed daily, and he was very particular. If not to his mind, he would say to Mrs. Danby, 'Can't you set a palette better than this?' Like Wilson, Turner used gamboge: this was simply pounded and mixed with linseed cold-drawn oil.

His brushes were of the humblest description, mostly large round hog's tools and some flat. He was said to use very short handles, which might have been the case with his watercolours; but I observed one very long-handled brush, with which I have no doubt he put in his effective touches in his late pictures. I was informed by his housekeeper that he used the long brush exclusively for the rigging of ships, &c. However, there were a great many long-haired sables, which could not have been all employed for rigging. She also said that he used camel's hair for his oil pictures; and formerly he showed my father some Chinese brushes he was in the habit of using. Mrs. Danby told me that when he had nearly finished a picture, he took it to the end of his long gallery, and put in the last touches.

I next inspected his travelling-box. Had I been asked to guess his travelling library, I should have said Young's *Night Thoughts*, and Isaak Walton; and there they were, together with some inferior translation of Horace. His library was select, but it showed the man. There was a red morocco pocket-book, which, from the wear and tear it exhibited, one might have imagined his companion through life. There were cakes of water-colour fastened on a leaf, the centres of which were worn away, the commonest colours, one a cake of verditer, one or two sable brushes and lead pencils, not in wood, with which he seemed to have drawn a few outlines in his sketchbook; these consisted of a few lines which he used to say no one could make out but himself. I have some doubts if he could have made them out himself without the assistance of other drawings, and he seems to have purchased detail-views of foreign scenery, of which there was a large assortment well thumbed; the drudgery of the art, of which masterminds avail themselves.

There is no doubt that in his early pictures he

used wax, from their having turned yellow; there was a jar of wax melted with rose madder and also with blue, which must have been used very recently, though it might have been for watercolours.

There was also a bureau of old colours and oils, which I looked over very carefully. A bottle of spirit-varnish and a preparation of tar, tubes of magilp, old bladders of raw umber and other dark earths, all Newman's, from whom might be learned what colours he used.

The above, with numerous unframed pictures around the apartment, were the contents of his painting-room, which had no skylight. It had been originally the drawing-room, and had a good north light, with two windows.(II, 278–83)

THE GRAND FUNERAL

Since Turner's death, some admiring artists wished to put a memorial tablet over the door of the house in Maiden Lane where he was born, but the Board of Works refused to allow it.

The Times gave the following account of his funeral:—

> The mortal remains of the great artist who has just been removed from us, full of years and honours, were received within the walls of St. Paul's on

Tuesday, December 3rd, and borne to their final resting-place in the catacombs. Whatever hesitation might have been felt by the mass of those who gazed on the later efforts of his brush in believing that he was entitled to the highest rank in his profession, none of his brethren seemed to have any doubt of his decided excellence, and the best of them all have ever readily admitted his superiority in poetry, feeling, fancy, and genius. Long ere his death he had the felicity of knowing that his name and his works were regarded with that reverential respect and estimation which is given to other artists by posterity alone, and his earlier productions have been placed among the classical ornaments of our choicest collections and galleries for many years. Even those who could only sneer and smile at the erratic blaze of his colour, shifting and flickering as the light of the Aurora, lingered minute after minute before the last incomprehensible 'Turner' that gleamed on the walls of the Academy, and the first name sought for upon the catalogue by the critic, artist, and amateur, as well as by those who could not understand him when they found him, was his also. Many of the most distinguished of our painters, and many private friends, paid the last tribute of respect to his remains, and followed his hearse yesterday, and a long procession of mourning coaches and private carriages preceded it to the cathedral.(II, 285–6)

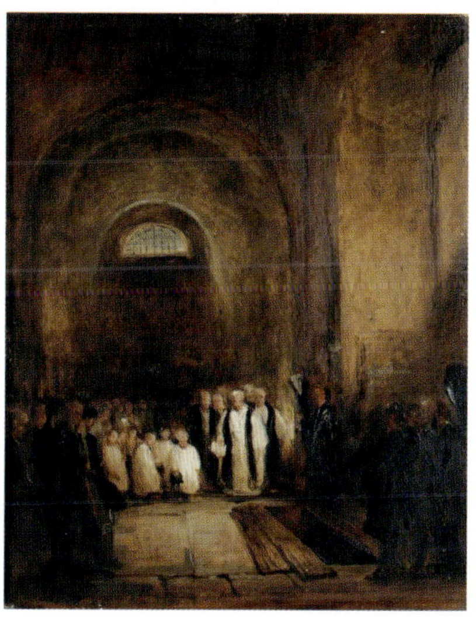

George Jones, Turner's Burial in the Crypt of St Paul's, c. 1852

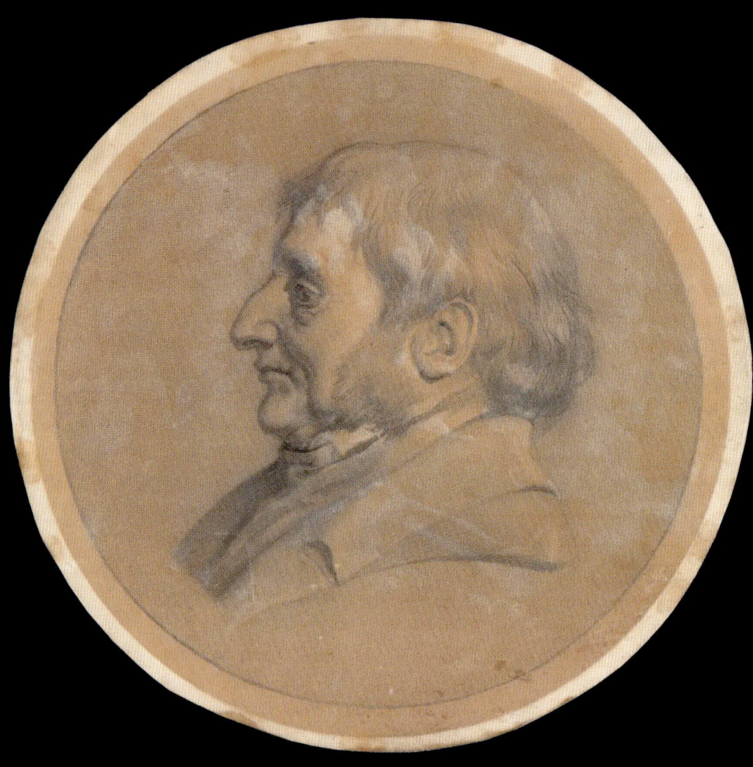

Daniel Maclise, A design for the obverse of the Turner medal, 1858

OLD MORTALITY: AN ASSESSMENT

But while thus expressing my admiration and astonishment at the genius of Turner, I should not be a lover of truth were I to conceal my opinion of his faults. In many respects he was born at an unfortunate period. He was compelled at first to be imitative in order to sell. He was now trying to see nature like Vandervelde—now to turn English hills into Poussin mountains—now to lap his canvas in Cuyp's sunshine; sometimes because the manner of these painters was more like nature than he could yet reach, but more often because buyers would not look at any picture that was not in the Vandervelde or Claude manner.

Later, there fell upon Turner a baser spirit, that of rivalry; not the wish to paint like Claude, because Claude's manner sold, or because Claude often obtained a serenity of air that was pure and exquisite, but because he was determined to show that he could paint better than Claude, with more grandeur and more thought.

Turner, born in a Claude atmosphere, nursed at the foot of a Vandervelde, and nurtured on Thomson and Akenside as his poetical food, lived long enough to see a new and daring sect of reformers arise in art—men whose creed emerged from the Gothic reaction, and was a pushing forward of the old Wordsworthian lines into new regions of convention.(II, 341)

Nor can I (as I am making a clean breast of it) conceal either the fact that, whether from carelessness, fatigue, or experiment. Turner's colour was often weak, and sometimes downright bad. In his Yorkshire drawings his blue distances have often a disagreeable green tinge about them. In some of the *England* series there is a violent foxy tone, very hot and oppressive. In the Roman oil pictures there often prevails a mustardy yellow, which perhaps seemed beautiful at the time, but is now quite out of tone. Vermilion shadows in flesh I have not a word to say for; nor do I like the opacity of his Vandervelde period more than I do the crude staring whites of the architecture in some of his later Venetian pictures.

> 'Turner is exceedingly unequal,' says Mr. Ruskin, most frequently in elaborate compositions from redundant quantity. Sometimes from over-care, as very signally in a large and most laboured drawing of *Bamborough Castle*.* Sometimes his eye for colour seems to fail, as in *Rome from the Forum*,† *Cicero's Villa*,‡ and *Building of Carthage*, sometimes criminally, from taking licences, or indulging in

* Private collection † Tate, London ‡ Private collection

> conventionalities. His dry sea that does not wet the boat in one of his storms is specially reprehensible, and so is the occasional foxy colour, as in his drawing of *Oxford*,* in Mr. Munro's collection. His *Blenheim*¶ is an almost unique instance of failure in composition, as the Duke's house is the last thing the eye observes. There is sometimes, too, a livid purple about his colour which is far from pleasing.[(II, 342–3)]

I have tried carefully, yet without malice, to show that Turner was not immaculate; that with all his genius there was no finality in him; and that, with all his knowledge and industry, a genius may still arise who may combine great truth and quantity with better drawing of the figure, less classic convention, and a more exact delineation of nature. His faults in linear perspective were not unfrequent, although he had made that science his special study; his colour was subject to aberrations, and in oil painting his work was too often experimental and perishable. He too often used dangerous vegetable colours and uncertain vehicles; his skies darken and crack, his distemper pictures wash out. Indeed, I sometimes fear that in time we shall have, after all, to turn to that wonderful *Liber* as the great monument of his genius.

It must not be thought that Turner always drew such

* Ashmolean Museum, Oxford ¶ Birmingham Museums, Birmingham

distorted, doll-figures as in the *Phryne*, the *Exile*, &c.* In the drawings of his best period the figures are always firmly, expressively, and intelligently drawn, often with admirable grace and truth. The figures in the *Liber* are generally beautiful to line and composition. The life-studies in Turner's sketch-books are not unworthy of a professional figure-painter. The *Venus and Adonis*† in Mr. Munro's gallery is ostentatiously well drawn. In his best moments no one knew better than Turner how to express momentary action in a figure. In the illustrations to Scott there are figures worthy of any landscape-painter, and a thousand times superior to those puerile inanities of Claude, which are so feeble and so unreal. In his later pictures Turner's sense of form became utterly weakened, partly, perhaps, from a lessening of mental power, and still more from his sensual sacrifice of every other quality to that of colour.

The fatal conventionalisms of an artificial and past age had too deep a hold on Turner's mind. The dreams of a false and obscene mythology that he could not understand, and with which the great world never did and never will sympathize, excited his imagination. He could not appreciate our real national architecture. The Gothic ruins he spent half his life drawing, never really touched his heart as they did Scott's and Wordsworth's.

He had, too, a fatal belief of the necessity of rearranging

* Both Tate, London † Private collection

Nature. Few of his later works are faithful representations of the places they pretend to describe. He was always remaking the world according to some ideal theory of his own.

I think, after all, that Turner was a better water-colour than oil painter. He never acquired the built-up solidity of Titian's handling, or the vigour and dash of Velasquez. To the last he was rather a 'niggler' in oil, often brown and heavy, oftener still flimsy and fantastic, in execution, confounding the shadow and the substance, heightening the colour, and exaggerating the reflections and subtleties of Nature.

I am sure that, with the exception of the *Polyphemus* and the *Temeraire*, his water-colour drawings were more unapproachable than his oil, more ærial, more tender, more magical. I am not sure if the *Liber Studiorum*, for variety, grasp, versatility, and handling, is not, both in the etchings and the unfinished states, more wonderful than anything else he did.

Of his later works I am no defender. They are dreams, challenges, theories, experiments, and absurdities. The figures are generally contemptible. The colour, that of fireworks, rising sometimes almost to insanity, and occasionally sinking into imbecility. The eye is dim, the sense of form was lost, the outlines are gone, the sentiment only remains. They are certainly what no one else could do; but, then, no one wishes to do them.

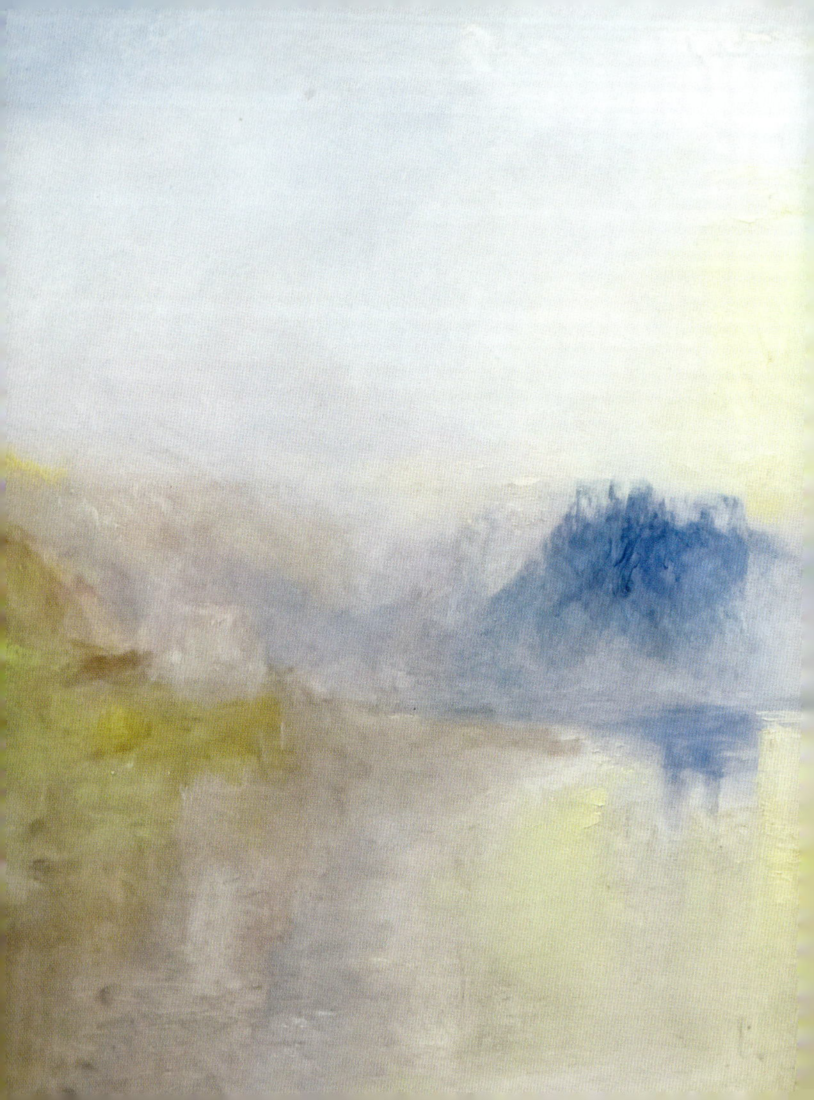

If I was, in as few words as possible, to try to describe the special characteristics of Turner's genius, I should not select the versatility that led him from poor English hedgers and ditchers to Jason on the war-trail and Ulysses triumphing at the sunrise, nor to the industry that produced twenty thousand sketches, but the wide sympathies that made him take as great an interest in a plain Scottish peat-bog as in the most gorgeous visions of Modern Italy, or the wildest depths of the Alps, the ærial perspective in which he revels in the *Modern Italy*, the *Bay of Baiæ* and the *Crossing of the Brook*, and the extraordinary 'multitude' and quantity which we see in his *Grenoble*, in the *Liber*, &c. Turner was the first to venture to place twenty miles of landscape within the four walls of a frame; he was the first to attempt all natural phenomena, first to give us storm and sunshine; in fact, to widen on all sides the hitherto narrow dominions of landscape-painting.(II, 344–7)

In writing these two volumes, I have felt as a restorer of a fine old Gothic church must feel when he is peeling the moss from the marred face of some calm stone figure. I have concealed no faults, because I love truth. I have detracted from no virtues, because I respect the memory of Turner. I know that I shall offend some fanatics in his

Previous pages: Norham Castle, Sunrise, c. 1845

praise, by owning that I do not like the theoretical, obscure, and sketchy pictures of his old age; others, more discriminating, by confessing that I think him a greater water-colour painter than an oil-painter, and showing that he, too, often exaggerated and revised nature. His enemies will be annoyed that I have not shown him pure soot; his older friends that I have not clothed him in shining silver.

I can only plead that I have rejected no evidence and suppressed no fact, and it is for my kind countrymen to consider on their verdict, which I am sure will be an impartial one.[II, 348–9]

List of illustrations

All works are by J. M. W. Turner and oil on canvas unless stated otherwise.
Measurements given height before width.
Turner's spellings have been retained.
Images from holding institutions unless noted.

NOTE ON THE TEXT

As many of its first readers noted, Walter Thornbury's two-volume *Life of Turner* of nearly 900 pages, published on 8 November 1861, was padded out with long quotations from other authors, or historical material about the artist's era, and institutions and places associated with him. Another much-criticised flaw was Thornbury's tendency to repeat stories, sometimes to completely different effect. In this selection of extracts I have dispensed with extraneous material to concentrate largely on incidents (arranged here roughly in chronological order) that have subsequently become part of standard accounts of Turner's career and private life, regardless of whether they are verifiable or not. Indeed, some of them have been shown to be flawed (at best) or downright impossible, such as the celebrated account of Turner supposedly watching the *Temeraire* tugged up the Thames in 1838. The interested reader is encouraged to explore more recent biographies, or the *Oxford Companion to Turner* (2001), to corroborate anything they read here. I have retained some of Thornbury's characteristic page headers as section titles to help pinpoint specific narratives. Thornbury's sloppy, uncorrected details are supplemented in square brackets. References are to the volume and page of the first edition. I. W.

First published 2026 by
Pallas Athene (Publishers) Limited
2 Birch Close, N19 5XD
www.pallasathene.co.uk
© Pallas Athene 2026
ISBN 978 1 84368 286 8
Printed in China through WorldPrint
Series editor: Alexander Fyjis-Walker
Editorial assistants: Patrick Davies and Caroline Brooke Johnson